W9-DGI-177

...PANTS ON FIRE

...PANTS ON FIRE

How Al Franken Lies, Smears, and Deceives

ALAN SKORSKI

WND Books
An imprint of Cumberland House Publishing
Nashville, Tennessee

There are so many deserving people to whom I would like to dedicate this book, so I will. To the great blessings in my life—my wife, daughters, family, and friends, and to those to whom I owe a debt I will never be able to repay for the freedom I now enjoy—the brave men and women of the U.S. Armed Forces.

... PANTS ON FIRE
A WND BOOK
PUBLISHED BY CUMBERLAND HOUSE PUBLISHING
431 Harding Industrial Drive
Nashville, Tennessee 37211

Cover design: James Duncan Creative, Nashville, Tennessee

Library of Congress Cataloging-in-Publication Data
Skorski, Alan, 1962–
--pants on fire : how Al Franken lies, smears, and deceives / Alan Skorski.
p. cm.
Includes bibliographical references and index.
ISBN-13: 978-1-58182-480-3 (hardcover : alk. paper)
ISBN-10: 1-58182-480-7 (hardcover : alk. paper)
1. Franken, Al. 2. United States—Politics and government—2001– I. Title.
PN1991.4.F73 2005
791.4402'8092—dc22

2005025206

Printed in the United States of America
1 2 3 4 5 6 7 8 9 10—09 08 07 06 05

Contents

Introduction

When Al Franken smears or calls someone a liar, people listen. Even Mike Wallace, of *60 Minutes*, while interviewing Bill O'Reilly on September 26, 2004, couldn't resist invoking Franken's slurs against O'Reilly. In mid-August 2005, by some coincidence, the *New York Times* and the *San Francisco Chronicle* both followed Franken's lead in charging that O'Reilly accused Cindy Sheehan of treason. Both the *Times* and the *Chronicle* issued retractions. Franken wrote an entire book smearing Rush Limbaugh. He's also accused Fox News's Brit Hume, Bill O'Reilly, Sean Hannity, Ann Coulter, and even President Bush of being liars, hypocrites, evil, obscene, cheaters, lazy, shameless, dishonest—and this is when he is being charitable. Franken repeatedly makes these charges, in a variety of ways and in a variety of forums, including speeches, TV appearances, and radio broadcasts.

By smearing and sliming his adversaries time and again, Franken has become a hero to the Left, which reveals and illustrates its intellectual depth and high standards. His behavior has also earned him a lucrative position as the host of the marquee show on the left-wing radio network Air America. In reality, when people talk about Air America, they are talking about Al Franken. What a great title for a network that constantly bashes America!

While blasting his opponents—I think of them as his intellectual superiors—as shameless liars, Franken simultaneously portrays himself as this ultimate truth-teller (or UTT) and generally gets away with it. His claims and personal accolades have never seriously been challenged by the mainstream media. Coincidentally, this is the same media he criticizes regularly for not shining the light on the "distortions" and other "misdeeds" of conservatives.

Even conservative or Right-leaning journalists—with few exceptions—haven't taken the time to do the research that shows that Franken, not his conservative targets, is the one guilty of deceitful, dishonest disseminations.

Franken not only portrays himself as the Ultimate Truth Teller; he also positions himself as the "Super Truth Dude." He declares, "If a right-winger tells a lie, I'll be there," as he bellows out his sinister laugh, MWHAHAHAHAHA!

Being Super Truth Dude does not mean that Franken merely tells the truth. "I hold myself to an impossibly high standard when it comes to telling the truth," he says. Unlike regular folk, who merely *tell* the truth, Franken maintains standards unknown to mere humankind: *impossibly high standards.*

• • •

In writing a book about lies and liars, it's important to establish what a lie is and what the accepted boundaries for telling a lie are. I would propose that a fair-minded definition of *lie* is "intentionally telling an untruth with the purpose of trying to cover up or get away with something." Telling your wife that her new dress does not make her look fat may not be true, but it's still something harmless; and you had better be ready to say it or be willing to accept the chill that will come over your marriage for a while if you tell her something else. Telling your boss that your alarm clock didn't work so you can play an early round of golf is a lie. Period.

Franken, however, has a different take on what a lie is. In fact, the title of the last chapter of his book *Lies and the Lying Liars Who Tell Them* is "What Is a Lie?" He doesn't exactly give a definition of the word *lie,* but here is what he *does* say:

- "Calling someone a liar is a serious charge." <I agree.* On March 17, 2005, *Newsweek* senior editor Jonathan Alter told Franken, "You and I disagree a little bit on how often that

**Note:* Here and throughout the book, text contained in angled brackets (<>) is my own commentary.

word, 'lie,' should be thrown around. I don't like to toss it around quite as often as you do.">

- "Yes. Lying is a serious matter." <Obviously, except when he does it.>
- "And all the lies, small and large, add up." <Yes, they do. That's why I show Franken's small lies and his large ones. They "add up.">
- "I'm a bad liar, I never lie. That is unless it's absolutely necessary." (p. 261)

This book, though, is about more than just Franken's lies. It is about what Bill O'Reilly calls Franken's career as a *smear merchant*. Franken, of course, doesn't believe he smears anyone. But to anyone who has observed Franken for any length of time, it is quite obvious that smearing is one of Franken's primary weapons and something he relishes.

A lie does not necessarily have to have any victims. "The dog ate my homework" harms no one. But a smear damages reputations, which is precisely what Franken delights in doing.

Take for example, Franken's smearing of Rush Limbaugh in his book *Rush Limbaugh Is a Big Fat Idiot*. (Where does Franken come up with these clever book titles?) In the beginning of the book, Franken completely distorts the meaning of one of Rush's well-known terms, *feminazi*. Hearing this reference at first can cause someone to gasp, "Omigod, Rush is calling women Nazis." And it is exactly this misconception and fear that Al "I-maintain-impossibly-high-standards" Franken plays on.

How misleading and deceitful is Franken's own definition of *feminazi*? Franken tells his readers on page 5 (paperback edition), "Listening to him spew about feminazis and their women-as-victim ideas . . . feminists who believe that all heterosexual sex is rape." But Limbaugh's actual definition of a *feminazi*, which Franken and his researcher just happened to have missed or ignored, is stated quite clearly on page 296 of his first book, *The Way Things Ought to Be:*

> *Feminazi:* Widely misunderstood by most to simply mean "feminist." . . . A feminazi is a feminist to whom the most important thing in life is ensuring that as many abortions as possible occur.

> There are fewer than twenty-five known feminazis in the United States.

Did Franken lie about Rush when he incorrectly stated to his readers what Rush means by *feminazi*? Did he and his assistant just happen to miss this section of Rush's book? Did they also just happen to miss the many radio shows where Rush has repeatedly defined what a feminazi is? No! He *smeared* Rush. He distorted Rush's satirical term for an extremist feminist to persuade his readers who do not listen to Rush's radio program that Rush is a "typical conservative woman hater."

This example illustrates how Franken has little or no desire to tell the truth about his enemies. Finding out what Rush considers a feminazi was easy. All Franken needed to do was turn to the back of Rush's book.

But if Franken is so wrong and seemingly so willing to distort something as inconsequential or trivial about Rush and some of his satirical terms for his favorite targets, like "ultra-extreme fanatical abortion-loving feminists," why should we believe that Franken or his Harvard researchers exerted any stronger effort to get to the truth on more important issues or exposés on President Bush, Bill O'Reilly, Sean Hannity, Ann Coulter, or other conservatives? The answer is: we shouldn't.

Here's another seemingly unimportant distortion. Franken tells his readers that Limbaugh's *dittoheads* are "those who *blindly* follow what Rush Limbaugh says." But Franken's "thorough research" once again results in another distortion. On page 295 of *The Way Things Ought to Be,* Rush defines a dittohead as simply, "an avid listener of the EIB Network." That wasn't so hard to find, but I suppose it's easier and more fun to lump twenty million conservative listeners and Rush fans into one group of rabid "Jim Jones zombies."

In the grand scheme of things, it doesn't really matter if Franken and the Left misuse or abuse terms like *feminazis* or *dittoheads*. I merely cite it as evidence of the truth about Franken's "truth-telling" and as an example of what is to come: much larger and more outrageous lies, smears, and distortions perpetrated by Franken.

To be fair, Franken does not define what *he* believes is a lie, except to say that conservatives "get away with it." Within the pages of this book, you will find that Franken's working definition of a lie seems to be anything a conservative says that he doesn't like. For instance, if Rush says that the United Nations (the holy temple of all things Democrat) is an anti-Semitic and anti-Israel institution, Franken will call him a liar. On other occasions, whenever a conservative says something that Franken thinks he can twist and spin out of context, he plays the "you're a lying liar" game.

Nearly every day, whether on his radio show or in some other public forum, Franken portrays himself as the "paragon of truth" while accusing the "right wing" of being "shameless, hypocritical . . . lying." Get the picture? Franken tells the truth. His adversaries, all of whom are great Americans, are all compulsive liars.

Here's another example of how Franken twists other people's words. At both the May 31, 2003, Los Angeles Book Expo America and in his book *Lies and the Lying Liars Who Tell Them,* Franken claims, "Even John Fund [Rush's good friend and ghostwriter] said my last book on Rush was honest."

Did Franken really think he was going to get away with that? It only took one call to John Fund, *Wall Street Journal* editorial board member, to verify his statement. Fund chuckled about Al using him as a reference and replied that he had heard Franken was making that claim. "At most," Fund told me, "I said his book wasn't as vicious as I thought it would be." I guess in Franken's world "not as vicious" means the same thing as "honest."

So I find myself asking whom I believe: Al Franken, who distorts and smears people, in this case Rush Limbaugh, or Rush's good friend and writing collaborator John Fund? Hmmmm. I'll have to get back to you on that one.

• • •

A good many of the "lies" Franken claims to expose are petty and lame. One example of this occurred when he accused Bill O'Reilly of lying (years earlier) about whether he or *Inside Edition* won a Peabody Award or a Polk Award. As you will read later, Franken gets so giddy whenever he talks about this subject that he tells different people different versions of the story. By the time a person finishes reading about it, one can't help wondering if Franken isn't angry that *he* didn't win the award.

An even more "damning" lie, according to Franken, was when Ann Coulter told an interviewer for the *New York Observer* that she and Franken were friends. Ooohh, what a lie. Lest you think that all of Franken's attacks against Coulter are this infantile, consider a much more egregious transgression Franken was able to uncover.

On page 9 of *Lies and the Lying Liars Who Tell Them,* Franken writes, "Well, in the entire 206 pages [of *Slander*] she never actually makes a case for *any* conservative issue." Ann might have been busted here, but either Franken missed the subtitle of the book or his fourteen Harvard researchers forgot to tell him that the subtitle of the book is *Liberal Lies About the American Right.* Since her book is about liberal lies about conservatives, exactly where or under what heading would he expect her to promote conservative ideals? It's not as though the name of her book was *Why America Is Great: Because of Conservatism.*

To expect a book about liberal lies to make the case for conservative ideas is like complaining that in Franken's nearly four-hundred-page book about conservative lies there isn't *one* word about Al's favorite knish stand. Just think about it. With thousands of knish stands in Manhattan, Al didn't come up with one story?

Franken really gets into trouble with the truth, though, when he accuses Rush, in many public forums, of "pulling numbers from his butt" when he stated that "the majority of minimum wage earners are teenagers." Franken claims that his staff researched the data from the Bureau of Labor Statistics to refute Rush's claims, but he has a problem here. I, too, checked the bureau's statistics, and Franken lied about their data. I mean, he *really* lied. Maybe the problem is not with Franken but with his researchers, who, judging by their competency, *ought* to be paid minimum wage.

Franken alleges there is "no liberal bias in the media," citing a study by the Pew Charitable Trusts to back his claims. In chapter 9, "Hummus and Liberal Bias," I show how Franken and his fourteen Harvard researchers distorted and totally misrepresented the findings of the polling data and study conducted by Pew.

Franken also cites a passage from Rush Limbaugh's *The Way Things Ought to Be* as evidence that Rush *hates* poor people. In chapter 6, I show how Franken took a satirical passage from the chapter "Demonstrating Absurdity, by Being Absurd" and deceptively presented it to portray Rush as someone who *does* hate the poor. How ironic that a professional satirist does not even recognize satire when somebody else writes it.

Franken attacks and smears Bill O'Reilly by claiming that he lied about the show *Inside Edition* winning a Peabody Award. In this book I show how Franken lied to his audience and readers by citing news articles that don't back Franken's claims in any way. Even more absurdly, Franken cited a news column that he *never read* as evidence to attack O'Reilly as a "pathological liar."

Franken accuses Ann Coulter of "lying with footnotes" by "citing a source and misrepresenting what it says." I prove over and over again that Franken himself is guilty of citing a source but totally misrepresenting what it says. Franken writes that this form of lying is "how to lie with footnotes #3" (on page 13 of *Lies and the Lying Liars Who Tell Them*). I call this form of deception a *Frankenism*. It's easier to remember than "how to lie with footnotes #3."

Al Franken on Truth

People have asked me, "Why write a book on Franken when so many liberals lie and smear conservatives?" While that is true, Al Franken is the *only* liberal who has made it a cottage industry, earning himself millions of dollars in the process. He lies, smears, distorts, manipulates, and attacks high-profile conservatives while professing to maintain the highest levels of truth, honor, accuracy, and decency himself.

Furthermore, Al Franken is the recognized face of the progressive radio network Air America and the activist wing of the Democratic Party. Without Franken, these institutions lose their credibility and standing with the hard Left. And as Al prepares to run for the U.S. Senate in 2008, don't the voters of Minnesota deserve to know the "real" Al Franken? By confronting the credibility of his claim to be truthful, I am laying down the gauntlet to the media in the hope that they will be a little more skeptical of his claims, particularly with the release of his new book and his statements at his public appearances.

Franken's poison has begun to seep into the language of Democratic leaders. Consider these recent examples:

- "I haven't (apologized) for calling him (Bush) a liar."—Senator Harry Reid (D-NV), April 2005
- "It's very hard to stop people who have never been acquainted with the truth."—Senator Hillary Clinton (D-NY), June 6, 2005

So how did Franken manage to create his cottage industry, earning millions of dollars and bamboozling the masses? Just read below:

- "Telling the truth is something I take seriously, and I try to hold myself to an impossibly high standard" (chapter 43, *Lies and the Lying Liars Who Tell Them*). While Franken professes to hold "impossibly high standards" of speaking truthfully, he makes no such claim of "impossibly high standards" when it comes to intellectual honesty, as will be evidenced throughout this book.
- "Because with fourteen researchers, I could do something that my targets seem incapable of doing—get my facts straight." (note from the author, *Lies and the Lying Liars Who Tell Them*).
- "I don't want to make it personal, and O'Reilly really has. He's gone after me and said I'm a smear artist. He has not pointed to one thing I've said that isn't true. . . . First of all, I'm funny. . . . It's done for comedic purpose. And I don't lie." (Interview with Howard Kurtz, CNN, August 28, 2003)
- "The difference between my book and those books on the Right is that mine is based on truth. . . . I believe truth is the most important thing. And that's what I'm doing." (Interview with Lou Dobbs, CNN, September 15, 2003)
- "He's very serious about honesty and integrity, and he doesn't let people off the hook. . . . He holds himself to a very high standard, and holds other people to the same standard." (Ben Wikler, one of fourteen Harvard Team Franken researchers and Al Franken's radio show producer in an e-mail response to me, March 26, 2004)
- "We are scrupulous about our facts." (Said twice by Franken on October 18, 2004, at the National Press Club)
- "Right-wing radio and Fox News manipulate their audience. I

try to serve my audience." (Franken at the National Press Club, October 18, 2004)

- "I don't lie." (*The Al Franken Show,* October 11, 2004)
- "Telling the truth is a moral concern." (*The Al Franken Show,* November 15, 2004)
- "Rush Limbaugh pulls information out of his butt. . . . I tell the truth. . . . These people just lie and lie . . . they have no shame. . . ." (Just about every day on *The Al Franken Show*)
- "I do tell the truth. And when I—and if I do get caught or if I do say something wrong, I admit it." (Franken, in an exchange with O'Reilly at the May 31, 2003, Los Angeles Book Expo America)
- "We tell the truth on the show." (Al Franken, speaking at the State Theatre in New Jersey, April 4, 2005)
- "Their [conservative talk radio] level is lying. We don't manipulate our audience. We serve our audience." ("A Conversation with Al Franken" in Portland, Oregon, May 10, 2005)
- "One of the great things about working with Al is that he has a serious adherence to facts. We don't say anything unless it's been researched, and we have a whole team of producers and researchers. If we say something on the show, we have documentation." (Franken cohost Katherine Lanpher, on QC Times.com, April 9, 2005)

I encourage you to refer to these Franken quotes and testimonials about him (especially the last one from Katherine Lanpher) regularly as you read the book. Then you will understand why it is so important to document Franken's lies and smears and, frankly, to always be a little leery of a man who always says, "I'm honest and I tell the truth."

Franken makes much of his fourteen Harvard researchers, known more affectionately as Team Franken throughout his book. It seems to be his defense mechanism, his way of saying, "There's no way that I lied or made any mistakes in my book." And yet, as I became more involved in my research, I found more and more lies, mistakes, discrepancies, sloppy research, and other sins that Franken would find intolerable if committed by conservatives. I wondered who these "fourteen Harvard researchers" were.

Franken's Foray into Talk Radio

From the late 1980s through the mid 1990s, conservative talk radio, led by Rush Limbaugh, grew by leaps and bounds. During this period, mainstream media dismissed the growth of Limbaugh and other conservative talk-show hosts as a short-term phenomenon. In 1992 they said that Rush would have nothing to talk about if George Bush lost. In 1996 they claimed that Rush would have nothing to talk about if Bill Clinton lost. As Rush has proven, it doesn't matter who is in power as far as the success of his show is concerned.

Frustrated by consistent losses at the polls, in 2004 Democrats and left-wing progressives put together their own talk radio outfit and called it Air America. The Left believed that Air America was desperately needed to compete with their conservative counterparts in order to, according to former Sen. Tom Daschle, "get our message out."

Get our message out? Are you kidding? Do you really need a radio program to say "Republicans are Nazis," "George Bush is Hitler," "Tax cuts equal apartheid," "Bruce Springsteen rocks," or "Americans should turn off their air conditioners so I can fly around in my corporate jets"?

Franken transformed himself from a *Saturday Night Live* writer and so-so comedian to a full-time bitter and often confused activist dedicated to responding to conservative talk radio and media. Franken relishes hearing others say he is "the liberal Rush Limbaugh" so he can say, "No, I'm not. I tell the truth."

Prior to his last political book, Franken was a virtual "nobody" in the arena of political punditry. He was elevated to "somebody" status by attacking the stars of the conservative and traditionalist movement. How long will he be allowed to grow (albeit at a slow and painful rate) his radio audience, give his opinions on cable news and other outlets, and receive awards that he clearly has not earned before his own credibility is legitimately challenged?

This book is based on my research of Franken's last two books on Rush Limbaugh and the conservative establishment and conversations with people he cites in those books. I engaged in more than thirty e-mail exchanges with him—he didn't include any Stuart Smalley jokes in his responses—monitored, recorded, and took notes on his daily radio program, and monitored his Web site and blogs, as well as his television appearances. Whereas Franken's "truth" comes from saying he had fourteen researchers, my truthfulness is validated by correctly citing the sources of my information.

Franken on Civility

Throughout this book you may come across Franken quotes that have already been mentioned. I repeat myself because Franken's smear tactics and hypocrisy bear repeating; they are applicable in so many different scenarios. For example, in his interview with CNN's Lou Dobbs on September 15, 2003, Franken claimed that his book is "bringing people together."

In the book he writes that the way for Democrats to win is to be "funny and attractive." But anybody who actually follows Franken knows that "bringing people together" and "funny and attractive" are not what Franken practices. Al "I Never Lie" Franken appears to say one thing to large audiences and something else when he thinks that only his loyal followers are listening.

For instance, on March 3, 2005, he participated in an online chat room in which he fielded questions from liberal college students. Here is an exchange between Al and a student about how liberals should fight back. Remember, this is from the man who says his goals are "bringing people together" and being "funny and attractive."

> Mr. Franken,
> I'm wondering what your advice is to combat the increasing number of right-wing funded organizations and publications on campus. . . . Is it best to take these groups on publicly and expose them for who they are, or just ignore them and not risk giving them extra publicity?

At 5:27 p.m. Al Franken answered the student:

> Out-organize them. Get involved in Campus Progress, which is hosting this webchat; get involved in MoveOn and host parties; expose any lies in their publications; beat them in debates; and remember—scorn and ridicule, scorn and ridicule.
> (source: http://www.thegreatsatan.com/archives/000212.html)

Scorn and ridicule? Funny, I didn't read that in any of his writings. What happened? Didn't funny and attractive work? Would Stuart Smalley approve of scorn and ridicule?

The Challenge

This book takes the fight to the guy who has challenged and begged the right wing to prove he lied.

In an October 2004 appearance on Howard Stern's show, Franken told Stern how he had recently addressed a college crowd about the upcoming elections and offered to debate some Republican hecklers who had been outside protesting his visit. Franken lamented how the students rejected his challenge. On that same program, he announced that he is prepared to debate any Republican.

Franken has even stated publicly that he is prepared to offer Bill O'Reilly $10,000 if he can refute his charges against him. Well, maybe O'Reilly doesn't need the money, but I accept the challenge.

Sean Hannity has described Michael Moore and Al Franken as "the two biggest losers in the Democrat party." Bill O'Reilly has said: "Franken is *more* dangerous than Michael Moore." So I say, let's compromise and just label Franken as a dangerous loser.

Following the Kerry loss in 2004, a number of high-profile Democrats acknowledged that Michael Moore did not help their elective efforts. Indeed, some of them suggested that he may have been the reason John Kerry lost.

Franken, on the other hand, is still viewed as their great hope for countering Rush Limbaugh and the "right-wing machine." At his farewell party on February 10, 2005, Democratic National Committee Chairman Terry McAuliffe singled out Al Franken for recognition for his contributions to the Democratic Party. On behalf of Republicans nationwide, I, too, would like to thank Al Franken (and Howard Dean) for his contributions to the Democrats.

After this book is published, Franken will still be defended by the extreme and irrelevant MoveOn.org types and other left-wing groups of the Democratic Party, whose existence is, in part, dependent upon the survival of Franken and Air America. However, the media and "mainstream" Democrats will have to acknowledge that things aren't so kosher in Frankenville.

I Am Embarrassed

I am embarrassed for everybody associated with the production of Franken's "lying liar" book. I am embarrassed for the parents of Team Franken, whose reputations will be forever tainted by their association with Franken's book of . . . uhmmm, lies and smears. And I am most embarrassed for Alex Jones, the director of the Shorenstein Center at Harvard University, who stood by Franken.

I am embarrassed for Robert Redford, who allowed himself to be hoodwinked into letting Franken take an hour* of broadcast time on Sundance channel. I'm also embarrassed for Al Franken's publishers at Dutton, who, according to Franken (June 17, 2005) have very strict guidelines for their authors to be truthful and accurate. (Franken made these comments while admonishing the publishers at Penguin [which owns Dutton] for publishing Ed Klein's book, *The Truth About Hillary*.)

In an interview broadcast on *CBS News Sunday Morning* on May 8, 2004, Franken said, "I stand up to bullies. I stand up to liars." In this book I stand up to Al Franken, the biggest bully and liar of them all.

---

*It's actually three hours: one of the show and two of repeats.

1 Franken Gets a Letter from a "Fan"

On his November 10, 2004, broadcast, Franken read an e-mail from a fan who had written to apologize for having been so *wrongheaded* for so long about Al Franken, thanks in part to things he alleges people like Bill O'Reilly, Sean Hannity, and Ann Coulter had said about him.

I couldn't help but be a tad suspicious about a letter that began:

> Dear Mr. Franken,
> I would like to begin by saying I'm a Hispanic male, married with two children, United States Navy submarine sailor. A Texan, a registered Republican who did vote for George Bush.

(The only thing missing from his opening was how his house is decorated with elephants).

He then went on to say that ever since listening to Franken's radio show the day after the 2004 presidential election and running out to buy *Lies and the Lying Liars Who Tell Them,* he now sees the world in a whole new light.

He wrote of his ability, he thought, to "smell a line of bull from a mile away," but felt embarrassed that he had been so taken in by the Right. All this, mind you, after listening to Franken's radio show for just a few days and reading through half his book. (Can you imagine if this sailor ever fell into enemy hands—he'd spill his guts in no time!)

He closed with: "Even though you've never heard of me, I'm sure you are aware of many . . . who hate you only because of what Ann Coulter, Bill O'Reilly, and the big fat idiots of the world say about you. Thank you, Mr. Franken. (Name not said on the air)"

After Franken read this letter, he said, "Now this is what we're trying to do on this show. This is why we're important and why Air America is important. Doing it with respect. Respect for the truth. Fighting back against the bastards, the O'Reillys, the Coulters, and the Hannitys." That's funny! My reaction to the letter was just "Aaach!"

On the surface, this piece of "fan mail" seemed somewhat suspicious. How convenient that Franken would get an apology letter from a Hispanic (minority) naval officer who used to hate Franken but now loves him, and who formerly loved O'Reilly, Coulter, and the others but now hates them. (Sounds like someone who is very emotionally stable.) And also a registered Republican who voted for President Bush? I would think Franken's staffer could just as easily have played the role of an elderly black woman whose benefits had been cut recently because of the evil Republicans. At least that would be more believable.

I, too, read Franken's book as part of my necessary research for this book. While this alleged "naval officer" may not have had the time I had to research every smear alleged by Franken, enough information is available online to refute or at least raise questions about Franken's allegations. At the very least, this "naval officer" could have written the people Franken attacked, just as he found the time to write Franken, to get their side of the story. Wasn't he the least bit curious as to whether these attacks on conservatives were even true? Was he so impressed with Franken writing "I don't like Ann Coulter" that he threw aside all his long-held beliefs? Was the logic of Franken's take on the Peabody/Polk Award mistake so impressive that the "officer" was overwhelmed with regret over voting for Bush? Or was he so easily "persuaded" because Franken claimed that he used fourteen Harvard researchers?

If Mr. Name Withheld is a *real* person and not just a Franken lackey, I dedicate this book to him and to all Americans of goodwill (and questionable judgment) who are so easily persuadable by people like Michael Moore and Al Franken.

Franken was especially pleased with the "fan's" closing sentence, in which he talks about what Ann Coulter, Bill O'Reilly, and Sean Hannity "say about" Franken. I've got news for you, Al. Coulter, O'Reilly, and Hannity *don't* talk about you (unless of course you count making jokes about you, in which case I stand corrected).

2 Polks, Peabodys, and Videotape

No self-respecting author could write a book about Al Franken without writing about the shot that was heard across the country in the spring of 2003. It was that day when Franken descended from the heavens to bear witness to the people that Fox News superstar Bill O'Reilly told a lie. This was no ordinary lie. No, it was the kind of lie that would bring serious repercussions for all involved.

Apparently, some years earlier while promoting his book *The No Spin Zone,* O'Reilly told his audience (in response to a question) that *Inside Edition*, a program he had once worked for, had been the recipient of the prestigious Peabody Award. In fact, thanks to Franken's many hours of painstaking research, it was learned that *Inside Edition* had won the prestigious Polk Award, not the Peabody.

Liberals like Franken were horrified to hear of O'Reilly's mistake. He had misspoken about an award! Thanks to "Super Truth Dude" (STD) Al Franken, a terrible injustice was brought to our attention.

It's not as if the American people are an unforgiving people. If a man, hypothetically speaking of course, is a leader in the racist Ku Klux Klan, we can forgive him and elect him to be a United States senator. If a man, hypothetically speaking of course, drives his car off a bridge and into the water, leaves the scene, and allows his girlfriend to drown, we can forgive him and elect him to the United States Senate as well. But when a man misattributes one journalism award for another, by gum, it's time to draw the line.

So the American people punished O'Reilly to make an example of him by making *The O'Reilly Factor* the most-watched program on cable news. In case someone thought this punishment wasn't severe enough, Americans listen to his radio program on more than four hundred radio stations across this country every day. Let's see now, how many stations is Franken on these days?

But enough of this churlishness! If truth-telling Al Franken says O'Reilly lied, then we owe it to him and everybody who listens to him to read the entire story for ourselves.

On May 31, 2003, book buyers and sellers, publishers, and authors gathered at the annual Book Expo America in Los Angeles, California. One event featured three authors who were there to promote their new books. For those who could not attend, it was broadcast later on C-Span.

Molly Ivins, author of *Bushwhacked*, another anti-Bush book (as if the marketplace weren't flooded with them already), went first and gave the audience a presentation on her book that lasted about fifteen minutes. She was aggressive and to the point, but not nearly as nasty as I expected. She held her own in a very dignified manner.

Then Bill O'Reilly took his turn to promote *Who's Looking Out for You?* The audience listened attentively as he explained the value and content of the book and made a rather persuasive case for buying and reading it. It worked for me. His presentation was nonpartisan. He shone light on *both* political parties and the powers that be without stooping to personal attacks.

Then it was Franken's turn to promote his new book, *Lies and the Lying Liars Who Tell Them.* It wasn't too long into his sales pitch that he explained to the luncheon and C-Span audience why Bill O'Reilly—who was sitting just a few feet away from him—deserved to be called one of the "lying liars" portrayed on the cover of his book. Just as Franken had undoubtedly hoped, O'Reilly got really upset, as any man of honor would, especially someone like O'Reilly, whose success is based on the trust between him and his viewers and readers. Soon the two men were into a raucous exchange onstage in front of the Book Expo crowd and national television audience. Franken got what he wanted: a cheap publicity stunt to promote his book.

What big lie had Franken exposed? "I've been on the air for six years," O'Reilly later said, "and this is what he has on me. That I once misspoke and claimed that *Inside Edition*, a show I once anchored, won a Peabody Award instead of a Polk."

This was *the confrontation* that made Franken a national figure, at least in the world of political demagoguery. Following this heated confrontation, many of the left-wing Web sites and blogs hailed Franken as their new hero.

CNN, MSNBC, and the other networks invited Franken on their programs to talk about his book and the blowup with O'Reilly. C-Span did everyone the courtesy of playing this segment over and over again as well. I, too, watched the repeats. I never get tired of hearing Al Franken say, "I'm a nice person. I'm honest. And I tell the truth."

If nothing else, the event itself was what great performances are made of. It had everything. It had drama and adventure. It had moments of suspense, anticipation, anger, and even laughter. Most of all it had Al Franken falling all over himself in lies, distortions, and smears against Bill O'Reilly.

It is amazing how Franken could take such an innocent misstatement that O'Reilly readily acknowledged to any reasonable person willing to listen (such as Lloyd Grove of the *Washington Post*) and turn it into a series of tales that even he contradicted at every opportunity. It was also amazing to read how Franken's version of events changed from what he said at Book Expo America to what he wrote in his book, to what he told Lloyd Grove and Buzzflash.com and other left-wing audiences, and to what he e-mailed me.

A Case Study of How Character Assassination Can Elevate You to Left-Wing-Icon Status

Is Al Franken honest? Does he maintain "impossibly high standards"? Does the left wing demand honesty and integrity from its leaders? Here's a case study on how he smeared Bill O'Reilly.

Remember what Franken charges: that conservatives lie, misrepresent the context of a story, do not thoroughly research a story, and blur the subject. Franken began:

"A couple of years ago, I was watching C-Span, which I love to watch. And I see Bill promoting his book, *The No Spin Zone*. And the format was actually like this [Book Expo], with a moderator . . . and the moderator said something like 'You hosted a show called *Inside Edition* that was kind of a tabloid.'

"'Tabloid Show?!' O'Reilly was indignant. 'We won two Peabodys!' <Clearly he is defending the integrity of *Inside Edition.*>

"'Well, still, you gotta admit, it was a tabloid show.'

"'I beg your pardon, but the Peabody is only the most prestigious award in journalism.'

"'But you have to admit, *Inside Edition* was something of a tabloid show.'

"'So you want us to give the Peabodys back?'

"So I'm watching this . . . and thinking, *Inside Edition* never won a Peabody. So I Nexised Peabody and *Inside Edition,* and I do get three hits. They're all Bill saying on his show that *Inside Edition* had won Peabodys." <*Note:* Franken admits that Bill was talking about *Inside Edition,* not himself, winning the award.>

Franken continues:

- **August 30, 1999—O'Reilly:** I anchored a program called *Inside Edition,* which has won a Peabody Award. <Who did he say won the Peabody? *Inside Edition* or himself?>
- **May 8, 2000—O'Reilly:** Well, all I've got to say to that is *Inside Edition* has won, I—I believe, two Peabody Awards, the highest journalism award in the country. <See the previous reply.>
- **May 19, 2000**—(with guest Arthel Neville):
  Neville: You hosted *Inside Edition. . . .*
  O'Reilly: Correct.
  Neville: Which is considered a tabloid show.
  O'Reilly: By whom?
  Neville: By many people.
  O'Reilly: Does that mean . . .
  Neville: And even you . . .
  O'Reilly: We throw the Peabody Awards back? We won Peabody Awards. <Yes, he says "we." Only a nitwit would interpret this,

> especially after reading the two prior comments, as anything other than defending the integrity of *Inside Edition.*>*

Later, Franken alters the story when speaking with left-wing webmeister BuzzFlash (June 12, 2003). "Well, it isn't just that Bill O'Reilly claims he won a couple of Peabody Awards. Whenever he was asked about *Inside Edition* and it being sort of a tabloid show, O'Reilly would indignantly say that they had won two Peabody Awards. 'Who says we're a tabloid show?'"

At the Book Expo, Franken said O'Reilly was responding to charges that *Inside Edition* was "tabloidish." Above, he says that O'Reilly claimed *he* won Peabodys. Second, saying "whenever" makes it sound like he is frequently challenged to defend *Inside Edition* against charges that it is a tabloid. According to Franken's *own* research, he was asked once by Arthel Neville and once while promoting *The No Spin Zone.*

• • •

Back to the Franken address at the Expo:

> "So I go to the Peabody Web site and look for *Inside Edition* and Peabodys, and there aren't any. So I'm thinking, what could they have won it for? 'Swimsuits: How Bare Is Too Bare?' Or Something on Madonna—on the father of her first baby? <Okay I'll give Franken this one. It was kind of funny.>
>
> "So then I called the Peabody people and asked the woman on the other end of the line, 'Yeah, did, by any chance, the show *Inside Edition* ever win a Peabody?'
>
> "There was some laughter on the other end. 'No, *Inside Edition* has never been the recipient of a Peabody Award.' <She was probably asking herself, "Who is this?">
>
> "So I called Bill. <In his book, Franken writes that he congratulated Bill on his success.>
>
> "'Yeah, what is it, Al?'

---

*On page 71 of *Lies and the Lying Liars Who Tell Them,* Franken wrote, "I'd found four separate incidents where he had claimed to have won Peabodys, three of them in Nexis." Re-read the three Nexis findings and see if O'Reilly claimed to have won Peabodys.

"'Okay, I saw you the other night on C-Span, and you said *Inside Edition* had won a couple of Peabody's.'

"'That's right. We did.'

"'Well, maybe you should check that out with the Peabody people. Because they don't think you did.'

"'I'll call you back.'

"About ten minutes later, Bill was on the line. 'It was a Polk.'

"'A Polk?' I asked.

"'Yeah. Just as prestigious as the Peabody.'

"I said, 'So there are *two* most prestigious awards in journalism?' <At this point, *I* would have hung up on him.>

"'Fine,' I said. 'But, Bill, don't you think it's a little odd that you got it wrong about a *journalism* award?'

"'Okay, Al, if you want to go after me, go after me.'

"So, I did. <What a schmuck.>

"I called Lloyd Grove at the *Washington Post*'s 'The Reliable Source' column. Lloyd ran with it on March 1, 2001, after checking Nexis. He also offered Bill the opportunity to respond and quoted him saying, 'Al Franken is on a jihad against me. So I got mixed up between a Peabody and a Polk Award, which is just as prestigious.'

"I thought Bill's reaction was odd. He hadn't said, 'Omigod! How embarrassing! I can't believe I've been saying that! Thank you so much, Al, for calling me. Now I won't humiliate myself by making that mistake again. Thank you so much for calling me rather than taking it public.' Instead it was, 'Go after me if you want.' <Note to Al: Revenge is a dish best served cold. What does that mean anyway?> Okay. So that was over. He got caught making a mistake, and was kind of a jerk about it. Fine."

Franken continues:

". . . Hang on. A couple other papers picked up the Peabody story from the *Post*. *Newsday* ran a March 8 column by Robert Reno titled 'Some Factors About O'Reilly Aren't Factual.'

"On March 13, O'Reilly introduced that night's Personal Stories segment: 'Attack Journalism.'

"'This is personal to me, because some writers are really violating every tenet of fairness in what they're saying in print about your humble servant.'

"His guest was Michael Wolff, the terrific media columnist for *New York* magazine. O'Reilly and Wolff began by discussing the definition of 'attack journalism.' O'Reilly, it was clear, considered himself an expert on attack journalism, but not for the reason you might think.

O'Reilly: If you lie about someone it goes right up on the Nexis, where everyone can read it. . . . I'll give you an example. Guy says about me, couple of weeks ago, O'Reilly said he won a Peabody Award. Never said it. You can't find a transcript where I said it. You—there is no one on earth you could bring in that would say I said it. Robert Reno in *Newsday,* a columnist, writes in his column, calls me a liar, all right? And it's totally fabricated. That's attack journalism. It's dishonest, it's disgusting, and it hurts reputations.
Wolff: It's also incorrect journalism, if it's wrong . . .
O'Reilly: It is wrong.
Wolff: Okay, well, then the guy made a mistake.
O'Reilly: No, come on. He made a mistake that's—lives forever in the Nexis. And did he write a column the next day saying he made a mistake?
Wolff: Well, obviously, obviously, obviously he should—usually, I find, if someone's made a mistake, if you ask them to correct it, they do correct it.
O'Reilly: No, not in this society anymore.

"So Bill, I'm sorry . . . I call you a liar . . . one of the many people, who do lie, in my book."

This is the entire story, as told by Franken at the Book Expo, then written by Franken in his book.

A BRIEF SYNOPSIS TO THIS POINT:

1. We have Franken astutely picking up on O'Reilly's making a mistake about which prestigious journalism award *Inside Edition* had won several years earlier, a Peabody or a Polk.
2. Acting juvenile, Franken calls O'Reilly to correct him on his error, then taunts him after making the correction.

3. Franken then leaks the story to Lloyd Grove of the *Washington Post* in an effort to embarrass O'Reilly.
4. Franken then blurs the story from "we won" a Peabody to "I won" a Peabody. When Franken called O'Reilly after speaking with the Peabody lady, he only questioned O'Reilly about *Inside Edition* winning one. He never questioned him about allegedly claiming to have won the Peabody himself.
5. Then Franken accuses O'Reilly of "attacking" "honest reporter" Robert Reno, a reporter whose columns, in *my* opinion, are among the most vicious I have ever read. That is saying a lot, since I also regularly read the *New York Times* columns of Paul Krugman, Bob Herbert, and Maureen Dowd.
6. After several years of *The O'Reilly Factor* being on TV, the only thing Franken could come up with to attack O'Reilly was that he mixed up the Peabody and Polk Awards. Franken then concluded by saying O'Reilly "got caught making a mistake."

After reading Franken's rendition of events, I decided to check out Grove's article for myself. I couldn't believe that the *Washington Post* would have a Franken sycophant in its employ.

I decided to see what Lloyd Grove said in his *Washington Post* gossip column on March 1, 2001. Here is a portion of that column:

> Investigative humorist Al Franken thought something was amiss when Fox News star Bill O'Reilly . . . claimed that his previous show, the syndicated tabloid *Inside Edition,* had won the coveted George Foster Peabody award. . . .
>
> "I called Bill and he was nice enough to get back to me," Franken told us. "Turns out he's been confused: In 1996, *Inside Edition* won a Polk, which does start with a 'P.' You know, it's one thing to get your facts wrong on Fox. That's expected. But lying on C-Span? I don't think you should do that."
>
> Yesterday O'Reilly told us: "Al Franken is on a jihad against me. So I got mixed up between a Peabody Award and a Polk Award, which is just as prestigious. Is this an illogical mistake? My comment is: We did good work. There was no intention to mislead. I really don't understand what Franken's problem is."

So Lloyd Grove basically repeated what Franken told the Book Expo audience with one caveat. At the Expo Franken acknowledged that O'Reilly made a mistake on the Peabody/Polk story, but when he talked to Lloyd Grove, he called it a lie.

When I read the Grove column, I was a bit mystified. Grove certainly didn't accuse him of lying, and he didn't he seem to take the same umbrage with the award confusion that Franken took. So I called Grove, who now works at the *New York Daily News*.

> **Skorski:** Good afternoon Mr. Grove. My name is Alan Skorski. I am doing research on Al Franken. I read your article from 2001 about the O'Reilly Peabody/Polk thing.
> **Grove:** Yes?
> **Skorski:** I was just wondering—I didn't get the sense, from your article at least, that you were accusing O'Reilly, as Franken has, of lying about the award.
> **Grove:** O'Reilly wasn't lying. It was an honest mistake.
> **Skorski:** Yeah, okay, but Franken is writing and telling audiences that O'Reilly lied about the Peabody Award, and your article, which he refers to, doesn't suggest that he was lying.
> **Grove:** Yeah, I know. Franken just enjoys needling O'Reilly.

Needling? I'll have to check my dictionary and see if *needling* falls under the definition of "impossibly high standards."

Remember, in his chapter titled, "What Is a Lie?" Franken wrote, "Calling someone a liar is a serious charge. . . . Telling the truth is something I take seriously."

Even before I called Grove I began emailing Franken myself and asking, "What was the big deal? O'Reilly has been on TV for years, and this is the best you've got?"

Franken responded promptly, in a June 2, 2003, e-mail:

> The point of the Peabody-Polk story was not that he mistook a Polk for a Peabody. The point was that after he acknowledged that he made the mistake in the *Washington Post,* a columnist from *Newsday* wrote that he had done that. And then, he attacked that columnist and denied ever having said it in the most vehement terms.

After I replied, Franken e-mailed me again, on June 3, 2003.

> Reno wrote a piece in *Newsday* citing the *Washington Post* article, and a few days later O'Reilly attacked Reno on the air for lying. He said something to the effect: "This guy Reno says I claimed to have won a Peabody"—he claimed on several occasions which I documented in my speech and which he admitted to in the *Post* article. . . . "I defy anyone to find anywhere that I said I won a Peabody."
>
> This guy is a liar. If anyone is pathological, it is O'Reilly. That was the point of the story about the Peabodys. Once again—only a week after conceding that he had been in error, he attacks the guy as a liar for saying he had made the error.

After I replied to this, Franken sent a third e-mail, this time on June 8, 2003:

> If you still don't think that bashing the guy from *Newsday* the way he did rises to the level of lying, I don't get it. He called the guy a liar, said that it was a total fabrication, and defied anyone to find an instance where he had said he had won a Peabody. This is about ten days after acknowledging that he had in the *Washington Post.*

Franken once again blurs the charges against O'Reilly. By Franken's *own account* at the Expo luncheon, O'Reilly clearly stated that *Inside Edition,* not O'Reilly himself, was the recipient of the Peabody Award. And this was only to defend the show's integrity against charges that it was a tabloid show. As Franken said in a June 13, 2003, interview with Buzzflash.com, "Whenever he was asked about *Inside Edition* and it being sort of a tabloid show, O'Reilly would indignantly say that they had won two Peabody Awards."

When O'Reilly attacked Reno as a liar and said, "I defy anyone to find anywhere that I said I won a Peabody," O'Reilly was being truthful. He *never* said, "I won a Peabody" (and Franken acknowledges that in writing himself). This is not a question of splitting hairs. There is a big difference between a show winning an award and an *individual* on the show winning an award. Franken attempts to confuse his readers by blurring the two.

It is interesting to look at some of the highlights of Robert Reno's column that originally appeared in *Newsday*, March 8, 2001, in light of how much was later made of it:

> To be fair to him, Bill O'Reilly, the ranting Fox-TV star and surprise best-selling author, has never pretended he grew up in a trailer park or suffered through a potato famine.
>
> But he's actually done everything else to stress a humble, blue collar pedigree as pure as any dog pound mutt's. . . . Yes, O'Reilly went to Harvard. He never lets you forget it.
>
> O'Reilly also has repeatedly boasted of his Peabody awards, not exactly the attitude of a maverick who shuns the approval of the media grandees who heap these Peabodys and Pulitzers on each other annually in an orgy of mutual congratulation. Actually he has never won a Peabody.
>
> He explains that he got it confused with the Polk award, which, incidentally, he also never received but which had been won after he left the show.
>
> But enough of this churlishness. If O'Reilly says his old dad never earned more than $35,000 a year, maybe it ought to give him total freedom to claim suffering, lower-middle-class martyrdom and the right to speak for America's proletariat. . . .
>
> This is more than the Irish or the blameless, upstanding residents of the nation's trailer parks should have to put up with.

Reno's personal assault on O'Reilly not only illustrates his personal meanness about O'Reilly, it also exposes Franken of not only lying about *O'Reilly* but also lying about the people Franken *claims* O'Reilly lied about.

Reno dedicated just seventy-five words to the Peabody story—which he got *all wrong*—and Franken later claimed that it was written as a follow-up to the Grove article.

In February 2004, I e-mailed Franken to ask him if he had actually *read* the Reno article. This is important, because on June 3, 2003, he e-mailed me that Reno had *cited* Grove as the source and basis of the Peabody/Polk story, which he did not do. Further, the Reno story, which Franken claims is the basis for his attack on O'Reilly, had nothing to do with the Grove article or the Peabody/Polk Awards other than referring to the awards in passing.

On February 2, 2004, Franken responded:

> I can't remember exactly what I wrote you last about Reno, but I doubt I said he cited Grove. It just came on the heels of Grove's article and I assumed it was the impetus for Reno's article.

After I replied, Franken wrote on February 3, 2004:

> I'm assuming Reno Nexised the references to O'Reilly.

Remember that on June 3, 2003, Franken had e-mailed me, "Reno wrote a piece for *Newsday* citing the *Washington Post* article." But the truth is, Reno *did not* cite Grove's article, nor did he suggest that his column was a follow-up to Lloyd Grove's column.

I also called Lloyd Grove back to ask him about the Reno article and how his story, according to Franken, was the impetus for Reno's column.

> **Skorski:** Listen, Franken claims that Robert Reno wrote an article for *Newsday* and cited your article as the source. Has Reno ever called you to verify the story, or anything like that?
> **Grove:** Reno never called me, and we have never spoken about the story.

In his e-mails to me in June 2003, Franken became aggravated with me for not ceding his point and wrote that the whole point of the Peabody/Polk story was to expose O'Reilly as "pathological" for admitting to the *Washington Post* his mistake and then calling Reno, whose article was based on the story, a liar.

But as is clear above, the Reno article had nothing to do with the Grove story other than mentioning the Peabody Award in passing. Reno falsely wrote, "O'Reilly also has repeatedly boasted of his Peabody awards." Eager to smear O'Reilly, Franken does not write in his book or tell the Expo audience that O'Reilly boasts of *his* Peabodys. He does, however, make that claim to BuzzFlash, which is ironic given his claim in that interview about how meticulous he is about truth and accuracy.

In my own Lexis/Nexis searches, the only time O'Reilly mentions the awards is in reference to *Inside Edition* itself. He neither states nor implies that he personally won awards. There is a clear distinction.

In e-mails dated February 2 and 3, 2004, Franken defended his referencing Reno's article by writing, "I *assumed* Reno's article was based on Grove's story" and "I *assumed* Reno had done his own Nexis research." How does one make the claim that he has "impossibly high standards" and that he used "fourteen researchers . . . I get my facts straight" and then rely on "assumptions" to prove a point? This brings several questions to my mind:

1. Why didn't Franken or his fourteen Harvard researchers take the time to read Reno's article, which Franken cites as evidence that Bill O'Reilly is a pathological liar? I mean, as Franken himself says, "calling someone a liar is a serious charge."
2. After receiving a hefty advance on his book, did Franken not have the three dollars to archive Reno's article?
3. Isn't it remarkable that of all the stories from his book Franken could have chosen to talk about in promoting *Lies and the Lying Liars Who Tell Them* at Book Expo, he selected one that was completely dishonest from beginning to end? Franken has repeatedly challenged O'Reilly to prove that he smeared him. Here is the proof.
4. Who reveals the symptoms of being "truth challenged" and a "pathological liar"? Bill O'Reilly, who admitted mistaking one prestigious award for another in defending a program he had anchored many years earlier? Or Al Franken, who, based on "assumptions," repeatedly cited Robert Reno's article (which did not say what Franken alleged it said) to attack O'Reilly?

"What a Horrible Person!!!"

This chapter appears early in the book because his conflict with O'Reilly put Franken on the map. Until then, he was known as "that guy from *Saturday Night Live*" and "the guy who wrote that book on Rush Limbaugh."

Franken continues to distort other things O'Reilly says or does every chance he gets. While the preceding story took place in the spring of 2003, the following smear was made against O'Reilly on a much more serious subject in the spring of 2005. Apparently, old habits never die.

Yes, I think Al Franken is a horrible person, but that is not the point of the following.

Since June 6, 2005, Franken has been on the Sundance Channel at 11:30 p.m. for a one-hour nightly televised program that rebroadcasts various segments of his radio show. On June 8, 2005, Franken blasted O'Reilly for telling his television audience that "Senator Biden called for the closing down of Gitmo and our military prison system," by editing portions of Biden's *actual* interview with George Stephanopoulos from the preceding Sunday to make it look like Biden said something he really didn't say. I was sort of listening with only one ear—not quite the same as fighting with half my brain tied behind my back—when I first heard it, and it sounded like Franken may have been onto something.

But when I watched the segment on television and saw how Franken had put it together, I could see what O'Reilly had *actually* done. All I could say was, Holy crap! O'Reilly was *not* guilty of pulling a Michael Moore—editing a film to change the context of a story—as Franken had suggested.

The story is fascinating. On June 6 Senator Biden appeared on ABC's *This Week* and was asked by "Stephy" Stephanopoulos about the current news stories alleging torture by our troops against terror suspects in the U.S. military prisons. Biden told him he had introduced a bill that would set up a commission to review the entire military prison system and report back to Congress. I don't know if we need yet another commission, but still, his idea seemed fair enough. I suspect that the actual reason he wanted a commission was to use it to inflict political pain on the Bush administration.

At this point conservative readers are likely in agreement with me over what I believe were Biden's *actual* intentions. Undoubtedly, liberal or left-wing readers are thinking, "There you go again. Accusing Democrats of being against our troops and country." Not so fast. Read on.

As I suspected, my suspicions were not unfounded. As a follow-up, Stephy asked Biden if he thought Gitmo and Abu Ghraib should be shut down.

In responding to the question, Biden paused briefly, then said *that he would like to wait for the commission's report, so it wouldn't be just him calling for the closing* (emphasis mine). In other words, he was saying, "Yes, I want them closed down. I just need some cover from another agency."

Way to be a stand-up guy, Joe!

Now Franken came into the picture. He played a clip of O'Reilly playing a clip of Biden saying that he supports closing down the prison system. Franken, on Sundance, played a side-by-side video of Biden's interview on *This Week* and O'Reilly's replaying of it on *The Factor,* showing that O'Reilly edited some portions to make it look like Biden said something he really didn't say.

In the ABC video Biden said that he would like a commission to come and "make recommendations to the Congress." Later, he restated his position, declaring he wanted it "to support shutting down the prisons." On *The Factor,* all we heard was Biden saying *he* supports closing down the prisons, without mentioning the role of the commission.

The problem is, the role of the commission wasn't the point of O'Reilly's "Talking Points Memo." What O'Reilly pointed out, correctly, was that Biden had joined with the chorus of those who wanted to hurt the president and our anti-terror efforts by supporting the prison closings. The context was left unchanged. Just some words that didn't change the story were edited out. Period!

"What a horrible person!" Franken exclaimed (of O'Reilly).

However, the context remained consistent. In both clips we clearly understand that Biden supports closing down the prisons, which in practice would be handing a victory to the terrorists and their sponsors, not to mention left-wing groups like Amnesty International who seek to undermine our country.

Toward the end of the segment, Franken continued his assault on O'Reilly for calling on the president to appoint a commission. He edited the part that showed appointing a commission was *Biden's* idea, implying that somehow O'Reilly was stealing Biden's idea.

Bill O'Reilly doesn't have to steal any ideas from anybody, but if he *were* going to take somebody else's idea, it's doubtful he would steal one from Joe Biden. The clear and obvious distinction between the two proposed commissions was that Biden wanted a commission to hurt the president, undermine our war on terror, and release a report recommending that we shut down our prison system. On the other hand, O'Reilly's proposal was for the president to go on the *offensive* by appointing a commission in order to exonerate our prison guards and put all the rumors and innuendo of abuse and torture to bed once and for all.

But the sliming and distortions don't end there.

Just as Franken sought to embarrass O'Reilly by running to Lloyd Grove with the Peabody story, he ran to Howard Kurtz of CNN and the *Washington Post* to peddle this tripe about O'Reilly's "scandalous" editing practices.

On June 21, 2005, Franken brought up the O'Reilly/Biden episode again. This time he added a new wrinkle. He told his audience that when he approached him, Kurtz, replied, "Well, you kind of expect that from Fox News." This Kurtz quote made Franken euphoric, and he repeated it several times.

I was surprised. Kurtz has always come across as a professional, not as someone who would resort to Franken-style cheap shots. So I e-mailed Mr. Kurtz on June 22 to ask him about the quotes Franken had attributed to him. It seems that not only did Franken get caught falsely smearing O'Reilly and Fox News, but he also lied about what Howard Kurtz had told him.

Kurtz wrote:

> I did not say that, by the way. What I said is that these charges are made against Fox News (and others) all the time and that in my job I have to be careful about focusing only on the most egregious examples. I looked into the matter—having been called by Biden's office, not Franken—and decided there wasn't enough for me to write. I didn't think O'Reilly should have cut out Biden calling for an independent commission and then called for one himself, but I didn't find the editing to be terribly unfair, given the way Biden's remarks were widely reported.

---

*As I wrote in the Introduction, when Al Franken smears or calls someone a liar, people listen. His poison reaches media beyond our borders and continent. The UK's *Guardian,* on June 27, repeated Franken's smears against O'Reilly and Fox News, and the misattributed comments by Howard Kurtz.

3 "If I Get Caught in a Mistake, I Admit It"

—Al Franken to Bill O'Reilly at Book Expo America, May 31, 2003

It is fairly common knowledge that if you lie often enough, you will get caught. If you are Al Franken and you get caught, you either say you were joking or accuse your accuser of lying. It is also common knowledge that if you lie to enough people, you will often start to forget what you have said and to whom you have said it. Remember how Franken couldn't remember and became a little confused over what he told his audience at the Los Angeles Book Expo versus what he wrote in his book versus what he told BuzzFlash versus what he e-mailed me about the Peabody/Polk Award attack on O'Reilly?

Following the Peabody/Polk Award smear, which exposed Franken's lies, distortions, incorrectly cited sources, and misrepresentations of what those sources said, came even more evidence of Franken misleading his audience.

Franken's main charge against O'Reilly regarding the Peabody/Polk Award was that he attacked columnist Robert Reno by calling him a liar for writing that "O'Reilly said *he* won a Peabody."

Franken made his exposé on O'Reilly the cornerstone of his effort to unmask conservatives as liars and frauds. The length Franken was willing to go to hurt O'Reilly was mind-boggling.

Franken and I exchanged several e-mails on the subject. See if you can find any evidence that Franken admitted or even considered the possibility that he *may* have made a mistake, as he claims he does when he is wrong (see the title of this chapter).

On February 2, 2004, 11:45 a.m., I e-mailed Franken, "Reno wrote that O'Reilly claimed to have won the Peabody. By your own admission, O'Reilly never claimed he won. He said *IE [Inside Edition]* won. There is a big difference."

Franken's response at 8:19 p.m. was, "O'Reilly said several times 'WE won two Peabodys. Do you want us to give OUR Peabodys back?' What part of the first person plural doesn't contain 'I'?"

My reply at 10:19 p.m. was:

> You cite three separate claims (in your book) by O'Reilly:
>
> - "August 30, 1999: I anchored a program called *Inside Edition,* which has won a Peabody Award." <*Note:* He says *Inside Edition,* not "I" or "we.">
> - "May 8, 2000: Well, all I've got to say is *Inside Edition* has won, I—I believe two Peabody Awards." <Again, *Inside Edition,* not "I" or "we.">
> - "May 19, 2000: In an interview with friend and colleague Arthel Neville, he said, '. . . We throw the Peabodys back?'" <Jackpot! There's Franken's "we." Franken also cited these three quotes at Book Expo.>
>
> You give three examples. One uses "we" and so you use *that* as evidence that O'Reilly lied to everyone? Two things wrong here. One, for a guy who has claimed numerous times that you hold yourself to "an impossibly high standard," this is grasping at straws. Secondly, if you talk to anybody in New England this week, you will find millions of people saying, "*We* won the Super Bowl" [*Note:* This exchange took place following the New England Patriots' winning the 2004 Super Bowl.]
>
> At the LA Book Expo, you quoted O'Reilly as saying, *IE* won the award, as he was trying to defend *IE* as a news program, not tabloid.

Franken responded on February 3, 2004, 1:11 a.m.:

> I also heard O'Reilly use "we" when he said it on C-Span, which is not Nexusable. If O'Reilly had used the "we" in the same way New

Englanders say, "We won the Super Bowl," it would have been quite easy for him to explain in response to the Reno article that, "I can see how someone might have thought I was saying I won two Peabody's but I meant we in the sense that I still feel part of my old program and I meant that I was proud they won two Peabody's. I can see how Mr. Reno could have easily gotten the impression that I was claiming to have won something personally that I had not, but the truth is I was just defending the show I had worked for." He easily could have said something like that. Instead, he went after the guy, calling it "disgusting," etc.

I replied on February 3, 12:54 p.m.:

Al, I will address your response in greater detail later. But two things here. You said yourself at the Book Expo that O'Reilly was responding to a question as to whether *IE* was "tabloid" or legitimate news. He was clearly defending the integrity of *IE* by mentioning the Peabody, and not trying to elevate himself.

You seem to want to have it both ways. You say you have the "highest standards of truth," but you also twist people's words to satisfy your agenda. This is the second time you have written, "O'Reilly *should have* . . ." The first time was when you wrote that "he *should have* thanked me for telling him that he made a mistake about winning the Peabody, so that he wouldn't embarrass himself in the future," and now he *should have* been more clear in his response to Reno.

No other author I am aware of makes claims of "highest standards of truth" and then twists people's words.

I can't believe that after attacking O'Reilly at the Book Expo, and then on several interviews, including "Buzz Flash," on his attacks on Reno, that you never bothered to read the Reno article yourself.

I could write a book attacking people based on "assumptions." But if I did that, I wouldn't talk about "high standards of truth."

Franken responded on February 3, 8:54 p.m.:

I repeat. He said, "We won two Peabodys." Not "'they' won

two Peabodys." And he said it several times. "You want us to give our Peabodys back?" "We won Peabodys."

He and they didn't win Peabodys. A reporter for *IE* won a Polk for a report he did a year after O'Reilly left.

He also continues to lie. He now says he had nothing to do with Fox's lawsuit against me. . . . He has made false claims regarding the relative sales of our books and Hillary's book. . . . Worse still, on Terry Gross's show he made outrageous false statements. . . ."

The final response from me was on February 3, 9:20 p.m.:

Al, you are changing the subject. You and I had countless e-mail exchanges [which began in early June 2003] about the Peabody-Polk thing. You grew impatient with me because I wouldn't address O'Reilly's attack on Reno.

Where is the "we" coming from? I read Grove's article. O'Reilly consistently referred to *IE* to defend its integrity and you know that. The fact that the show won an award after he left would be further evidence that he didn't win (nor would he claim to have won). At the Book Expo, YOU said he responded to a question about *IE* being a tabloid.

You admitted that you didn't read Reno's article, so how could you defend him?

It is obvious that I am very persistent (and need to get a life), and Franken does not accept that he makes mistakes, or in this case flat-out lies, when he gets caught. This is another charge he frequently makes against conservatives.

Toward the end of our exchanges, he jumped from the Peabody/Polk argument to Fox's lawsuit against him, to Hillary's book sales, and then to other O'Reilly "false accusations," changing subjects when he can't win an argument. This is another tactic, by the way, he frequently accuses conservatives of using.

• • •

One can prove once and for all that Franken *knew*—yes, he *knew*—that O'Reilly was defending the integrity of *Inside Edition* and that he (O'Reilly) never claimed to have won the award himself. This is provable by using Franken's own words. This means Franken lied and did not simply make a mistake.

On page 67 of *Lies and the Lying Liars Who Tell Them,* Franken writes, "But what on earth could *Inside Edition* have won a Peabody for?" He does not write, "But what on earth could O'Reilly have won a Peabody for?"

On page 68 he writes, "So I went to my Nexis and put in 'Peabody Award' and '*Inside Edition.*' They were all Bill O'Reilly claiming that *Inside Edition* had won a Peabody."

He does *not* write, "I put in Peabody Award and Bill O'Reilly," and all were Bill O'Reilly claiming that he had won a Peabody. This is ample evidence that Franken knew he was being deceptive about O'Reilly and lying about him.

On page 68 Franken writes, "Next I went to the Peabody website . . . No *Inside Edition.* Franken does *not* write, "Next I went to the Peabody website . . . No Bill O'Reilly."

On pages 68–69 he writes, "I called the Peabody people, and asked the woman on the other end of the line, "Yeah, did, by any chance, the show *Inside Edition* ever win a Peabody?" He does *NOT* write, "I called the Peabody people . . . 'Did, by any chance, Bill O'Reilly ever win a Peabody?'"

On page 69 Franken writes about calling O'Reilly on the phone, "I saw you the other night on C-Span, and you said *Inside Edition* had won a couple of Peabodys." He does *not* write, "I saw you the other night . . . and you said you had won a couple of Peabodys."

• • •

The blowup over the Peabody/Polk Award was what helped put Franken on the map. It was played over and over again on different networks and Web sites and made Franken a major league left-wing smear merchant.

Al Franken lied about Bill O'Reilly. I caught him. He admitted nothing.

Maybe that's where I went wrong. Maybe Franken *does* admit when he makes a mistake. It's when he lies and gets caught that he doesn't admit it.

What Did He Know, and When Did He Lie About It?

While this could easily be another example of Franken lying when he says, "when I get caught . . . I admit it," this is much more serious. This is a bald-faced lie; a cover-up.

The *New York Post* reported extensively over the summer of 2005 of how a Bronx-based tax-funded organization, the Gloria Wise Boys and Girls club, had loaned close to $1 million to Air America to help get it off the ground. That in and of itself is scandalous. Since when did it become the role of social services organizations to become investors in liberal propaganda ventures? And why hadn't Air America repaid the loan?

Evan Cohen, who served on the board at Gloria Wise, was also one of the original owners of Air America, whose role it was to raise enough money for the network to survive for a few years even without the networks having to turn a profit (how prophetic).

As I closely followed the story, I just couldn't find any wrongdoing on Franken's part. And besides, we all know how much Franken cares about the little people, so there is no way he could be involved in a scheme that swindles underprivileged kids and seniors.

But as was reported by the *Washington Times* on September 11, 2005, Al Franken signed a notarized document (dated in the fall of 2004) titled "AAR Liabilities." The document—again, signed by Franken—notes $875,000 claimed by the Gloria Wise Boys and Girls Club, of which $167,000 was transferred in late 2003 and another $708,000 was transferred in March 2004.

Furthermore, as noted by conservative pundit Michelle Malkin, according to a November 2004 settlement agreement between former Air America head honchos Evan Cohen and Rex Sorensen and Air America's current owners and investors at Piquant LLC, Al Franken was smack dab in the middle of negotiations over the debts owed by the liberal radio network—including the Gloria Wise loan.

Now we know that O'Reilly misstating one journalism award for another is a dastardly lie, but really Al, taking money from the kids and then lying about it?

4 Air Un-America

"Today is both an ending and a beginning: an end to the right-wing dominance of talk radio, and a beginning of a battle for truth, a battle for justice, a battle indeed for America itself . . ."

—Al Franken's opening monologue on March 31, 2004, Air America's debut

Little did Franken know that three weeks later it would be a battle for Air America just to pay its bills.

The Air America radio network was launched in 2004 as the liberal response to what had been, until then, conservative-dominated talk radio. Given who and what is on the network, it might be more appropriate to call it "Air Un-America." No, I'm not saying "Un-America" because they are liberals.

The marquee show of the network, *The Al Franken Show,* airs in the 12:00 p.m. to 3:00 p.m. time slot to challenge conservative talk radio king Rush Limbaugh. I'll never forget the time Franken told his audience, "I'm often compared to Rush Limbaugh." Yeah, right, and I'm often compared to Tom Cruise.

Other than sharing the same time slot, there are no comparisons between Limbaugh and Franken. Rush Limbaugh had one hundred affiliates after just three months on the air with a concept—talk radio—that hadn't proven itself in the marketplace. Franken, who had the groundwork laid for him, had only fifty-one affiliates after one year. As of April 6, 2005, Al Franken was on fifty-three affiliates, while conservative Bill Bennett, whose radio show was launched a week after Franken's, had 116. Rush Limbaugh has talent on loan from G-d. In my opinion, Franken doesn't believe in G-d, which probably explains why G-d hasn't loaned him any radio talent.

The show did not start off being called *The Al Franken Show.* It was called *The O'Franken Factor.* Isn't Franken clever? Fox News has *The O'Reilly Factor,* so Franken thought he would get a lot of laughs if he mimicked it. How did *Saturday Night Live* ever let him get away? And while O'Reilly's credo is "the no spin zone," Franken's credo is "the no sense zone."

For all of the left-wing bellyaching and whining that they don't have a voice in talk radio, their first "star" started off by looking for a fight with Fox News star Bill O'Reilly. On his radio program and at the Air America launch party, Franken announced that the reason for calling his show *The O'Franken Factor* is: "There's really one reason and one reason only, and that is to annoy and to bait Bill O'Reilly."

In August Franken announced a new name for the show, stating, "Since we've done everything we can to get O'Reilly to sue us—it's obvious he won't—we've accomplished what we wanted, and from today on we will be called *The Al Franken Show.*" Ironically, Franken has charged author Ed Klein, who penned *The Truth About Hillary,* of being greedy and seeking quick cash, and yet he admits he wanted to get sued again, ostensibly to make money off the publicity.

But the name of the program really doesn't matter. Franken's show was malicious, dishonest, dull, and boring when it was called *The O'Franken Factor,* and it has remained malicious, dishonest, dull, and boring since the name change.

• • •

So what can Franken's fans and listeners expect from the three-hour show? Daily news? Brilliant analysis? Reports from around the nation? Interesting dialogue with callers and guests? Clever and witty parodies? Gut-busting comedy? If you answered *no* to all of the above, you were correct. Yet this was the show that was supposed to be a counter to Rush Limbaugh.

Though Franken took to the airwaves at the end of March, I didn't actually listen to his program until the July 4 weekend. With it being a holiday weekend, Limbaugh's program was a repeat of "the best of Rush." So I tuned in Air America, figuring, "How lame and annoying could Franken's show be?"

I was soon to find out. Franken's first guest that day was popular Libertarian talk-show host Neal Boortz. Turned out, this was a Franken repeat as well. The original broadcast was June 2, 2004.

One of the first questions out of Franken's mouth was, "Why did you lie about me?"

This was the first time I had listened to Al since I had read his book about "liars" and exchanged numerous e-mails with him. "Here we go again," I thought. "Everybody that argues with Al is a liar." My next thought was, "Why have a guest on if you're just going to ask him why he lied about you?" If Franken was truly incensed, why wouldn't he just call him or send him a nasty e-mail?

Within a few uncomfortable moments, Boortz realized he was being sucker punched, and Franken had no objective for the interview other than to embarrass him. So Boortz wised up and hung up on him.

When I spoke to Boortz about this episode, he explained that he was actually offering to help Franken by letting him host a segment on his program, which has a much wider listening audience. "And typical of Franken, this was the thanks I got," Boortz told me.

The Franken Show is kind of like a soap opera: if you miss a few weeks of the show, after one or two episodes you are pretty much caught up. It's just that predictable: the same stuff every day recycled in new packaging. No different from a soap opera. Franken opens up with the "lies of the day," and some clever and well-thought-out quip like "Right-wing liars, we're watching you." Oh, how *scary*!

During my earliest days of listening to the show, I found Franken's obnoxious name-calling an attention grabber: "Bush is a liar." "Rush is a liar." "O'Reilly just lies and lies." After a while, it becomes the same old thing. How many times can you listen to "Guess what Rush said . . . ?" before you get bored?

Even the title, *The Al Franken Show,* is deceiving. The show is not about him. It's about the people whose success he envies! So he uses his platform to lash out. Some more appropriate names for the show might be, *The I Hate Bill O'Reilly Show, The I Hate Some Other Well-known Conservative Show (Whose Fame I've Made Money Off Of),* or *The I Can Make Fun of Our Troops Because I Do USO Tours Show.*

So how does Franken keep his audience for three hours a day? He doesn't have to. He has three or four guests every day who have either written a book or an article that is venomously anti-Bush, and he just turns the show over to them for long monologues. Sure Franken has input; after all, it is his show. He might interrupt his guest with an intelligent question like, "Why do you suppose Bush is lying about this?" This no doubt makes Al feel like he's part of his own program and gives him that feeling of intellectual superiority and master of nuance.

Early in the show, Franken has a segment called the "Oy, Oy, Oy Show," which is about as funny as he gets. The segment, which is introduced with Jewish Hasidic music in the background, is a three-minute lighthearted look at the day's headlines. Franken's cohost, the adorable Katherine Lanpher, who forces herself to laugh at Franken's dumb jokes (or appears to be required to do so under the terms of her contract), reads a headline. Franken, playing the role of an older-sounding, tired Jew with some plumbing problems, says "Oy." Occasionally he'll respond to a headline with "Oy, the bastids." This is his *funny* way of keeping it Jewish. The segment concludes with him asking "So, uh, how are things in Israel?" Franken stopped asking about Israel toward the end of 2004, but he invokes something or somebody else who *is* Jewish, as with the conclusion of his June 1, 2005, segment when he said, "This was sponsored by ginkgo *jew* loba."

I'm not one to play the anti-Semite card, but I can't imagine the level of rage that would explode if a Limbaugh or Hannity had such a Jew-mocking segment on their show. What I find particularly offensive is that Franken, who by his own admission is a "very reformed Jew," meaning that he is completely nonobservant of anything related to Judaism or the Torah, makes fun of the stereotypical Jew to an audience that, like him, is far left and looks down with scorn on observant Jews. This reminds me of the *Seinfeld* episode in which Jerry accuses his dentist friend, Tim Watley, of converting to Judaism just so he can get away with his frequent "Did you hear the one about the rabbi?" jokes.

Franken Advances Black-Jewish Relations

On May 16, 2005, in another "hysterical" episode of the "Oy, Oy, Oy Show," Al the Jew referred to black people as horses. The segment began, as it always does, with the adorable Katherine reading a headline to her Jewish friend Al. On this day she began with news from Bob Woodward that there could be a dark horse in the race for president in 2008. So Al asks, "J. C. Watts?"

The adorable Katherine, feigning indignantion, replied, "Al, no!"

Franken—ever the comedian—continued, "Bill Frist isn't a new name . . . George Allen isn't a new name . . . and Woodward said the 'dark horse' was a 'he' so it can't be Condaleeza Rice."

How do you suppose the Left would react if a conservative talk show host did a skit comparing "dark horses" to black people? If he were still alive, Jimmy "the Greek" could tell you if liberals have a sense of humor when comparing black people to horses. But apparently no one on the left, where the outrage always comes from, takes offense when Al Franken does it on Air America.

Franken has a daily guest from the Center for American Progress (CAP), a left-wing think tank founded by former Clinton chief of staff John Podesta. Its main function, it seems, is to attack the Bush administration or other high-profile conservatives based on unconfirmed or questionable news stories and innuendos. One of CAP's deputy directors is Christy Harvey, who is introduced with a Franken serenade that goes, "Talk to me; talk about the right wing's dishonesty. . . ." Isn't Franken a funny guy! When Christy is not available for the daily Bush bash, CAP sends in their benchwarmer, David Sirota,* who formerly served as spokesman for Bernie Sanders, the self-proclaimed Socialist congressman from Vermont. Franken thinks it's hilarious to introduce Sirota as a "sexy, sexy wonk."

---

*Sirota left CAP during summer 2005, but he is still a regular guest on Franken's show.

I already knew that some wealthy dopey left-wingers were flushing millions of dollars into the Air America money pit, but I wanted to see just how closely the New Left's activist wing of the Democratic Party is tied to it. When I Googled the Center for American Progress, I got a better picture of who these folks were and what they were all about.

When I noticed that the first few links claimed that CAP was a "nonpartisan" think tank, I wondered if I might have gotten the name wrong. After all, it would be kind of dishonest to represent yourself as nonpartisan when your primary function appears to be attacking George Bush and other conservatives. Reading on, I learned that it was founded by former Clintonoid (my term) John Podesta. How odd, I thought, that a liberal think tank founded by Podesta and whose representatives attack President Bush daily on the "I tell the truth" Franken show call themselves nonpartisan. When I found information about the founders, directors, and staff of CAP, I discovered that almost all of them are Democrat retreads, many with ties to the Clinton administration.

One of the links describes CAP as having been created in 2003 as an answer to the conservative Heritage Foundation. The distinction is that the Heritage is an actual think tank, and the CAP is a bash tank. Big difference, fellas.

The area of their site called "About Us" calls the CAP a nonpartisan research and educational institute dedicated to, among other things, "responding effectively and rapidly to conservative proposals and rhetoric with a thoughtful critique and clear alternatives."

Does this sound nonpartisan to you?

Why would Franken, who holds himself to an "impossibly high standard of truth," have as his daily guest or associate himself with someone who comes from an organization that misrepresents its political leanings? This is a rhetorical question, of course.

One of the most ridiculous and disingenuous segments of the program features Franken's partner and cohost, the adorable Katherine, introducing Franken's high school buddy Mark Luther with "time for our resident dittohead." Rush's theme song is played as background music, once again illustrating how obsessed Franken is with Rush Limbaugh.

In this segment Luther, a Rush listener, responds to a clip that Franken has selected and vetted before putting it on the air. Basically, it's a sandbag. Even worse, it is an insider's look at how Franken treats his "friends."

Out of Rush's three-hour radio broadcast and countless news stories and analysis, Franken will select something innocuous, often taken out of context or irrelevant, giving his friend a few seconds to respond. Franken, of course, has had plenty of time to prepare for the moment. When Luther can't respond or tells Al that he can't defend Rush's comments, Franken yells at him and questions his pride for listening to someone like Rush. Franken really loses it, however, when on the rare occasion Luther is actually prepared to respond and defends Rush's positions. These replies fluster him, and in no time Al responds with something like, "Time's up! Gotta go."

This is another example of Franken's hypocrisy. In his book he attacks Fox News, and *Hannity & Colmes* in particular, for claiming that they are fair and balanced when, in his opinion, they are anything but. But what is fair or balanced about having a team of researchers select seemingly "gotcha" clips, then having a guest—who has no idea what the clip might be—defend the statements?

Franken: Liberals Don't Support Negative Media Coverage of the War

Of course he would say that. This is the same man who says there is no liberal bias in the media and who counts on continued bad news out of Iraq so he can bash President Bush every day.

One example that illustrates Franken's "fairness" occurred on January 3, 2005. Franken demanded that Luther justify Rush's "unfair attacks" on the media for supposedly, according to Franken, gleefully reporting negative information about our war efforts in Iraq and for giving the Left the reports they enjoy so much.

> **Franken:** And Rush puts a spin on this . . . that the Left doesn't support our troops . . . that the Left wants our guys to die . . . this is really ugly.
>
> **Luther:** I think you got him there. I'm not going to argue with you.
>
> **Franken:** You can't just shine me on all the time.

I can't really blame Luther. After all, how much time was he given to study these Franken assaults or to evaluate whether Franken's charges were even accurate? As for Franken's charge that Rush makes up his claim that the media only reports and "the Left is only interested in bad news coming out of Iraq," Accuracy in Media published a report on the subject on December 25, 2004. It quoted an unidentified soldier who complained to Secretary of Defense Donald Rumsfeld:

> Everything we do good, no matter whether it's helping a little kid or building a new school, the public affairs sends out the message that the media doesn't pick up on. How do we win the propaganda war?

Rumsfeld's reply was instructive:

> Everything we do here is harder because of television stations like Al-Jazeera and Al-Arabia and the constant negative approach. You don't hear about the schools that are open, and the hospitals that are open, and the clinics that are open, and the fact that the stock market is open and the Iraqi currency is steady and the fact that there have been something like 140,000 refugees coming from other countries back into this country. They're voting with their feet because they believe this is a country of the future. You don't read about that. You read about every single negative thing that anyone can find to report. I was talking to a group of congressmen and senators the other day, and there were a couple of them who had negative things to say and they were in the press in five minutes. There were 15 or 20 that had positive things to say about what's going on in Iraq and they couldn't get on television. Television just said we're not interested. That's just—sorry.

Another story reported by Accuracy in Media dated January 13, 2005, was titled "American Troops Cheer Attacks on U.S. Media."

> Vince McMahon, chairman of World Wrestling Entertainment (WWE), told American troops in Iraq before Christmas that when

> he returned to the U.S. he was going to look up the "negative media nay saying types, and I'm going to say that you said that they can go straight to hell."
>
> His comments were met with cheers and thumbs-ups.
>
> Those who saw on TV McMahon's speech and the reaction of the troops to McMahon's strong attacks on the media saw powerful evidence that many of our troops are seething with anger and resentment over media coverage of the war.

I would love to ask Al Franken, "Which is more important to you: bad news coming out of Iraq so you can attack President Bush or supporting our troops, whom you claim to 'love and support' when they say they are getting shafted by the U.S. media?"

Franken has other weekly guests. All of them are from the extreme Left: Joe Conason from *Salon* and the *New York Observer;* Paul Krugman, the infamous and overrated Bush-bashing columnist for the *New York Times;* and David Brock of Media Matters.

Krugman is an economist who teaches at Princeton University, but he can't seem to make his points without getting help from people like Al Franken and Media Matters. In an August 2004 debate with Bill O'Reilly, hosted by Tim Russert, O'Reilly accused Krugman of knowing nothing about economics. Krugman, who had learned well from his good friend Franken, called O'Reilly a liar, denying he ever made the statements attributed to him by O'Reilly. O'Reilly had reminded Krugman of his repeated predictions of economic catastrophe if President Bush's tax cuts ever occurred, a catastrophe that obviously hasn't materialized. Krugman denied he ever made them. Here is a brief exchange from that encounter:

> **O'Reilly:** Mr. Krugman was dead 100 percent wrong in his columns, uh, two years ago when he said the Bush tax cuts would lead to a deeper recession. You can read his book and see how wrong he was.
>
> **Krugman:** Actually, you can read it. I never said that. I said it would lead to lousy job creation.

O'Reilly: Column after column after column. You made the point, in your book, okay, that these cuts, these tax cuts were going to be disastrous for the economy.
Krugman: Nope. . . .
O'Reilly: They haven't been.
Krugman: Uh, uh, I'm sorry. That's a lie. Let me just say, that's a lie.
O'Reilly: It's not a lie.
Krugman: It's a lie.

Turns out O'Reilly was right. On April 22, 2003, Krugman predicted in his column published in the *New York Times:*

> Aside from their cruelty and their adverse effect on the quality of life, these cuts will be a major drag on the national economy. . . . It's clear that the administration's tax-cut obsession isn't just busting the budget; it's also indirectly destroying jobs by preventing any rational response to a weak economy.

Since Krugman claimed not to have predicted a deeper recession after the tax cuts, O'Reilly cleverly asked him if he instead predicted the economic growth of the last year. Krugman was flustered, no doubt knowing he was checkmated. He stammered out this remarkable confession: "Compare me . . . compare me, uh, with anyone else, and I think you'll see that my forecasting record is not great."*

Another occasional guest on the Franken show is someone who, for the sake of convenience, we'll call "Benson." Benson maintains and operates an anti-O'Reilly Web site. As is typical of many left-wing sites and blogs, Benson's site is replete with the F-word. A typical Benson attack is one in which he criticizes Bill O'Reilly's answer to an e-mailer who read his book *The O'Reilly Factor for Kids*. Benson attacks O'Reilly for responding in a "gay-like, limp-wristed" manner.

Benson's vulgarity and crudeness don't end there. Besides using the F-word with regularity and using derogatory language about

---

*The source for this exchange and analysis is "The Dead Zone," by Don Luskin, on *National Review Online,* August 9, 2004.

gays, it seems that this guy—Franken's friend—also takes it upon himself to defend those who regard the three thousand victims of the 9/11 attack at the World Trade Center as legitimate targets. He actually defended Ward Churchill's obscene comments that the WTC victims were "little Eichmanns." That's right, a regular guest on the Al Franken show attacked O'Reilly for exposing Ward Churchill as a vile anti-American monster, and Franken sat on his butt and said nothing. I'm not even sure which is the greater offense: Franken's silence as his regular guest defends Churchill's comments or his neglecting to go after Churchill himself as O'Reilly did.

Here is Benson's shameless defense of Churchill on his February 11, 2005, posting:

> Bill's spent all week talking about some guy in Colorado named Ward Churchill, of whom I've never heard because I follow the real news, which tends to be about important things. Apparently Churchill is a professor who thinks that America is an evil empire. Wow. Fancy that. But never one to stop beating a rather dull horse, Bill's been interpreting the existence of crazy people on the campuses of hippie universities as the final sign of the coming apocalypse.

How about that? Ward Churchill is "just some guy from Colorado." That Benson had never heard of him shows how ignorant he is since many media outlets *did* cover the Churchill controversy. O'Reilly spent as much time on it as he did because Churchill was in the news just about every day for one infamous statement after another. Also, Churchill was exposed as a fraud for claiming to have Indian lineage as a member of the Keetowah Cherokee tribe when in fact he had none. Furthermore, his fabricated Indian "background" on his résumé helped him earn tenure as a professor at the University of Colorado.

On May 26, 2005, Franken finally took an interest in the Churchill issue but only to attack Bill O'Reilly. His complaint was that O'Reilly had pointed out that the *New York Times* had put the Abu Ghraib story on its front page close to fifty times, consistent with its bias against the U.S. military action in Iraq and in an attempt to damage our efforts to win over the hearts and minds of the people of the Middle East. Franken then cited a report that O'Reilly talked about Churchill's hateful and vitriolic denigration of the victims of 9/11 twenty-five times. So what was Franken's point?

In case Franken wasn't keeping count, O'Reilly has also done many stories on other issues people care about—like the agencies that raised millions of dollars for the families of 9/11 but weren't passing the money on to them. He has also done countless stories on "Jessica's Law." Do you want to attack him for that also, Al? He also did many stories on Florida's incompetent Child Services agencies and on Islamic Jihad front man Sami Al Arian, a professor from the University of South Florida. Thanks to people like Bill O'Reilly and conservative columnist Debbie Schlussel, Al Arian was fired and is now facing trial.

But let's take a look at those *really, really* important stories that Franken has done repeatedly on his show:

"O'Reilly is a jerk." <Now that's important.>
"Limbaugh lies and lies and . . ." <Can't forget those.>
"Coulter is a bitch." <Almost forgot, until Franken reminded us.>
"Hannity is an immoral bastard." <As opposed to a moral bastard?>

Oh, yeah, and he likes to repeat the stories about U.S. troops (whom he loves, don't forget!) peeing on the terrorists' Korans. Is it any wonder that liberals are so much more informed on the most important issues of the day than ignorant conservatives are?

Hello? Anybody There?

What about the callers to the Franken show? Unlike Rush or Sean, whom Franken tries to imitate and who take many calls throughout their shows and put "liberal callers" at the top of the list, on a good day Franken takes an average of one to three calls per show. Most days he has none. The overwhelming number of these calls are from Franken supporters. Only rarely does a caller opposed to Franken ever get through.

Franken likes to gloat that his show is getting good ratings in a couple of states. One would think that if he had a "popular show," he would have more than a couple of calls a day. Sometimes, though, he can't even get people who agree with him to call the show.

At 2:35 p.m. on January 12, 2005, Franken's cohost, the adorable Katherine, said, "We're going to take calls now." For the next four minutes Franken blathered on about Armstrong Williams and the Department of Education controversy. At 2:39 Katherine asked, "Are there any callers out there?" By 2:45 p.m., ten minutes since they opened the phone lines, there had yet to be a caller to the show. So Franken continued to rant about the Social Security "surplus," citing the Congressional Budget Office (CBO) as a "conservative organization." He usually calls the CBO nonpartisan, but whatever.

When Franken went to a commercial break at 2:49 p.m., still nobody had called. At 2:53 p.m., eighteen minutes after the phone lines were opened, Al and Katherine took their first call. Franken sounded relieved.

This is what happens on *The Al Franken Show* hosted by "the liberal Rush Limbaugh," the go-to guy for the Democrats. This is the same guy Senator Tom Daschle said would go toe-to-toe with conservative talk radio, the guy who was going to energize the disenfranchised.

For those of you who, like me, had thought Al Franken's show would be as funny as *Saturday Night Live* or Stuart Smalley, or at the very least an informative show promoting liberal ideas, I'm sorry. His program fails in every way.

Air America Hate Speech

For years, the media elite have tried to portray conservatives and conservative talk radio hosts as haters and mean-spirited. In contrast, liberals are compassionate and tolerant. And they just love everybody.

Here are just a few examples of how "nice and tolerant" Air America hosts are:

- "I hate this country. America is the number one terrorist country in the world."—Mike Molloy, nighttime host, March 24, 2005
- "The difference between Bush and Hitler is that Hitler was elected."—Randi Rhodes, the actual talent on Air America, from a promo I heard during a commercial break on Franken's show.

- "Sure Yasser Arafat was controversial, but so was Ronald Reagan."—Saturday night hostess Laura Flanders, criticizing the *New York Post* headline "The Ara-fat lady sings" for making fun of Arafat's zaftik (Yiddish for "portly") widow
- "Let's go to Brit Hume, the horrible scumbag, who many people consider somewhat responsible for the fact that his son committed suicide."—Sam Seder, cohost with Janeane Garofalo, the *Majority Report* July 7, 2005

Trash TV meets Trash Radio

I tip my hat to Air America for surviving its tumultuous first year. Then they sank further into the gutter by bringing trash TV host Jerry Springer in as the lead-in program to Al Franken's show. His show debuted on April 1, 2005.

Is the man who brought such family tragedies as "I love my wife, but find my 300-pound transsexual mother more attractive" into our living rooms every day going to give Air America the credibility it has been searching for?

Franken's Formula for Success

In *Lies and the Lying Liars Who Tell Them,* Franken writes, "We have to fight back. But we can't fight like they do. The Right's entertainment value comes from their willingness to lie and distort. Ours will have to come from being *funny and attractive*" (italics added).

I will admit that at one time Franken was funny. Who can forget his hysterical Stuart Smalley segments: dishing out self-help advice to guests like Michael Jordan or Al Gore? But that was a long time ago. He isn't funny anymore. As for his claim that liberals need to be attractive . . . well, uh, did I mention that Franken used to be funny?

So Why Are Al's Ratings in the Toilet?

"No they're not. I beat Rush in Portland, Oregon." That's *always* his answer. Every talk-show host strives for that coveted number one position in the all-important Portland market.

One of the things that always annoys me when I watch a conservative host interviewing a conservative guest is when they ask, "What do the Democrats have to do to win back the people?" "Don't answer! Don't tell them!" is how I usually react. So I have to admit I'm being a little hypocritical for giving Franken some free, constructive criticism about his show.

For starters, his biggest problem is not understanding his audience. Sometimes he seems oblivious to the fact that he even has one. Let me explain.

In 2005, Franken took his show on the road on the Left Coast from Monday, May 9, through Friday, May 13. He began in Seattle on Monday. Two of his guests were Ron Sims, the county executive of Seattle's King County, and the other was Dan Savage, editor of Seattle's newsweekly *The Stranger.*

Question: Have you ever heard of these people? Do you care who they are, much less what they have to say? You see, the "talented" talk-show host Franken, who often speaks of his respect for his readers (and I'm assuming his listeners), thinks his show is a performance for the fifty or so people who come out to watch him broadcast his program. It doesn't dawn on him that the other *hundred* or so listeners he has on his other fifty-three affiliates couldn't care less about Kings County in Seattle.

On Wednesday of that week he did the broadcast from the Crest Theatre in Sacramento, California. His guests included Gil Cedillo, a state senator from East Los Angeles, and assembly member Jackie Goldberg, who was there to talk about the state's education issues.

Same problem as before. Nobody outside the Franken groupies watching him live cared about these guests or their fields of expertise.

What really annoyed me was listening to him tell the same jokes every day. As far as Franken was concerned, every day was a different (live) audience. For his radio listeners, however, every day it was the same joke, different venue. If the joke wasn't funny when he told it in Seattle, I'm not going to laugh when he tells it in Sacramento.

On Thursday, in San Francisco, one of his guests was a Professor Mark Danner, who also authored the book *Torture and Truth: America, Abu Ghraib, and the War on Terror.* Gee, do you think that book is pro- or anti-America?

Ratings

Frankly, I never understood the difference between a 2.6 or 1.4 or "10-4 good buddy" when networks release their ratings and market share. And since I have yet to pick up my copy of *Ratings for Dummies,* I was lucky enough to find a list of the actual numbers of listeners for various radio shows in the *New York Post*'s July 25 issue, written by John Mainelli.

So here are actual numbers of listeners (at any given time) to a variety of radio shows heard in the New York City region:

RUSH LIMBAUGH	139,000
SEAN HANNITY	103,700
BOB GRANT	87,000
MARK LEVIN	74,300
BILL O'REILLY	72,700
AL FRANKEN	61,400

Now, for Franken, this is somewhat of a quandary. On the one hand, he has often boasted that he has exceeded the predictions of Rush Limbaugh, Sean Hannity, and Bill O'Reilly when they said that "nobody would listen to liberal talk radio."

Granted, 61,400 is a lot more than "nobody." But it's also a lot less than Rush's 139,000 or Sean's 103,700. And when you consider that New York City is the mecca of liberalism, it should give even more pause to the geniuses at Air America.

But here's what I find even more humorous. Franken trails O'Reilly by more than 11,000 listeners even though Franken has a two-hour head start (Franken is on from noon to 3:00 p.m., and O'Reilly is on from 2:00 to 4:00 p.m.). Furthermore, O'Reilly's show in NYC isn't even a live broadcast, it is actually a rebroadcast of his noon to 2:00 pm program.

So congratulations, Al. You proved everyone wrong. You got more people than "nobody" to listen to your daily vitriolic character assassination radio show, and you even come within 11,300 listeners of a radio show that isn't even live.*

Al Likes Anniversaries

I love anniversaries. They can mark an annual passing with great

---

*The full list is of the top twenty talk-show hosts in New York City, according to Arbitron. Al Franken is number 16.

blessings or good feelings. For Al Franken, anniversaries are just another opportunity to undermine this country.

On April 28 and 29, 2005, Franken talked about the one-year anniversary of Abu Ghraib. To cover his "I love my country" ass, he wrote on his blog, "And no, Rush, that doesn't make it a celebration, and it doesn't make us happy."

At first I laughed at Franken's posting. Does he really think Rush listens to his program or reads his blogs? Remember, Al, it's you trying to make money off Rush, not the other way around. You need him. He doesn't need you. But I digress.

What other anniversaries did Franken remember to celebrate? Another way of saying it is, what other anniversaries did he use in order to insult the United States and this administration?

He did remember the one-year anniversary of the launch of Air America. That was fun.

Guess which anniversary he *didn't* remember or celebrate: the anniversary of the fall of the statue of Saddam Hussein, which took place on April 9, 2003. Not only did he not take the time to remember this great historic event, which would have been a great topic just two weeks after Air America's birth, but he neglected to remember the fall of the statue on its second anniversary on April 9, 2005. Shame!

Then came December 13, 2004. It was the one-year anniversary of U.S. troops' capture of Hussein in a spider hole in Tikrit without firing a single shot. What did Franken talk about on this anniversary? The president's plan to destroy Social Security and Bernard Kerik's nanny problems.

Franken had no time to discuss the fall and capture of the evil tyrant Saddam Hussein, but he took two days to remember Abu Ghraib.

In early May, while countries around the world remembered the end of World War II, the defeat of Nazism, and the liberation of the Nazi death camps, Franken found more important topics to talk about, like blocking the Bolton nomination and energy independence.

There's always next year.

The Future of *Air Un-America (AUA)*

When Rush and other conservatives said that AUA wouldn't succeed, which Franken loves to remind his audience, it was because they were misled into believing that AUA was going to have a "liberal" format. No one told them it was going to be character assassination or bash-America radio. That's totally different.

When we were in school, we all learned something like, If A = B and B = C, then A = C. Makes sense to me. Applying this commonsense theory to Al Franken and Air America, here's how it plays out. Since Air America = Al Franken and Al Franken = lies, smears, and distortions, then Air America = lies, smears, and distortions.

I have yet to see this formula lead to success anywhere in the business or corporate worlds. Then again, since Franken and Air America believe corporations are evil, maybe this will be to their liking in the end.

Now that *Air Un-America* has survived its first year, can it make it a second year? The answer is yes, with one caveat: that Rush Limbaugh, Sean Hannity, Bill O'Reilly, and Ann Coulter don't take a hiatus. If they were to take a one-month vacation at the same time, AUA would implode. They would cease to exist. What would they talk about? Would Franken have to resort to "Guess what Rush lied about last month?" or "Can you believe what O'Reilly said last month?" I have to believe that even Franken's adoring fans would get bored and move on to something else.

However, that scenario seems improbable. It would be interesting to see what would happen if each of the hosts and hostesses of *Air Un-America* were to make a pledge not to mention the names of Limbaugh, Hannity, O'Reilly, or Coulter in any way for an entire month and see what happens to their programs. And that also means their callers, too.

Do we have any takers?

5 Dittoheads vs. Dunderheads

One thing we can all agree on is that Al Franken is obsessed with Rush Limbaugh. Yes, it's awkward to hear one guy talk about another guy with such frequency, but if it sold books, I guess Franken thinks it'll grow his radio show. Tune in *The Al Franken Show* on any day and you'll hear something like:

> "Last week Rush said . . ."
> "I'm frequently compared to Rush. . . ."
> "Here's what Rush said . . ."
> "Rush has the largest radio audience. . . ."
> "It's Rush this, Rush that . . . Mommy, why can't I be like Rush?"

He even plays a liberal dating service commercial using a Rush impersonator on his program. His can't be a healthy obsession.

Except for Bill O'Reilly, Franken seems to be most irritated by Rush Limbaugh's legions of adoring fans, known as "dittoheads." Even though Franken wrote *Rush Limbaugh Is a Big Fat Idiot* and claims to monitor Rush's show every day, he distorts who and what dittoheads are. According to Franken, "Dittoheads are those who blindly follow what Rush Limbaugh says." In the back of *The Way Things Ought to Be,* Rush has an entire chapter defining the terms and phrases associated with *The Rush Limbaugh Program*. According to Rush, a dittohead is simply an avid listener.

I know this is just a small lie, but, as Franken himself writes, "Little lies and big lies add up."

I believe Franken's obsession with Rush is in part based on Franken's jealousy that Rush has legions of supporters and followers with a branded nickname: dittohead. This is something we can easily remedy.

Let me suggest an appropriate nickname for Franken's devoted fans. How about "dunderheads"? There, Al, now you have another way to compare yourself to Rush: fans with a branded nickname.

Let's be clear on just what it takes to be a dunderhead. You, too, can be a dunderhead if:

- You believe Al Franken is a skilled radio talk-show host.
- You believe Franken's radio show is funny (and are able to give examples when asked). On second thought, if you're a dunderhead, you think everything Al says is funny.
- You believe that Franken's cohost, the adorable Katherine Lanpher, isn't forcing herself to laugh at Franken's "jokes." (On June 6, 2005, after a Rush joke, Katherine asked him how many times he's going to use *that* line.)
- You believe that Al Franken doesn't lie, smear, or engage in character assassination.
- You believe, like Franken, that Americans shouldn't have to work more than forty hours a week to make a good living.
- You believe that Franken carefully researched Rush Limbaugh and other conservatives before writing about them.
- You don't think Franken has "sweaty thighs" for Ann Coulter.
- You don't believe that Franken is jealous of Sean Hannity's success.
- You believe that Al Franken can sway elections and rally progressives.
- You believe that trashing President Bush is patriotic.

Let me recap what distinguishes Rush Limbaugh's listeners and fans (twenty million) from Al Franken's listeners and fans (twenty thousand—heh, heh, heh). Dittoheads are rational individuals who can think for themselves and are avid listeners to the Rush Limbaugh program. Dunderheads are angry, bitter, self-delusional individuals who think that Al Franken is funny and informative. And, oh yeah, that he has high ratings.

The NOW Gang

Rush has referred to a small group of bitter and vocal angry feminists as "feminazis." Partly because of Franken's distortions, liberals who don't listen to Rush believe that he calls all women feminazis. Since Franken claims he listens to Rush and has read Rush's books, why does he lie about what a feminazi is?

Franken writes about "listening to him spew about 'feminazis' and their 'women-as-victim' ideas. Limbaugh was railing about how feminists believe that all heterosexual sex is rape."

Since Franken claimed to have listened to Rush's radio program before writing his screed against him, was he taking a potty break during Rush's feminist updates? These comical, satirical segments expose this most extreme small group of bitter women who say things like, "We're fierce, we're feminists, and we're in your face." Are these the typical feminists Franken claims he is acquainted with?

The actual definition of *feminazi* is found in *The Way Things Ought to Be:* "Widely misunderstood by most to mean 'feminist.' A feminazi is a feminist to whom the most important thing in life is ensuring that as many abortions as possible occur. There are fewer than twenty-five known feminazis in the United States." (It would serve the jihadists and homicide bombers right if these twenty-five feminazis were part of the seventy-two virgins awaiting them in "paradise.")

Again, why does Franken lie? Why does he mislead his readers and listeners? Could it be that he wants to demonize Limbaugh to a group of dunderheads whom he knows don't or won't listen to the Limbaugh program? Does Franken want to imply that a leading voice in the conservative movement has serious issues with compassion toward minorities, and women in particular? Is this what Franken means when he says, "I bring people together"?

More Franken Lies—This Time About Judges and Another Smear Against Rush Limbaugh

The preceding portion of this chapter merely exposes Franken as a buffoon who is clearly jealous of Rush's success. What is more important, though, is exposing the depths of smear and character assassination—not to mention the lack of respect Franken has for his listeners who claim to seek the truth—to which Franken will go.

During the "resident dittohead" segment on May 23, 2005, Franken once again got Mark Luther to concede that "Rush doesn't always tell the truth." There is no way for Luther to know if Franken is lying or not because, remember, Franken has time to prepare for a segment, whereas Luther has to respond to it immediately.

On this particular day, Franken played a clip of Rush saying something to the effect that all of Bush's minority nominees are getting the Clarence Thomas treatment: cruel and humiliating abuse at the hands of white elitist Democrats against any minority who has "forgotten their place" and are conservative.

Franken then went on to name Bush minority nominees who passed right through the Senate confirmation hearings. Of course, this proves once again that Rush lies. Luther, a beaten man after a year of Franken's pummeling, didn't know what to say, except that he will be a little more skeptical when listening to Rush.

Poor Mark Luther. When is he ever going to learn that when Franken says he has researched a subject, his facts are probably wrong or distorted?

I played back the audio portion of this segment a few times just so I could get the names of these minority nominees who were given the red-carpet treatment by the Kennedy-Leahy-Schumer cabal. I wanted to see what the story really was.

Big shocker! Franken once again deceived his audience, not to mention his *friend,* Mark Luther.

FRANKEN LIE #1

First there was Judge Barrington Parker Jr., an African-American. No Clarence Thomas treatment. What happened? Were the Democrats changing their stripes? Were they being fair? Not quite. In fact, Judge Parker was first appointed by Bill Clinton in 1994 to the Circuit Court of Appeals, and it would be somewhat awkward for Democrats to rough up someone who had been nominated by Clinton, especially since he was a liberal.

FRANKEN LIE #2

Franken then named Judge Roger Gregory, another African-American Bush nominee, who sailed through the confirmation process. Wrong again, Al. Let me retract that. "Wrong" would imply a mistake, an accident. Al, you got caught lying again. Judge Roger Gregory was a recess appointment made by Bill Clinton on December 27, 2000, and a pro-choice liberal whom President Bush re-nominated as a good-faith gesture to the Democrats.

FRANKEN LIE #3

Franken went on to name a Judge Edward Prado, a Hispanic who, like the two judges above, was also easily confirmed. His story is a little different. Judge Prado had already been a sitting federal Judge since 1984. Second, though Judge Prado was appointed by a conservative, Ronald Reagan, Prado was enthusiastically endorsed by the liberal Congressional Hispanic Caucus for apparently telling them that he supports using the courts to elevate minorities, according to David Broder in the *Washington Post.* Miguel Estrada would not commit to this poition, so one Hispanic was approved by Democrats and the other wasn't.

So we see here, as we will see in later chapters, how Franken can take a story or an audio clip and distort its context, in this case leaving out the important fact that the approved minority judges were all *liberal*, even if they were nominated by President Bush. Rush was clearly talking about conservative minority nominees being blocked and given the Clarence Thomas treatment.

What say you, Dunderheads?

Franken Don't Know the Truth About Ruth

Though it is rarely talked about during political campaigns or even in most polls, no event brings out the howling, angry, left-wing mobs like judicial nominations. Wild accusations are made, like: "Conservatives want women to go for back-alley abortions." "Bush has declared war on working people." "Bush wants to impose a theocracy." Yada yada yada.

Yet in all this time in which the radical extremists Scalia, Rehnquist, and Thomas have served on the bench, women still get abortions, Leftists still burn flags, and the Bible is still considered more offensive than *Heather Has Two Mommies*.

Let's look, though, at what impact liberal judges have had on this country:

- U.S. District Judge Joseph Bataillon struck down a state amendment barring same-sex marriage or civil unions, nullifying a Nebraska measure passed by 70 percent of voters in 2000.
- In the 2000 presidential election, before any complaint had been filed by Al Gore, the Florida Supreme Court acted unilaterally in ruling that the secretary of state was forbidden from certifying the election.
- Federal Court Judge Thomas Marten ruled that privacy concerns trump the protection of children who are victims of sexual abuse. His decision came in a case filed by abortionists and other pro-abortion groups and individuals in response to Kansas State Attorney General Phil Kline's opinion that sexual activity in children under age fifteen is suspicious and should be reported for the child's well-being. Marten said, in essence, that the state has no compelling interest in protecting children from rape or other abuse, but it does have an interest in protecting privacy rights.
- The Ninth Circuit U.S. Court of Appeals ruled that it is unconstitutional to recite the Pledge of Allegiance in public schools.
- In *Atkins v. Virginia,* Justice John Paul Stevens rewrote the Eighth Amendment to outlaw capital punishment for those with low IQ scores.
- By the year 2000, the court even banned prayers before football games *(Santa Fe Indep. School District v. Doe).*

These are but a few examples of liberal judges run amok of the system and ignoring both the will of the people and the United States Constitution.

So you can just imagine the outrage that so many conservatives had when obstructionists like Pat Leahy (D-VT), Ted Kennedy (D-MA), and Chucky Schumer (D-NY) threatened to filibuster President Bush's judicial nominees because *they* were "out of the mainstream."

As these mindless Senate proceedings proceeded, one name kept popping up in my head: Ruth Bader Ginsburg, Ruth Bader Ginsburg, Ruth Bader Ginsburg. If only Orrin Hatch and the Republicans had known in 1993 what the Democrats had in mind for years later, they could have blocked this extremist from ever getting through the Judicial Committee.

Guess who else thinks Ruth Bader Ginsburg is a liberal extremist? That's right, Professor Rush. And guess who thinks that Rush is lying about her? That's right, Al Franken. And guess who proves that, once again, Franken is the one doing the lying? That's right, moi.

On June 1, 2005, during the now often predictable "resident dittohead" segment, Franken played the following audio clip of Rush:

> "You know, Ruth Bader Ginsburg is more extreme than any of these nominees that Bush has brought up. I went through this list of things she *actually* believes in, that came out in her testimony, such as getting rid of Mother's Day and Father's Day and replacing it with Parents' Day . . ."
>
> **Franken to Luther:** "She never actually said anything about Mother's Day and Father's Day for Parents' Day . . . anywhere."
>
> **Luther** (developing a backbone): So you think he is just fabricating this completely?
>
> **Franken:** I think it's an urban myth from conservatives. We got this from Thomas E. Mann, a Brookings Institute Senior Fellow on Government Studies. He told us . . . I now have it on the highest and closest authority that Ruth Bader Ginsburg has *never,* in any setting, proposed doing anything with Mother's Day. . . .

Franken then went on to belittle Luther by asking, "Don't you think that Rush should have researched this?"

So I did a Google search to see for myself, rather than rely on Franken's painstaking research. I put in the words "urban conservative myth" and "Ruth Bader Ginsburg" and "Franken smears Limbaugh." Wouldn't you know it, I got thousands of hits.

So I tried to narrow my requests to "Ruth Bader Ginsburg" and "Franken's crappy research." Again, way too many hits. So I gave it one last try and just inserted "Ruth Bader Ginsburg" and something about dropping Mother's Day and Father's Day for Parents' Day.

There it was: The quote from Ruth Bader Ginsburg that Franken said didn't exist. The so-called "urban conservative myth" appeared in a column on National Review Online, "Bench Warmers, Putting Judicial Nominees in Perspective, Part III," written by Edward Whelan, (May 20, 2005). There Whelan cites the "Report of Columbia Law School Equal Rights Advocacy Project: The Legal Status of Women Under Federal Law," coauthored by Ruth Bader Ginsburg and Brenda Feigen Fasteau in September 1974. This is what appears in the "nonexistent" source of Ginsburg's "mainstream" philosophy:

> Replacing "Mother's Day" and "Father's Day" with a "Parents' Day" should be considered, as an observance more consistent with a policy of minimizing traditional sex-based differences in parental roles.

6 Al Franken Hates Poor People

No, I don't really have any proof that Al Franken hates the poor. Al Franken has no proof that Rush Limbaugh hates poor people, either, but it didn't stop him from writing in his book that he does. But then again, *that* book was written before Franken declared, "I hold myself to impossibly high standards. . . ."

On page 15 of *Rush Limbaugh Is a Big Fat Idiot,* Franken cites a passage from Rush's book:

> The poor in this country are the biggest piglets at the mother pig and her nipples. The poor feed off the largesse of this government and give nothing back. . . .
>
> We need to stop giving them coupons where they can go buy all kinds of junk. We just don't have the money. They're taking out, they put nothing in. And I'm sick and tired of playing the one phony game I've had to play and that is this so-called compassion for the poor. I don't have compassion for the poor.

This is pretty vicious stuff, and it didn't sound like the Rush Limbaugh I know and admire. So I e-mailed Franken, asking him when and where Rush said this horrible stuff. Franken responded that it was from Rush's second book, *See, I Told You So*, and that he cited the source in his book. After flipping through the book and looking for chapters that this subject might fit in, I still couldn't find it. Finally, as my frustration grew, I did a Nexis search and found where Rush had made these "cold hearted comments." Here's what I uncovered:

First, Franken does *not* cite the source of this material in his book, contrary to what he e-mailed me. Second, the quote comes not from Rush's second book (which Franken had me toiling hours looking through) but from Rush's *first* book, *The Way Things Ought to Be.*

The obvious question is, why didn't Franken give the source for this quote in his own book? Wouldn't it have been a great way to nail Rush? Or maybe it's because Franken didn't want his readers to see that the passage came from a chapter called "Demonstrating Absurdity by Being Absurd."

Listen, dunderheads: Rush was writing *satire* here! The kind of satire Franken likes to hide behind so he can't be sued for malicious smears against other people.

If I didn't listen to Rush's program and read his books, when I read this quote I would have thought that Rush *is* a big fat "meanie." This is exactly what Franken was counting on—smearing Rush and others, knowing his readers will never question the personal attacks.

But I'd like to use this charge against Rush to make a bigger point about how dangerous Franken's smears can be. Remember, in the chapter dealing with the Peabody/Polk Award, when Bill O'Reilly was interviewing *New York* magazine columnist Michael Wolff on the topic of attack journalism, O'Reilly opined to his guest that lying "hurts reputations . . . and lives forever in the Nexis."

He was right.

On January 19, 1996, the *Washington Post*'s Phil McCombs wrote an article called "Al & The Rushmeister, " an interview based on Franken's book tour for his Rush Limbaugh book. McCombs wrote, "Where I think [Franken] really hits the jackpot, though, is when he actually quotes Limbaugh directly, as in: *The poor in this country are the biggest piglets.*"

See? O'Reilly was right. You write something about somebody, true or false, and it ends up in Lexis/Nexis, which is how I found this piece.

I called the *Washington Post* to ask McCombs if he had researched the "anti-poor" rantings of Rush or if he had just trusted Franken's truthfulness and painstaking research. According to the *Post*, McCombs has long been retired. Yet his culpability in smearing Rush lives on.

I can almost give Mr. McCombs a pass since *he* wasn't doing a book on Rush. Franken is another story. Not only does he not cite the source for the "piglet" quotation, he also leaves out the fact that Rush also did a complete segment of "*The poor are the biggest piglets . . .*" on an episode of his television program broadcast on February 14, 1994. Since Franken claims that he monitored Rush's television program as part of his research for his book, this is an inexcusable oversight. Or was it an oversight?

Here is a more detailed description of Rush's "hating poor people" from his television program. Rush addressed his audience:

> And on April 1st of 1992, I ran a little editorial, a ditto monologue . . . suggesting that we tax the poor. And I'd like . . . to revisit this, because it's relevant to a news item that happened just recently over the weekend.
>
> "The poor in this country are the biggest piglets at the mother pig and her nipples. They're the ones who get all the benefits . . . the one's who are always pandered to. . . . Do they pay any taxes? No. They don't pay a thing. They contribute nothing to this country. It's time to get serious about raising taxes on the poor. <Franken leaves the joke about taxing aid to the poor out of his book.> There's no reason that we have to have the level of poverty in this country that we have. Tax them. Let's balance the budget on the backs of the poor."
>
> Well, you can imagine when I did—it's April Fool's Day, and I did it—there's a lot more to it than—and those were just the excerpts.
>
> And people were just, how can you be so cold-hearted? How can you be so cruel? . . . That's just typical of you conservatives. . . ."

The audience is then shown a headline from the *New York Times*: "Clinton Considers Taxing Aid to Poor to Pay for Reform." Limbaugh continues:

> I—friends, I was only kidding. He took my suggestion. I was kidding. He's obviously read my book. He says, Hey, that Limbaugh guy's got a pretty good idea. We—we could tax the poor.

So Rush did an entire satirical skit on taxing poor people and balancing the budget on the backs of the poor. He did an elaborate segment on his television show and wrote about it in his book. In response, Franken takes a small portion of it and distorts it as Rush's heartfelt opinion about poor people.

This is yet another example of a *Frankenism:* cite a passage, then manipulate the story behind it. Or as Franken likes to call it: "How to Lie with Footnotes #3: Cite a source, but totally misrepresent what it says."

Smearing and Hypocrisy

We've already established the lengths to which Franken will go to smear his adversaries—saying things about them that aren't true with the sole purpose of trying to hurt them. But then there's the "combo platter": smearing and hypocrisy. It is no secret that Rush Limbaugh was addicted to pain-killer medication. These were prescribed drugs for a man who had major back surgery. So how does Franken refer to Rush? As a big hypocrite, because Rush has called for mandatory prison sentences for drug users. Never mind that Rush was referring to cokeheads and other degenerates who threaten society, Franken saw Rush's predicament as an opening to smear him and accuse him of hypocrisy. But who is the *real* hypocrite here? According to authors Tom Shales and James Andrew Miller, who wrote *Live from New York: An Uncensored History of Saturday Night Live,* Al Franken himself was a recreational (cocaine) drug user while on the set of *Saturday Night Live.*

Now I'm not calling for Franken to be incarcerated, but certainly, he is in no position to pontificate to Rush Limbaugh or any other conservative about hypocrisy.

Government Programs That Work

On page 10 of his screed against Rush Limbaugh, Franken once again tries to prove that Rush can say whatever he wants, and his dittohead zombies will eat it up without questioning or thinking about it.

Like many conservatives, for years Rush has complained about and shone a light on the inefficiencies and waste of government programs that supposedly help the less fortunate among us but in fact keep them enslaved to the government. Franken cites a passage from Rush's best seller, *The Way Things Ought to Be*: "With the exception of the military, I defy you to name one government program that has worked and alleviated the problem it was created to solve. Hmmm? I'm waiting. . . ."

Franken could have zinged Rush with a litany of programs that do work, but of course he didn't. Instead, he wrote about the programs that what he called the "bona fides" of conservative thinkers—from conservative columnist and preeminent thinker George Will to former Nixon speechwriter and quiz show star Ben Stein—say have been successes.

And what successful government programs did Will, Stein, and other conservative pundits articulate that Franken was able to counter Rush with?

- Rural electrification—George Will
- National Institutes of Health, youth summer jobs programs—John Kasich
- The FAA, lighthouses, and federal penitentiaries—Bob Dornan
- Public libraries, the FBI, and the GI Bill—Richard Viguerie
- Social Security, Medicare, Head Start, FDIC, and food stamps—Ben Stein

Other than Stein's programs, which, except for the the FDIC, are in financial ruins today, the others cited are not exactly what I think of when I hear the phrase "successful liberal programs."

If Franken's point was merely that there are government programs that *do* work, he glossed right over the programs that Rush believes are better served by the government rather than the private sector, as he wrote on page 264 in his best-selling *See, I Told You So*, another book Franken claims to have thoroughly researched:

- U.S. Patent and Trademark Office
- NASA

Besides, it's not that Rush is against government helping people so much as he is sickened by the waste and inefficiencies of these programs. On page 265 of the same book, Rush states that 72 cents of every welfare dollar go to bureaucrats rather than to poor people. This bothers Rush. It bothers me, and it bothers millions of other Americans who are sick and tired of being called heartless racists for not wanting to see their hard-earned tax dollars going to waste.

On the other hand, Franken, who didn't come up with any successful government programs on his own other than Rural Electrification, seems to think that government waste is a good thing—as long as their (phony) intentions are good.

7 Rush's Minimum Wages vs. Franken's Minimum Truths (Franken's #1 Lie Exposed)

—And protecting, preserving, and enhancing Social Security

One of the most contentious issues between Republicans and Democrats is thought to be the minimum wage and its impact on businesses and those it is intended to benefit. In reality, it's not that contentious. Ted Kennedy pretends to care about poor people by offering an extra $2 per hour over a two-year period to elevate "hard-working families out of poverty," which, when you think of it, is very generous from a multimillionaire who deducted thousands of dollars in tax cuts for his D.C. mansions. Adding $80 a week (40 hours at $2 per hour) to a worker's check is not going to bring anyone out of poverty. If you're a college student, it means you can take your girlfriend out for a nice dinner once in a while and still have some extra cash to fill the gas tank. But if you're supporting a family (the people whom Franken and Kennedy would have you believe are the intended beneficiaries of this cynical wage increase), if you were dirt poor before the increase, you will remain dirt poor after the increase.

In *See, I Told You So,* Rush presented an extensive section on the subject of minimum wage and its impact on job gains and losses, in a chapter called "The Case for Less Government." For you dunderheads, this was *not* a satirical chapter.

Rush's sources included reports from the Congressional Budget Office (CBO), the Public Service Research Council, the Employment

Policies Institute, and the American Economic Association, as well as entries from the *Fortune Encyclopedia of Economics*.

I mention these sources because Franken has said repeatedly that when talking about minimum wages, "Rush pulls numbers from his butt." Franken never talks about this story without making this charge against Rush. It probably is Franken's number one favorite "conservative lie" that he likes to excoriate more than any other.

In the summer of 2004, Rush said on his radio program that an increase in the minimum wage will not reduce poverty as much as Democrats claim it will, because "75 percent of the people on minimum wage are teenagers in their first job." Upon hearing this and believing it to be false, Franken had his staff research this data with the Bureau of Labor Statistics. Franken was exhilarated to discover that *aha!* "Rush is wrong. Rush lied. Rush pulls numbers from his butt!—60.1 percent of minimum wage earners are 'adults.'" It's time to take a deep breath and let Franken have his two minutes of victory.

First, it's easy to determine Rush's position on the minimum wage by referring to his best-selling book, *See, I Told You So,* which in a detailed presentation discusses the issues and myths about minimum wage: who earns it and its impact on families. From Rush's book:

> Myth No 2: *Many heads of households are subsisting on minimum wage salaries.*
>
> Minimum wage earners are entry-level positions, most often filled by teenagers. More than 50 percent are between sixteen and twenty-four years old. Most of those jobs, 63 percent, are part time. . . . About 80 percent of minimum wage employees live in non-poor households. About 20 percent come from households with annual incomes of more than $50,000.

Just How Big Is *Franken's* Butt?

Franken uses Rush's statement, "75 percent of minimum wage earners are teenagers," to trash Rush and his posterior at every opportunity. The interviewer's question doesn't even matter.

> **Interviewer:** So Al, how's it going?
>
> **Al:** Well, I'm not sure how things are going, but let me tell you what

> I am sure about. Rush Limbaugh said that 75 percent of minimum wage earners are teenagers . . . so he pulls numbers from his butt!
>
> Or
>
> **Interviewer:** Al, how's the weather outside?
> **Al:** The weather is great, but you know what is even greater? The size of Rush's butt.

On October 18, 2004, Franken was on a panel at the National Press Club with fellow talkers G. Gordon Liddy and Jim Bohannon. When asked by moderator Marvin Kalb how talk radio would impact the upcoming election, Franken, who must have been either unprepared or unwilling to answer this simple question, responded by saying, "I'm not sure how talk radio will impact the upcoming elections, but let me tell you about Rush Limbaugh. . . ."

Franken, who likes to incorporate his Rush Limbaugh impression while telling this story, said:

> Rush Limbaugh, a couple of months ago, discussing the minimum wage, said, "75 percent of the people on minimum wage are teenagers in their first job." I knew this wasn't true, so I had my researchers go to this little old thing (pause for effect) called the Bureau of Labor Statistics, and what they say is 60.1 percent of people on minimum wage are "adults." . . . Rush gets his numbers from his butt . . . and I get my numbers from the Bureau of Labor and Statistics.

As Franken sat basking in the glory of his attack on Rush and adulation of the audience, he said, "We are scrupulous about our facts" (said twice), to laughter and applause from the audience.

I, for one, know that whenever Franken "sends his staff to do research," it's like the blind leading the blind, so the red flags go up. So I went to the Bureau of Labor Statistics Web site myself. Here's what I found:

> Characteristics of Minimum Wage Workers: 2003: According to current population estimates for 2003, some 72.9 million American workers were paid at hourly rates, representing 59.6 per-

> cent of all wage and salary workers. Of those paid by the hour, 545,000 were reported as earning exactly $5.15, the prevailing federal minimum wage, and another 1.6 million were reported with wages below the minimum. **Together, these 2.1 million workers with wages at or below the minimum made up 2.9 percent of all hourly paid workers.**

A further breakdown by the Bureau shows that 7 percent of the *hourly paid workers* between sixteen and twenty-four years of age earn minimum wages, 9.9 percent of workers sixteen to nineteen years old earn minimum age, and 1.7 percent of those twenty-five years old or older earn minimum age.

I spoke with Steve Haugen at the Bureau of Labor Statistics and told him I was trying to resolve the debate between Limbaugh's and Franken's numbers. When I told him Franken cited the bureau as the source for his assertion that 60.1 percent of minimum wage earners are adults, Haugen asked me what Franken defines as an "adult." "What difference does it make?" I asked back. He replied, "The Bureau's statistics does not have a breakdown or category called adults." Uh-oh, Al.

"Furthermore, none of the Bureau's statistics on the minimum wage used the number 60.1 percent." Do you think they're still laughing at the National Press Club, Al?

So let's review the Franken lies regarding the so-called "Rush's Butt" and Franken's flawed research that someone like myself was able to refute:

- There is no category in the bureau's minimum wage study for adults.
- Only when pressed by Chris Matthews on MSNBC (one of the thousand times I heard this story) did Franken offer an age bracket for "adults" as being workers over the age of twenty. (It'll be interesting to see what Franken says the next time he goes on *Hardball* and says that Rush lies.)
- There is no age bracket in the bureau study for "workers over 20." The three brackets are: 16 to 19, 16 to 24, and 25 and over.
- None of the Bureau of Labor Statistics data on minimum wages uses the number 60.1 percent.

- Last, and perhaps most important, the Bureau of Labor Statistics does not provide data for the percentage of American workers who earn the minimum wage. Their study is of workers who are paid by the hour, which includes people who earn $10 an hour, $20 an hour, and so on. The Bureau *does* provide data on the percentage of minimum wage earners *only* as a percentage of hourly paid workers. Only 1.7 percent, not 60.1 percent, Al, of hourly paid workers who are "adults"—over the age of 25—earn the minimum wage or less. (source:www.bls.gov/cps/minwage2003.htm)

Below is a partial graph, which, as you can see, is not very user-friendly (especially if you're a Harvard researcher).

Employed Wage and Salary Workers Paid Hourly Rates with Earnings at or Below the Prevailing Federal Minimum Wage by Age (2003 Annual Averages)

	Number of Workers (in thousands)				Percent Distribution				Percent of workers paid hourly rates		
		At or below $5.15				At or below $5.15			At or below $5.15		
Age	Total paid hourly rates	Total	At $5.15	Below $5.15	Total paid hourly rates	Total	At $5.15	Below $5.15	Total	At $5.15	Below $5.15
Total, 16 years and over	72,946	2,100	545	1555	100	100	100	100	2.9	0.7	2.1
16 to 24 years	15,871	1,106	330	776	21.8	52.7	60.6	49.9	7	2.1	4.9
16 to 19 years	5,412	534	212	322	7.4	25.4	38.9	20.7	9.9	3.9	5.9
25 years and over	57,075	995	215	780	78.2	47.4	39.4	50.2	1.7	0.4	1.4

What is important here is that you see how Al Franken operates when he thinks no one is looking. Franken has repeated this story more times than I care to count, certainly more times than we spoke about the Peabody Award and possibly even more times than he talks about his USO tours. He has done this for no reason other than to hurt Rush and those people who listen to him and believe in him. This is Franken's way of mocking dittoheads who "blindly" follow whatever Rush tells them. Franken has used this story deceptively, just as he did when he wrote about Rush hating poor people, when he lied about the feminists Rush refers to jocularly as feminazis, when he purposely got it wrong on dittoheads, and in his other daily assaults on Rush.

Another person besides Rush who is vindicated by these facts on minimum wages is Franken's favorite punching bag and "friend," Mark Luther. The minimum-wage clip has been played countless times by Franken on his radio program. Each time Franken demands to know how Luther can continue to listen to someone like Rush who just "lies and pulls numbers out of his butt." At these times Luther reasonably responds that "Rush was probably trying to make a larger point, that increasing minimum wage leads to more layoffs."

As we've seen, Luther was right.

I wonder if the Bureau of Labor and Statistics gives out Peabody Awards for distorting their data? I'm pullin' for ya, Al.

Franken's Hypocrisy on Minimum Wages

Okay, we already know what a compassionate guy Franken is when it comes to minimum wages. Even if he got his statistics all wrong, we know where his heart is.

Currently, the federal minimum wage is $5.15 an hour, hardly enough to live on unless you're a college student and living at home. Franken has called on Congress to support Senator Ted Kennedy's proposal to raise the minimum wage by $2 an hour over the next two years. This no doubt will allow college students to move out into a place of their own and make a down payment on an expensive new sports car. So I was shocked to hear Al plug a new commercial for a group called Purple Ocean that was condemning Wal-Mart for not paying their workers a higher wage.

With Wal-Mart's annual profits being in the billions, you'd think they could afford to pay their workers more than just $5.15 an hour. But—guess what—they *do*! They pay their workers more than minimum wage. In fact, they pay more than Teddy Kennedy's paltry $2 an hour increase that Franken supports. From a May 4, 2005, *New York Times* article by Steven Greenhouse, "Wal-Mart, Choosing Sides Over $9.68 an Hour":

> With most of Wal-Mart's workers earning less than $19,000 a year, a number of community groups and lawmakers have recently teamed up with labor unions in mounting an intensive campaign

> aimed at prodding Wal-Mart into paying its 1.3 million employees higher wages.

Before revealing more tidbits from the article, let's look at this again. Compassionate Ted and sidekick Al attack conservatives for not supporting a $7.15 minimum wage bill because the current rate is not enough to survive on, but now their surrogates and supporters are complaining that $9.68, which is more than $2 *more* than their $2 proposed increase isn't enough. What's going on here?

Could it be that the minimum wage increase advocates are exploiting the poor for political gain? Are they misleading these workers at the bottom of the ladder into believing that they are just a few dollars an hour increase away from financial security?

Here's some more from Greenhouse's article:

> One worker who has been out of work for two years before joining Wal-Mart, Frances Browning, for example, once earned $15 a hour, but now at Wal-Mart, where she is a cashier in Roswell, Georgia, she is paid $9.43. She says she is happy to have the job.

That's right, a *cashier* making $9.43 an hour.

Later in the article the author writes about a younger worker who has a *different* attitude:

> Jason Mrkwa, 27, a high school graduate who stocks frozen food at a Wal-Mart in Independence, Kansas, maintains that he is underpaid. "I make $8.53, even though every one of my evaluations has been above standard," Mr. Mrkwa (pronounced MARK-wah) said. "You can't really live on this."

A high school graduate who stocks frozen food and makes $8.53 an hour but thinks he's underpaid has spent just a little too much time in the freezer.

According to the article, Wal-Mart says its full-time workers average $9.68 an hour, and with many of them working thirty-five hours a week, their annual pay comes to around $17,600. That is below the $19,157 poverty line for a family of four, but above the $15,219 line for a family of three.

That right there, ladies and gentlemen, is the problem. If you think that stuffing frozen chickens and ice-cream pops into a freezer for thirty-five hours a week entitles you to a big house in the suburbs and an SUV, you haven't the foggiest clue about what it means to take advantage of the opportunities afforded to you in America.

If you want to get ahead, how about taking night classes in a local college? It might increase or add to your skills so you can get a higher paying job down the road. How about getting a second job and working weekends to add to your income? Gee whiz! $8.53 an hour to stock food in the freezer!

This, unfortunately, is the attitude of too many in this country who have bought into the liberal mantra that the rich are the winners of life's lottery and working people are the losers.

Hello!!! Rich people work far more than thirty-five hours a week. Even Ted Kennedy and John Kerry work more than that.

So what's the real agenda of these anti–Wal-Mart activists? The article says:

> Labor groups and their allies are focusing on Wal-Mart because they say that the campaign will not just benefit its workers but also reduce the existing pressure on unionized competitors to reduce their own wages and benefits.

Shopping at a Wal-Mart in Long Island myself, I asked an employee, a single young woman, if she minded me asking her some personal questions about her employment and how much she earns at the Big Box store. She told me that she had been there just under two years and makes just under $12 per hour.

Not bad.

Franken Fights for the "Little Guy"

With friends like Al Franken, workers don't need any enemies. On his March 9, 2005, broadcast, Franken, together with daily guest Christy Harvey from the Center for American Progress, lambasted the Senate in general and Republicans in particular for voting down an increase in the federal minimum wage.

Harvey told Al that according to her research, senators, who had just denied poor workers a mere $2.15 an hour increase, earn the equivalent of $72 an hour (based on a forty-hour workweek). Franken correctly pointed out that senators work a lot more than forty hours a week. (It's good to see George Soros's millions of dollars going into solid research.)

But here's what liberals like Franken and Harvey don't get, or maybe they do but just don't care. When you raise the minimum wage, you cause all wages to rise. Only 2.9 percent of all hourly workers are paid the minimum wage. So if you increase what you are paying these 2.9 percent of workers, you will have to increase the hourly wage of the remaining 97.1 percent. This will lead to layoffs and small business failures.

Think about this one example. Suppose you are a small business owner with six employees. You pay your workers $10 an hour, almost double the current minimum wage. Now the government mandates that the minimum wage must go up to $7.30 an hour. Your workers are most likely going to demand a raise. They will rightfully complain, "You can't pay us just $2.70 more than a minimum wage worker. We demand to be treated fairly."

Now you either have to figure out a way to increase the price of your products or services without losing customers, or you must lay a worker or two off to compensate for your increased labor costs. What happens to the workers laid off because of the increased minimum wage? How will they get health insurance, pay the rent, or feed their families?

But people like Franken don't care about ordinary people. They use them as political pawns, and the easiest way to do that is through minimum wage laws that make the false claim that liberals are compassionate and Republicans are mean-spirited.

Protecting and Preserving Social Security

Those of us who want to solve the problem and are not primarily motivated by gaining a political advantage can look at the problem of Social Security and, once presented with all the facts, judge for ourselves what the best course of action is. People like Al Franken, on the other hand, look at the issue through a different prism: "How can I use this to attack President Bush and the Republican Party?"

One can easily see the different approaches in an obvious example: the UN oil-for-food scandal. Saddam Hussein had been allowed to steal billions of dollars intended to provide humanitarian aid for his people, and the people who made it all possible appear to have been paid off.

What was Franken's response? Was he outraged? Did he foam at the mouth in utter contempt for UN head Kofi Annan? Absolutely not! Rather, he denounced Republican Senator Norm Coleman for calling for Kofi Annan's resignation for dereliction of duty as the person in charge during the scandal.

Does Franken exhibit honesty or, as he likes to put it, "an impossibly high standard," when looking at complex issues that affect all Americans? Never! It is far more important to Franken for him to be able to use the issue to smear Rush Limbaugh or President Bush or any other Republican in sight.

Franken looks at Social Security reform the way he looks at other issues: as a weapon to attack President Bush.

During the first week of December 2004, the first month after the worst month in liberal history (President Bush's reelection), Franken was discussing Social Security reform with Senator Harry Reid (D-NV), the incoming minority leader. They both agreed that President Bush's only agenda in Social Security reform was to reward his friends on Wall Street by pushing for private retirement accounts. Senator Reid went on to say that the Republicans are "sounding alarms" when, in fact, according to the senator, "Social Security will be solvent until the year 2052."

Hearing Reid—who is of Social Security age himself but earns almost $200,000 a year in salary and benefits—say, "Everything is just fine with the system," made me pause. I could have sworn that during the economic prosperity of the Clinton '90s he, like many of the Democrats, was saying something else. Could this have been the same Senator Reid who had previously proposed that we *should* "tinker" with Social Security? In fact, on February 14, 1999, Reid had commented, "Most of us have no problem with taking a small amount of the Social Security proceeds and putting it into the private sector," during his appearance on *Fox News Sunday*. On July 11 of the same year on the same show, he had said, "I think we have to take care of Social Security."

On *The Al Franken Show* a day later, during the resident dittohead segment, Franken harangued his friend Mark Luther for supporting the Bush agenda when Social Security is doing just fine. When Luther asked him what his source was, Franken replied that he got the numbers from the "nonpartisan" Congressional Budget Office (CBO). Unless Luther had listened to Franken's show one day earlier, he wouldn't know that Franken got his information from the very partisan Senator Harry Reid. Another lie.

As always turns out to be the case, when you check the source of liberals' statements, the information is quite different from what they have claimed. The relevant portion of the summary on Social Security put out by the CBO itself is quite different:

> Today, 47 million Americans receive some form of Social Security benefit. As the baby boom generation begins to retire, that number will rise considerably. Under the laws that currently govern Social Security, spending for the program will increase from about 4.4 percent of the nation's gross domestic product (GDP) now to more than 6 percent of GDP in 2030, the Congressional Budget Office (CBO) projects. In later years, outlays will continue to grow steadily as a share of GDP, though more slowly. Over the long term, paying the Social Security benefits scheduled under current law will require economic resources totaling between 5 percent and 8 percent of GDP, CBO projects.
>
> At the same time, the federal revenues dedicated to Social Security will remain close to their current level—about 5 percent of GDP—in the absence of changes to the program. **Thus, annual outlays for Social Security are projected to exceed revenues beginning in 2019** [bold print mine for emphasis]. Even if spending ends up being lower than expected and revenues higher than expected, a gap between the two is likely to remain for the indefinite future.
>
> Only four approaches to narrowing that gap exist, and each of those approaches has drawbacks:
>
> - The benefits scheduled to be paid under current law could be reduced, lowering Social Security's contribution to the income of future beneficiaries.
> - The taxes that fund Social Security could be increased, drawing additional resources from the economy to the program.

> - The resources consumed by other federal activities could be cut to make up for the shortfall in Social Security. However, the aging of the U.S. population and increases in medical costs will also lead to higher costs for other entitlement programs, most notably Medicare and Medicaid.
> - Federal borrowing could be increased, which would also draw additional resources from the economy to Social Security. But that borrowing would need to be repaid by future generations, either through higher taxes or lower spending.
>
> Any changes to Social Security will have to be made in the context of the pressures on the total federal budget. CBO projects that spending for government health programs will grow even faster than spending for Social Security because of rising health care costs. In particular, increasing outlays for Medicare and Medicaid are projected to cause long-term shortfalls in the rest of the budget that will be even greater than Social Security's. Unless taxation reaches levels that are unprecedented in the United States, current spending policies are likely to result in an ever-growing burden of federal debt held by the public, which will cause a corrosive contraction in the economy.

The Social Security Act was signed into law on August 14, 1935. It was designed to pay workers a continuing income after they retired at the age of sixty-five. From 1940, when slightly more than 222,000 people received monthly Social Security benefits, until today, when almost 45 million people receive such benefits, Social Security has grown steadily.

In 1983, the National Commission on Social Security Reform was created in response to the actuarial unsoundness of the system. Among the changes was an increase in the retirement age from sixty-five to sixty-seven, to be enacted gradually starting in 2000. Payroll taxes were 10.8 percent. (When Social Security first started payments around 1940, payroll taxes were only 2 percent. Today they are nearly 13 percent of wages.)

In 1996, during the Clinton administration, the Social Security Trustees' Report stated that the Social Security system would start to run deficits in 2012, and the trust funds would be exhausted by

2029. All members of the advisory panel agreed that some or all of Social Security's funds should be invested in the private sector. Without such changes, the trustees warned, payroll taxes would have to be increased 50 percent, to 18 percent of payroll, or benefits would have to be slashed by 30 percent. (My source for this information is the Social Security Reform Center at Citizens for a Sound Economy.)

It's clear that Social Security is in trouble.

When Social Security was first implemented, approximately fifteen to sixteen workers contributed to the benefits of one retiree. Today only three workers support one retiree. It will not be long before the ratio will approach two to one. Furthermore, people live ten to fifteen years longer on average than they did sixty years ago. We have fewer people working to support more retirees who draw Social Security for a longer period of time.

Any way you look at it, the enemies of Social Security reform are trying to protect big government in order to satisfy their special-interest friends. If it isn't fixed, most Americans will be burdened by rapidly increasing Social Security taxes. So, as on many other issues, Franken is clearly out of his league when he talks about Social Security.

Democrats Put Politics Over People. So What Else Is New?

On March 4, 2005, a delegation of "say-no-to-everything-Bush" Democrats met at Pace University in New York to criticize the president's plan to preserve, protect, and enhance Social Security. It was carried live on C-Span. During the event, Senator Chuck Schumer blamed the "far, far right wing that just want to destroy Social Security because they hate government programs." Then came Senate Minority Leader Reid, who told the audience, "If we leave Social Security alone and do nothing, it will still be able to pay out 100 percent of the benefits for the next fifty years."

Amazingly, Reid himself frequently cites the CBO's numbers; and they state rather emphatically that unless something is done to change the system, by the year 2019 the government will be paying out more in Social Security checks than it takes in as taxes.

This isn't just about Republicans vs. Democrats or conservatives vs. liberals. On March 4, 2005, the very bipartisan group the

Concord Coalition put out a paper titled "Reform Should Not Wait for a Crisis." It said, in part:

> It is often said that our political system only responds to a crisis. If that is true, we are in for big trouble. Whether we use the term "crisis" or some less alarming term to describe Social Security's problems, the program does need the immediate attention of lawmakers.
>
> Social Security benefits are not immediately threatened nor are those of Medicare and Medicaid, the other two large entitlement programs for the aged. Yet, a broad bipartisan consensus exists that the projected growth of these three programs puts our overall fiscal policy on an unsustainable path. No one can say exactly when a crisis will hit, but by the time it does we will have likely burdened the economy with a debilitating amount of debt; leaving painful benefit cuts and steep tax increases as the only solutions. Waiting for this outcome, knowing full well that it is coming, would be an act of fiscal and generational irresponsibility.

"Social Security Reform Is a Reward for President Bush's Wall Street Buddies"

It's amazing just how many buddies liberals think President Bush has. Liberals accused him of invading Afghanistan and Iraq to benefit his oil "buddies." He gave tax cuts for his rich CEO "buddies." Wealthy lobbyist "buddies" paid for his inauguration, and now he wants to unravel Social Security to reward his Wall Street "buddies."

To date, no liberal Democrat has come forward to provide a single idea to help save Social Security other than to raise taxes (Robert Wexler D-FL), tax the existing benefits (Bill Clinton), raise the age for benefits (Democratic National Committee Chair Howard Dean), leave everything alone for the next fifty years (Senate Minority Leader Harry Reid), or just *tweak* it a little (less creative Democrats).

My Great Plan to Save Social Security Versus Franken's Calamity

These politicians who say there is nothing wrong with Social Security and if we leave it alone it will be fine for the next forty years will be living on their fat government pensions when they retire. They don't care how changes in Social Security benefits will affect ordinary people. They just want to use senior citizens to hurt President Bush. That's the Washington, D.C., way!

But Al Franken claims he has a plan. He has found a way to take the politics out of this debate and protect Social Security for our seniors and for generations to come. He calls it "the doughnut-hole approach."

Here's the Franken Krispy Kreme, lamebrain plan. We should raise the maximum level of income presently taxed for Social Security from $90,000 a year to $150,000 a year. (Occasionally he says the upper limit should be raised to $120,000.) Then we should raise taxes even more on people making over a million dollars a year, which he claims will make up the rest of the Social Security deficits or the rest of the funds.

I'm sure that sounds like a good idea to many people who think it will not take money from them and will put money in their pockets. However, Franken's "doughnut-hole" plan fails to address a serious problem: Social Security taxes amount to 12.6 percent of your earnings. At $90,000, this means the government takes $11,340 out of your pocket. If the amount is raised to $150,000 a year, the government will take $18,900 from your pocket. Raising the cap means less money for you to add to your IRA or put back into the economy in other ways.

Franken's plan screws people making over $90,000 a year, period. This, of course, is a typical left-wing tactic: tax those who make more than others and call it compassion.

My plan is called the "put up or shut up plan." Here is how it works: We *lower* the rate on Social Security from 12.6 percent to 9.6 percent but increase the pool by raising the amount of taxable income to $110,000 a year. This comes out to $10,560 a year, leaving families with an extra $780 in their pockets. Why does this plan work? It's simple. Republicans believe that letting people keep more of their money will stimulate the economy, and Democrats want targeted tax cuts for middle- and lower-class working families, so both parties can claim victory.

Where do we make up the money from the cuts under my plan? We raise the Social Security tax on entertainment-industry millionaires up to 25 percent. We need to raise it this high because there are many more people making less than $110,000 than there are people in Hollywood making over $1 million. Since Democrats believe that anybody making $200,000 a year is wealthy (thereby confusing income with wealth), anybody who makes over a million dollars a year is mega-wealthy and can afford to pick up the slack for working families.

This is a winning plan. Democrats get to give relief to middle-class Americans while simultaneously raising taxes on their liberal, guilt-ridden Hollywood friends. And Republicans get to watch Sean Penn, Barbra Streisand, Alec Baldwin, and Bill "I-don't-need-the-money" Clinton wiggle their way out. Everybody wins!

527's Attack Social Security Reform

The radical left-wing group Campaign for America's Future (CAF) has waged a vicious and completely distorted campaign against the Social Security reforms proposed by President Bush. One of these attacks was against the nonpartisan political watchdog group FactCheck.Org, an organization cited frequently by Franken during the presidential campaign and a group covered extensively in a subsequent chapter. FactCheck.org received national exposure when Vice President Dick Cheney cited them regarding John Edwards during the vice presidential debates in 2004.

Below are excerpts from an e-mail alert sent out by FactCheck (March 6, 2005) rebutting charges made by CAF that they were inaccurate in their assessment that "Wall Street does *not* benefit handsomely from the Bush reform proposal." Space does not permit me to include all of it here, but you can find the entire article, unedited, at www.factcheck.org/article312m.html.

> Nowhere in their rebuttal does CAF attempt to dispute our central finding, that **the federal Thrift Savings Plan pays the securities industry an average of only 16 cents on a $10,000 account,** an amount many times smaller than previously assumed. Nor did they dispute that **the leading academic proponent of the "windfall to Wall Street" idea said—when shown our new information—that it was a "fair statement" that private accounts as now proposed by Bush would provide very little profit to securities firms.**
>
> The Bush plan is *exactly like* the TSP (Thrift Savings Plan) in the only ways that matter to the securities industry: it would be centrally administered by the federal government, and workers

would be allowed to invest only in a few broadly diversified, passively managed "index" funds offered by Wall Street at what turns out to be extremely low cost. Nothing in the *Washington Post* story contradicted that. The *Post* story didn't address the question of Wall Street profits at all.

Our article: But it would still be a far better deal than the fees charged by most privately marketed mutual funds, and it wouldn't mean any higher fees for Wall Street. **The higher cost of administration for Social Security accounts would be for a larger federal bureaucracy to handle the paperwork—not for securities firms to manage the funds.** In fact, fees to the securities industry could quite possibly be even lower (in percentage terms) for the funds available under Social Security accounts than for the funds available under the Thrift Savings Plan.

FactCheck.org concludes that Wall Street is likely to squeeze out very little profit in private accounts as currently described by the Bush administration. And even **economist Austan Goolsbee—a prominent critic of private accounts—tells us "your statement is fair"** provided Bush sticks to the TSP model.

One final note: Our article may have left readers confused about the difference between revenues and profits. The 16 cents per $10,000 we mention is revenue—the net fees charged by Barclays Global Investors to manage TSP index funds. Barclay's profit—if any—would be less. Profit, of course, is what a company has left after deducting its cost of doing business from what it takes in.

Visa, MasterCard, and Discover: The Left's New Piggy Bank

When I was a kid growing up, we didn't have a lot of money. When I would ask my father for something, he would say, "I don't have the money." "No problem," I responded, "just write a check or charge it." When a grown-up thinks that credit cards are just like cash and that you can charge endlessly without any pain, the consequences can be devastating.

During the booming economy of the 1990s, this country saw a record number of personal bankruptcies from people who maxed out their credit cards and declared bankruptcy rather than paying back their debts. During the week of March 7, 2005, the senate debated new laws that would make it more difficult to declare bankruptcy and would force a person to pay back his debts. The Left was up in arms over the prospect that hardworking middle-class people would be forced to pay back money they owed to the *evil* credit card companies.

The anger directed at the Senate from Air America hosts Al Franken, Sam Seder, and Rachel Maddow was intense.

Franken complained that this new law would stifle entrepreneurs since new businesses might not start operating if loans had to be paid back when the businesses failed. After all, Franken opined, people would stop taking risks in creating their new businesses if they didn't have the option of declaring bankruptcy.

Oh! I get it. The credit card companies are supposed to float you thousands of dollars in venture capital to start a new business. If things don't work out, don't sweat it. "We here at Visa are always ready to give money away to people who want to start new businesses."

The issue gets a little more complicated and pulls at your heartstrings when you realize that the majority of the people declaring bankruptcy had maxed out their cards on medical expenses. This is one of the few times Franken's research may have been accurate. The Left tried to portray this as a clash between multibillion-dollar credit card companies and hardworking middle-class people who had to pay for their sick mother's lifesaving operation.

But let's take a closer look. First, most major medical procedures are outrageously expensive. Your credit card is not going to pay for a $100,000 or even a $50,000 operation. Most likely, it will have a limit of $10,000 or $15,000. Second, credit card companies do not demand repayment of the entire amount all at once. They make their money when you pay it back slowly in small increments. Third, there are many companies, including nonprofits, that specialize in helping people who are up to their eyeballs in credit card debt work out a payment schedule; the banks would rather have *something* back than nothing. A number of these credit-counseling companies even advertise on Air America. Fourth, if you can't borrow desperately needed money from family or friends, why would you automatically assume that the banks are responsible for your expenses, whatever your reason for them? Fifth, most, if not all, credit card companies offer a low monthly insurance program to cover your debts in case of emergency, or if you lose your job or ability to work.

A caller to an Air America program blamed the massive consumer debt on the credit card companies themselves; they "lured" people to use them. He went on to say that since these companies do background credit checks on prospective clients, it's their responsibility to know to whom they are extending credit. It is their own fault when someone defaults on a loan.

If that is true, that would seem to justify the hesitation most financial institutions have about moving into poorer neighborhoods. If credit card companies are going to be demonized for wanting their loans repaid and they are guilty for loaning the money in the first place, the banks have no reason to go into the inner city in the first place.

Of course, that would not sit well with the racial arsonist crowd, who demand that banks open in poor, minority neighborhoods. This is why I am proposing a new institution called "Bankin' with Franken." The slogan could be, "We here at Franken Bank have millions of dollars we earned for performing in crappy movies and TV shows, and as guilt-ridden white liberals we feel it our duty to give back to the people whose ancestors built this country for our racist forefathers. We've got money: come and get it!"

See? This the way we can solve the problem. A multimillion-dollar bank loans money to the poor and middle class with little or no hope they'll see it again, and the bank won't care.

Wow! And to think it took a conservative to come up with this idea!

Who Is John Murphy?

It seems that Al Franken has this uncanny ability to unmask those people he believes are "liars" as well as those he believes suffer from the affliction of "pulling numbers from their butt."

On his August 1, 2005, program, Franken once again cited data from the Bureau of Labor and Statistics that his researchers had uncovered while working on Franken's new book, *The Truth.*

Franken was talking about a July 27 episode of PBS's *Lehrer Report* where the topic was the impact of CAFTA on the U.S. economy. Taking the pro-CAFTA position was the U.S. Chamber of Commerce's John Murphy. According to Murphy, CAFTA would have the same positive effect as did NAFTA, pointing to the low

(July) 5 percent unemployment rate as evidence that these trade treaties in fact do work.

So what is the lie? Where are the butt-pulled numbers? According to Franken, Murphy lied when he said, "The 5 percent unemployment is the lowest that we've had in decades."

Here is what Murphy actually said on the program:

> Well, if you look at the record of the past 11 years under NAFTA, we've seen 21 million jobs created in this country; we've seen unemployment fall to 5.0 percent today, which is lower than it's been in decades.

According to Franken, not only did Murphy lie, but his assistant, Tom Mouhsian, is also a liar, because after Franken called him and told him that under Bill Clinton unemployment had been under 5 percent the last three years of his administration, the chamber refused to retract Murphy's statement that unemployment, at 5 percent, is lower than it's been in decades.

I knew that if I called the bureau myself again, I would catch Franken in another lie. I spoke with Randy Ilg, who went over the unemployment rates since 1970 through the present with me and agreed that even though there were several years (see the chart on the next page) that had seen unemployment below 5 percent, it would not be an honest statement to say that John Murphy lied when he said that we're at a rate now that has not been lower in decades.

Next, thanks to Franken's giving his direct phone number over the air, I was able to call Tom Mouhsian at the Chamber of Commerce to ask him about his exchange with Franken and if he was aware that he was being labeled as a liar over the Air America airwaves. He explained to me that Franken had faxed over the data of just the last few years of the Clinton administration (not the entire graph, which gives a much broader picture) and demanded a retraction of Murphy's claims. Aside from some of the nasty calls he had received from Franken's dunderheads, Mouhsian told me that when Murphy was on PBS, he was talking about the average over the last three decades and that indeed 5 percent is among the lower rates of unemployment in that period.

Here are the actual Bureau of Labor Statistics figures for unemployment rates by year since 1970:

1970 4.9 **1971** 5.9 **1972** 5.6 **1973** 4.9 **1974** 5.6 **1975** 8.5
1976 7.7 **1977** 7.1 **1978** 6.1 **1979** 5.8 **1980** 7.1 **1981** 7.6
1982 9.7 **1983** 9.6 **1984** 7.5 **1985** 7.2 **1986** 7.0 **1987** 6.2
1988 5.5 **1989** 5.3 **1990** 5.6 **1991** 6.8 **1992** 7.5 **1993** 6.9
1994 6.1 **1995** 5.6 **1996** 5.4 **1997** 4.9 **1998** 4.5 **1999** 4.2
2000 4.0 **2001** 4.7 **2002** 5.8 **2003** 6.0
(source: http://www.bls.gov/cps/prev_yrs.htm)

So let's review what happened and how Franken deliberately misled his listeners:

1. Franken changed John Murphy's statement from: "We've seen unemployment fall to 5.0 percent today, which is *lower* than it's been in decades," to ". . . which is at its *lowest* in decades." Murphy did not say, "These are the lowest unemployment figures we've seen in decades" or "We've never had such low unemployment numbers in recent memory." Franken, unsurprisingly, misleads his listeners by misstating what Murphy actually said and his clear intent. "Lower" and "lowest" do not mean the same thing, and since my kids, who are in elementary school, know that, I would expect a Harvard fellow to know that as well.
2. Since Franken made the point on both his radio program and his television program, where the graph could be used as a visual, that Murphy was talking about unemployment percentages in previous decades, it was quite dishonest and misleading to fax over just the three Clinton years to Tom Mouhsian when demanding a retraction from the Chamber of Commerce.
3. On the Al Franken Show blog, http://shows.airamericaradio.com/alfrankenshow/node/3054, they displayed the unemployment numbers under Clinton by the month, rather than by the year, as done by the frequently cited Bureau of Labor Statistics, giving the misperception that there were thirty-six (3 years x 12 months) consecutive periods in which the unemployment rate was below 5 percent, in a sad attempt to portray

John Murphy and the chamber as incredible liars. If you review the bureau's graph, you see that there have been only seven years since 1970 that unemployment was below 5 percent. Pretty misleading to your blog viewers, Al.

4. On his program, Franken lied to his audience about the unemployment rates during certain years. For example, he said that in 1988 (under President Bush the elder) unemployment was at 6 percent. As you can see, it was 5.5 percent, which is a significant difference according to Franken's oft-cited Bureau of Labor Statistics. He also went on to tell his audience that under Bill Clinton, unemployment rates were below 4 percent. Again, according to Franken's favorite bureau, the lowest unemployment numbers were never below 4 percent.
5. In Franken's zeal to once again call someone a liar and prove to his fans that he has an unbelievably talented research staff working on his new book, Franken, who has railed against CAFTA, unwittingly made the case on behalf of John Murphy, President Bush, and the Republican Party for why CAFTA *should* be supported. By pointing out and emphasizing the robust economy and low unemployment rates of the last three years of the Clinton administration, he proved that free trade treaties such as NAFTA, which was signed by Bill Clinton, and the soon to be passed CAFTA actually lead to higher employment numbers.

8 Who Benefits from Tax Cuts? We All Do

Democrats say, "Only the wealthiest 1 percent of Americans benefit from tax cuts."

This is one of my all-time favorite lies. Franken didn't start this one, but he likes to perpetuate it. On the face of it, the statement is absolutely ridiculous. It's so stupid that it probably doesn't quite qualify as a lie but as ignorance.

In the first place, the one thing that politicians from both parties have in common is their desire to get reelected. How do you get elected or reelected by promoting policies that pander to 1 percent of Americans?

And just who are these wealthy 1 percent? Are they really George Bush's buddies? Did George Bush run for president, travel all over the country, get gray hair, and shed some pounds just to give a helping hand to Ken Lay (whom Franken calls "Kenny boy") and the wealthiest 1 percent of Americans?

Besides, many of these really rich people are *liberals:* multibillionaires like Warren Buffett and George Soros, multimillionaire rock stars Bruce Springsteen, REM, Matthew Davis, John Mellencamp, and Hollywood leftists Barbra Streisand, Ben Affleck, Jennifer Aniston, Christie Brinkley, Harvey Weinstein, and Steven Spielberg. All of these people are just some of the wealthy 1 percent who supposedly are George Bush's pals just because they're rich. Bill Clinton is among them, too. Who can forget his reminding us over and over just how rich he is and how generous the tax cuts he received were. And "I don't even need it!"

According to Franken, George Bush and Republicans like him only care about the 1 percent of this country. Maybe he just isn't smart enough to understand that a significant number of this 1 percent who are Democrats are out to destroy him.

On the back jacket and in chapter 1 of *Lies and the Lying Liars Who Tell Them,* on his radio program, and in public forums, Franken accuses President Bush of "just lying" when he said, "The vast majority of my tax cuts go to those at the bottom."

In his book and at Book Expo America, Franken entertained the audience with his different renditions of what President Bush said regarding his proposed tax cuts for all Americans who pay taxes.

Chapter 35 of *Lies and the Lying Liars Who Tell Them* is called "By Far the Vast Majority of My Tax Cuts Go to Those at the Bottom." He claims that this is a Bush lie and has repeated the charge over and over. On October 29, 2004, Franken told his audience that Bush lied when he made that statement. Franken then played a clip of Bush saying, "the vast majority of the help goes to those at the bottom." Any honest person can see for themselves that these are two different statements.

But Franken seems to offer his readers (and listeners) contradicting versions of what the president said. At the bottom of page 2 of *Lies and the Lying Liars Who Tell Them,* Franken quotes Bush as saying, "[b]y far, the vast majority of help goes to the people at the bottom end of the economic ladder." And Franken's deceptions continue. In the very next paragraph, Franken writes, "By far, the vast majority . . . goes to people at the bottom." Franken continues, "The truth is that *the bottom 60 percent got 14.7 percent.*"

Here is a perfect illustration of Franken's shell game. He gives us three very similar-looking versions of what the president says, then replies to just one of them—the one that makes the president look dishonest. By cleverly using an ellipsis in the quote: "By far, the vast majority . . . goes to the people at the bottom," Franken makes it look like the president is promising that the "vast majority" goes "to the bottom." Then he gets his little zinger in there about the bottom

60 percent. But that's not what President Bush was saying. I'll explain in just a moment. But in the meantime, let's play the Franken game and examine every word under a microscope so that we can find differences in statements that look identical on the surface but are in fact very different in meaning.

In chapter 35 Franken asks his readers to get into the mind of the president in order to understand what he may have meant when he said "vast" and "majority." Well, I'm not trying to distract my readers from the proper context of the story as Franken was. Why worry about the facts when you can deceive with satire? The issue is not about "vast" or "majority," but it is about the benefits to the working class who do benefit when the economy is strong.

When *evil, rich* corporations thrive, it means more jobs, more health benefits, and better wages to the workers. The workers' tax cuts are smaller, but it is because they are paying less taxes than their rich friends or bosses.

The word *help* as used by President Bush changes the entire context of the statement. Let's understand one thing here. People who are rich (and I'm talking millionaire rich, not $200,000 a year Democrat rich) will always be rich, regardless of the tax codes. They have the accountants and the lawyers who know how to protect their assets. John Kerry and John Edwards did it. So does Ted Kennedy.

So who suffers when new tax regulations are introduced and enforced? It's simple: the "vast majority" at the bottom. If you raise taxes on big corporations, the CEOs will still be millionaires; but if the company has to cut back, lay people off, or move the company out of town, who gets hurt? The "vast majority" at the bottom.

California Governor Arnold Schwarzenegger has made cutting taxes for businesses one of the top priorities for his state. Is it because he sides with big business over working families? No. It is because by making California a business-friendly state with lower taxes and fewer regulations, he is encouraging California companies to stay there and companies from other states to move there as well. These big companies hire more employees, which means more people have health care, more people pay taxes and buy stuff, which helps—surprise!—everyone, including those at the bottom.

On page 353 of *Lies and the Lying Liars Who Tell Them* Franken writes that President Bush "gives tax cuts to his supporters

. . . and leaves millions of children behind. He calls himself a compassionate conservative. That's the biggest lie of all." But President Bush has increased education spending by 58 percent in less than four years, more than Bill Clinton or any of his predecessors did in their entire administrations.

It can be said that President Bush does give tax cuts to his supporters because in the last two elections, especially in 2000, President Bush received millions of checks from supporters in small amounts of $10 or $25, while Democrat donors tend to be the fat cats. According to *Political Money Line,* the wealthiest of the wealthy give overwhelmingly to the Democrats. So by giving tax cuts to all taxpayers in every bracket, George Bush's tax cuts mean that Franken is actually telling the truth when he says the president gives tax breaks to his supporters, but somehow I doubt that's the kind of answer he had in mind.

According to Democrats, the rich are not entitled to tax cuts, but more cuts should be given to the middle class and the poor. As someone who has grown up and lived most of my life in the lower middle class, I should embrace the Democratic agenda. After all, if I can get back more money from the government than I'm entitled to *and* screw over the rich, then why shouldn't I want more tax cuts for myself?

It is my dream to become rich, and when I do I can guarantee you that the Democrats will have had nothing to do with it. Resenting rich people won't put money in my pocket. Demonizing the more prosperous among us won't pay my rent or mortgage, either.

For those of you, rich or poor, who want to have a better understanding of just how dishonest the Democratic approach to tax cuts is, consider this one example:

A greedy rich person walks into a restaurant and orders a meal. The bill comes out to $30, including a generous tip. He only has a $100 bill. So the kindly single-mom waitress brings him $70 change.

Now a middle-class guy walks into the restaurant. He obviously can't afford the expensive steak like the rich guy could, so he orders a couple of hot dogs and a soda. His bill comes out to $6, including tip. The middle class guy pays with a $10 bill and his change is $4.

Fair-minded people would agree that both of these customers

were given the correct change and were satisfied with their meals. But wait, a Democrat has witnessed everything and accuses the restaurant of being a cold-hearted and mean-spirited conservative Republican because the rich customer got $70 back in change and the poor customer, who definitely needs the money, got only $4.

Translating this story to tax cuts: tax cuts are not goodies for the rich. They are not bonuses, either. And they are not favors from the president. Tax cuts are refunds of part of what you paid to the government returned back to you, the rightful owner. Period!

It infuriates me to hear fabulously rich politicians who did not earn their wealth denouncing the rich in this country as the "winner's of life's lottery." Maybe in the case of John Kerry that's true. After all, as Ann Coulter says, it takes a real talent to become a kept man. But most of the wealthy people in this country worked hard, made smart decisions, and earned every penny of the money they made.

How can anyone actually believe John Kerry when he says he wants to fight for the middle class? When did he ever fight for them? When did Bill Clinton?

In 2000 former Goldman Sachs Chairman Jon Corzine spent $60 million of his own money to run for the United States Senate in New Jersey. In reality, he risked $60 million to get a job that pays $160,000 a year and would make him one of one hundred senators for a political party that is not in power.

Is Corzine really interested in fighting for the poor and middle class, or is he interested in the power that comes from being a senator? How many poor and underprivileged children could have benefited from the $60 million this wonderful, compassionate Democrat spent while buying a Senate seat?

In *The Many Faces of John Kerry,* David Bossie quotes John Kerry from a January 17, 2004, campaign speech in Iowa: "As president, I will scrub the tax code . . . to remove every single loophole, every single incentive, every single provision that rewards Benedict Arnold CEO's and corporations for moving profits and American jobs overseas."

Oh, really?

Kerry himself has used tax loopholes for his own benefit. As the *Boston Globe* reported on June 19, 2003:

> Kerry took a loss in tax shelter in 1984 to avoid political fallout. . . . Documents obtained by the *Globe* detail John Kerry's 1983 investment of between $25,000 and $30,000 in offshore companies registered in the Cayman Islands. The document, dated December 13, 1983, signed by Kerry, shows his pledge to purchase 2,470 shares of Peabody Commodities Trading Corp. through Sytel Traders, registered in the Caymans. (source: http://www.boston.com/globe/nation/packages/Kerry/Images/days/tax1.htm)

On August 23, 2004, Al Franken was a guest on *The Donnie Deutch Show.* Franken said that the Republicans "are capitalists who look out for their own and hurt ordinary people." Does that mean that John and Teresa Heinz Kerry are Republicans? Are the Clintons Republicans? Are the overwhelming majority of Senators who claim to be Democrats really Republicans?

9 Hummus and Liberal Bias

What does hummus have to do with liberal bias? Let's ask Al Franken.

The first chapter of *Lies and the Lying Liars Who Tell Them* is called "Hummus," and in it Franken writes, "Asking whether there is a liberal or conservative bias to the mainstream media is a little like asking whether Al Qaeda uses too much oil in their hummus. . . . The problem with Al Qaeda is that they're trying to kill us."

Understand now?

This is one of the techniques Franken uses when he wants to distract the audience from a serious issue or question. He gives a smart-aleck response.

But he's right, Al Qaeda does want to kill us. And yet Franken and his friends got their underwear in a bunch when U.S. prison guards forced these hummus-eating killers to wear panties on their heads.

Ironically, there were no reports of hummus residue found on the rubber dingy used by the Islamo-bombers who blew up the USS *Cole* or any of the missiles fired at the Khobar Towers (the U.S. barracks) in Saudi Arabia.

Franken continues, "The mainstream media does not have a liberal bias . . . ABC, CBS, NBC, CNN, the *New York Times*, the *Washington Post*, *Time*, *Newsweek*, and the rest at least try to be fair." Yes, he actually said that!

To prove his nonsensical point that there is no liberal bias in the media, in chapters 1, 7, and 8 of his book, Franken compares percentages of positive and negative stories written about both Bush and Gore during the 2000 campaign to refute all charges that the press is liberal. He does this in part through a liberal use of Frankenisms. He cites a source to prove a point, promotes this source as impeccable and unimpeachable, quotes one passage accurately, and then distorts the rest of the information to suit his agenda.

According to Team Franken's "research," a study from the Pew Charitable Trusts Project for Excellence in Journalism showed that during the 2000 campaign the positive press for Gore was 13 percent compared to Bush's 24 percent and the negative percentages were 56 Gore and only 49 for Bush. According to Franken, that is irrefutable evidence that there is no liberal bias in the mainstream media. In his endnotes (which, by the way, he criticizes Ann Coulter for using because "nobody goes to the endnotes to verify information") he gives the web address for the Pew results and report (http://www.journalism.org/resources/research/reports/campaign2000/lastlap/default.asp).

Knowing how Franken and his researchers work, I decided to study the Pew report myself. At the bottom of the first page of the study, it indeed reports what Franken cites as his evidence: Gore received much more negative press than Bush did. This is where accuracy ends and Frankenisms begin.

Curiously, Franken doesn't talk about the actual methodology of the Pew report. Instead, after showing the graph of the percentages of negative press for Gore, Franken substitutes the Pew research with his lies and deceptions. For seven pages he tries to prove that the media not only spent more time on irrelevant stories and in pack mentality, but also piled on what most people referred to as Gore's exaggerations.

- Remember how Al Gore invented the Internet?
- Remember Al Gore's claim that *Love Story* was based on him and his wife, Tipper?
- Remember Al Gore's claims to have discovered the Love Canal environmental disaster?

Franken goes into great detail to deny that these claims were exaggerations at all. Further, he claims that, according to the Pew research, stories like these were the reason Gore's negative media coverage was so high. He blames the media for fixating on stories which were irrelevant, in contrast to Bush's lies, which were much more serious but were ignored by the mainstream media.

Here is an excerpt from a September 15, 2003, interview with Lou Dobbs on CNN:

> **Dobbs:** You don't think he [Gore] was an exaggerator?
> **Franken:** No, I don't think any more than anyone else. <So much for his demanding the high standards of others that he claims to maintain for himself.>

I reviewed the Pew study, and there was nothing in the report that claimed Gore's exaggerations, or "non-exaggerations" according to Franken, had anything to do with the high percentage of negative press Gore received. To make sure that I read their study properly, I called the Pew people. The woman I talked to confirmed what I had understood; it had nothing to do with the Gore exaggerations. In fact, it also had nothing to do with the "Internet story," the "*Love Story* story," Love Canal, or any other exaggerated claims Franken cited.

Franken does not cite the dates or times the Pew report covered to prove his findings. If he had, he would not have been able to fool his readers into believing that the media's fixation on Gore's exaggerations played any part in the study. For the record, the study examined the weeks of September 23–29, October 7–13, and October 14–20, which included the run up to the first debate coverage before, during, and after the second and third debates. It also included assessments of the vice presidential face-off.

Here are some highlights from the Pew research explaining their findings:

- Gore's coverage was decidedly more negative, more focused on the internal politics of campaigning, and had less to do with citizens than did that of his Republican rival.
- One reason for the hard time for Gore may be the penchant of the press to focus coverage around strategy and tactics.

- The study captured a time that some observers consider one of the most substantive moments of the campaign, the period of the debates. Yet the press assessed the debates not on the basis of the candidates' positions or their character but overwhelmingly on their performances.
- In particular, stories assessing the debates tended to focus on performance (53 percent) and strategy (12 percent) rather than on the philosophical differences between the candidates.

What does this mean? It's simple. During the first presidential debate Al Gore was heard by viewers and media alike rudely sighing heavily into his microphone while George Bush responded to the moderator's questions. During the second town-hall-style debate, Gore walked over into George Bush's "space."

Gore's performances in the debates were so poor and clownish that it was very easy for Darrell Hammond of *Saturday Night Live* to make fun of him and for the rest of us to laugh at him. In fact, his advisers made him watch the show to see how goofy he looked to millions of Americans.

That's why Gore lost to Bush: he performed and conducted himself inappropriately and in a manner unbecoming of a president during the debates. That's why the media didn't like him, even if they identified with him ideologically. And that is why Pew found so many negative stories about Gore in the media. His failure and high negative media coverage had nothing to do with stories about Love Canal, the Internet, *Love Story, or* the media piling on.

So this was another *Frankenism.* He cited an impeccable source, then distorted and manipulated the findings to accommodate his agenda while misleading his readers.

Doing my own research on Gore's negative coverage in the 2000 campaign, I found a study that Franken had not been able to manipulate. The Center for Media and Public Affairs (CMPA) issued a press release on October 18, 2000, titled "TV has bad news for Gore." Like Pew, CMPA reported that Gore's media coverage went negative after the first presidential debate for the reasons mentioned above. Their study was based on all stories broadcast from Labor Day through October 15 on the ABC, CBS, and NBC evening news shows.

According to CMPA research:

> Al Gore received about evenly balanced evaluations (48 percent vs. 52 percent negative) on network news throughout September, while evaluations of George Bush ran 2 to 1 (67 percent) negative. Since October 2, however, Gore's on air evaluations had been slightly worse than Bush's: 68 percent negative for Gore vs. 66 percent negative for Bush.

"During September," the report continues, "on-air assessments of Gore's election prospects were positive by a 6 to 1 margin (86 percent to 14 percent), while Bush's were negative by a 5 to 1 margin (83 percent to 17 percent)."

Press Coverage for 2004

It may come as a shock to Franken that in their study of the 2004 campaign, both the Pew and CMPA showed that Kerry received a much higher percentage of positive press than President Bush did. It's amazing how media bias did such a flip-flop in just four short years!

The 2004 CMPA study looked at stories broadcast from June 1 through September 2, 2004, on the ABC, CBS, and NBC nightly newscasts, as well as *Time*, *Newsweek,* and Fox News's *Special Report with Brit Hume*. They reported: "Evaluations of John Kerry were positive by a two-to-one margin, while evaluations of George W. Bush were over 60 percent negative." Some other interesting findings were:

- Among nonpartisan sources, Kerry's evaluations were almost 3-to-1 positive; Bush's were over 2-to-1 negative.
- Among the networks, the gap between the candidates was largest on NBC; the coverage was most balanced on ABC.
- Kerry's proportion of good press declined in August, but he still fared better than Bush until the GOP convention.
- Bush got better coverage than Kerry only during the GOP convention, which also was the only time he received a majority of positive evaluations.
- Based on CMPA's previous studies of primary and general election coverage, Kerry received the most favorable press on net-

work news of any presidential nominee since they began tracking election news in 1988.
- The report says that Fox News was about as negative toward Bush as the broadcast networks, though they were much more negative toward Kerry than the networks were.

With all the accusations from the Franken wing of the Democratic Party and the debunked documentary *Outfoxed* that Fox News shills for George Bush and the Republicans, CMPA's research showed that Fox News was just as negative on Bush as were Jennings, Brokaw, and Rather. The study also counters Kerry's accusations or inferences that his loss was somehow due to Fox News's influence.

Franken Testifies

In spite of all the evidence that proves Franken doesn't have a clue about the bias in the mainstream media, he and some other "equally qualified" friends were called upon to testify about media bias before a forum sponsored by Michigan Congressman John Conyers.

On May 24, 2005, Franken testified that there is no liberal media bias. What was his evidence? He introduced the Al Qaeda and Hummus story, which many on the panel found humorous. He also provided a study released by the University of Maryland, PIPA, that Franken has cited frequently to prove that not only is there a right-wing media bias, but that Fox News viewers are the least informed as a result of the network's misleading them. PIPA later released a statement in response to many on the left, including Al Franken, distorting their study and its findings. "Some have suggested that we have effectively claimed that we have demonstrated that Fox News, prompted by ideological bias, is misleading its viewers. We want to clarify emphatically that we are not making this assertion." In other words, while Franken was testifying—was it under oath?—he perjured himself by incorrectly citing the findings of a university study.

Another "highly qualified" witness to testify before the Conyers committee was his colleague Randi Rhodes. Her brief, yet informative, testimony was that she could provide evidence that Fox News's ratings were sinking and that they were losing money. Since they were losing money, there was no reason for them to stay on the air except to serve as a propaganda tool for the Republican Party and Bush White House.

One last witness was CAP Senior Fellow and author Eric Alterman, whose expertise comes from one of his books, *What Liberal Media? The Truth About Bias and the News*. Here is what he said (and I'm paraphrasing): Since CNN was able to get Republican columnist Robert Novak to sit on the conservative side for the show *Crossfire,* fairness would dictate that they find a liberal columnist to sit opposite him. All they could come up with were James Carville and Paul Begala, who are not columnists. So if there are so many "liberal" (biased) columnists, how come they couldn't come up with any?

Geez, I don't know, Eric. Maybe Joe Conason, Jonathan Alter, Richard Cohen, Bob Herbert, Maureen Dowd, Eleanor Clift, E. J. Dionne, David Corn, just to name a few, weren't at home the night CNN called. Or maybe CNN was looking for people with shaved heads and distinguished foreheads.

10 Liberal Media "Tries to Be Fair"

Franken states emphatically in *Lies and the Lying Liars Who Tell Them* that while there is a blatant right-wing bias at Fox News and the *Washington Times,* there is no liberal bias in the mainstream press. He goes on to write, "ABC, CBS, NBC, CNN, the *New York Times*—at least try to be fair."

Try to be fair?

For Franken and the rest of the "there is no liberal media bias" crowd, no matter how compelling the evidence, they will always deny that the *New York Times* and other big media have a liberal bent. If the *Times* had a screaming headline like LYING SOB PRESIDENT BUSH SENDS POOR KIDS OFF TO DIE IN IRAQ, they would deny that it is bias, but rather, that the paper is "just reporting the truth."

They claim that because the media didn't conspire to cover up Bill Clinton's sexual peccadilloes, there is no liberal bias. Liberals say that because Al Gore didn't get better media coverage, the charges of liberal media are bogus. Their reasoning defies logic and common sense.

In Arabic newspapers, which are run by the government, you won't read about government corruption. You won't read about Saddam's rape rooms in Iraq or the corruption of any other dictator in the Middle East. Is that because of pro-government media bias?

No! It's because those governments are tyrannical. The brutal dictators tell the editors what they can and cannot write.

There is a difference between liberal media bias and tyrannical dictates. Nobody in conservative circles has ever suggested that the *New York Times* "Pinch" Sulzberger is a tyrant or that he would have found the carcass of a dead horse in his bed if he didn't issue a news blackout on Bill and Monica.

While there is an American flag waving in the background of Fox News programs, I wouldn't expect to see the Democrat donkey waving in the backgrounds of the three major news networks, even though I believe they are biased. The biases are much more subtle than that.

A great many books written by Bernard Goldberg, Ann Coulter, Brent Bozell, Bob Kohn, and many others show that the Left dominates the mainstream media. Groups such as Accuracy in Media (AIM) and the Media Research Center (MRC) offer fresh examples of media bias every day. Former Clinton adviser Dick Morris also details the liberal bias from the *New York Times* in his book *Off with Their Heads.*

Even Daniel Okrent, the *New York Times* public editor, admits that his newspaper is biased toward the Left. I first heard of the Okrent confession in the summer of 2004 during a "Political Grapevine" segment of Fox News's *Special Report with Brit Hume.*

How awesome, I thought. Al "I get my facts straight" Franken says they "try to be fair," and the *New York Times'* own public editor says they are biased. I believe this is called a conundrum.

Then in November I saw a show on C-SPAN in which Okrent was interviewed. He talked about how a right-wing group had taken a quote of his out of context and posted it on their Web site. He said, "I was asked if the *New York Times* is a liberal newspaper, and I answered, 'Of course it is.' And now they put that up on their site with no context."

I was disappointed to hear Okrent's comments. This was just such a slam dunk against Franken's "At least they try to be fair." So I asked myself what Franken would do if he were predisposed to write something that suited his agenda, then found out that his information was wrong. He'd write it, of course. In contrast, I invested another $3 to archive Okrent's "taken out of context" article to see for myself.

The story appeared in the *New York Times* on July 25, 2004. Here are some excerpts from Okrent's article, which begins, "Is the *New York Times* a liberal newspaper? Of course it is." I'm quoting from the article extensively so that you can decide if Okrent admits liberal bias at the *Times* or if right-wingers quoted him out of context. He writes:

> For now my concern is the flammable stuff that ignites the Right. These are the social issues: gay rights, gun control, abortion, and environmental regulation, among others. And if you think the *Times* plays it down the middle on any of them, you've been reading the paper with your eyes closed. . . .
>
> But if you're examining the paper's coverage of these subjects from a perspective that is neither urban nor Northeastern nor culturally seen-it-all; if you are among the groups the *Times* treats as strange objects to be examined on a laboratory slide; if your value system wouldn't wear well on a composite *New York Times* journalist, then a walk through this paper can make you feel you're traveling in a strange and forbidding world.
>
> Start with the editorial page, so thoroughly saturated in liberal theology that when it occasionally strays from that point of view the shocked yelps from the Left overwhelm even the ceaseless rumble of disapproval from the Right. . . .
>
> But for those who also believe the news pages cannot retain their credibility unless all aspects of an issue are subject to robust examination, it's disappointing to see the *Times* present the social and cultural aspects of same-sex marriage in a tone that approaches cheerleading. From March 19, 2004: "Children of Gays, Marriage Brings Joy"; from January 30, 2004: "Gay Couples Seek Unions in God's Eyes."

Was Mr. Okrent quoted out of context? Is Franken right that the *New York Times* isn't biased and that they try to be fair? Okrent obviously doesn't think so.

I have to admit I was a little disappointed in Al. Whereas he wrote in his book that he personally made phone calls to the Peabody people—to attack O'Reilly—and *Newsweek*'s Evan Thomas—to attack Ann Coulter—there was no mention of a phone call to the *New York Times.* At the very least I expected something like:

> **Franken:** Yeah, uh, hi. Do you try to be fair?
> ***New York Times:*** Yes, yes we do.

You see, had he done that, I might have been persuaded that maybe they do try to be fair. Franken is either a nitwit or so blinded by his own biases that even in the face of overwhelming evidence he can still say there is no liberal bias in the media and they try to be fair.

In their 2004 annual report of the nuttiest or most obviously embarrassing liberal moments, the Media Research Center gave awards to those who fit the profile of "Admitting the Obvious Award for Acknowledging Liberal Bias," which went to *Newsweek* assistant managing editor Evan Thomas for a July 10 *Inside Washington Report:*

> Let's talk a little media bias here. The media, I think, wants Kerry to win. And I think they're going to portray Kerry and Edwards—I'm talking about the establishment media, not Fox—but they're going to portray Kerry and Edwards as being young and dynamic and optimistic and all. There's going to be this glow about them that some say is going to be worth, collectively, the two of them, that's going to be worth maybe 15 points.

Here is another example of how the "objective media" try to be fair. On October 8, 2004, Matt Drudge posted an internal ABC News memo on his site written by ABC News political director Mark Halperin. The memo admonishes ABC staff covering the Kerry and Bush presidential campaigns not to "reflexively and artificially hold both sides 'equally' accountable." Halperin admitted in the memo that "Kerry distorts, takes out of context, and mistakes all the time, but these are not central to his efforts to win." (In chapter 30, FactCheck.org presents evidence to the contrary.)

He continued: "The current Bush attacks on Kerry involve distortions and taking things out of context in a way that goes beyond what Kerry has done."

In August 2004 Halperin declared, "This is now John Kerry's contest to lose." (This was part of the Drudge post, but not part of the memo.)

When Drudge broke this story, the Left accused conservatives of taking the memo "out of context." Gee whiz, guys! What are we taking out of context?

Liberal groups defended Halperin's comments as being harmless, and that all he was trying to say is that the press needs to be *more careful*, that's all. Yes, be more careful next time not to get caught by Matt Drudge.

• • •

Back in the winter of 2004 I was watching a televised *New York Times*–sponsored debate. The panel included radio talk-show host and author of *Shut up and Sing* Laura Ingraham and conservative talking head Tucker Carlson on the one side, and Franken and Eric Alterman, author of *What Liberal Media Bias?* representing the liberal perspective.

Alterman actually said that the *New York Times* is not biased because "they endorsed Republican George Pataki for governor (against Democrat state comptroller Carl McCall), and he wasn't even that good a governor."

While Alterman may be correct about whether Pataki was a good governor, the fact is that he was running for a third term, was crushing his opponent in fund-raising and in every poll, and the Democratic Party had all but given up hope on winning that office. Furthermore, even though Governor Pataki is a Republican, he is very liberal on the social issues that the *New York Times* deems mainstream, such as abortion, gun control, and union support. The *Times* endorsement was nothing more than jumping on the bandwagon of a race whose outcome was already known. It is a little-known but true secret that many in the media like to take a little credit when a candidate they endorse wins.

But if that is what Alterman bases his thesis on, that's fine.

In October 2004 the *New York Post* endorsed Senator Chuck Schumer for reelection. Was I mistaken in thinking the *Post* is a conservative paper since since Schumer is well known as one of the most liberal and partisan Democrats in the United States Senate?

In his book *Off with Their Heads*, Dick Morris writes:

> In a *New Yorker* profile of Howell Raines, ousted from his job as *New York Times* managing editor because of his support of Jayson Blair, who made up quotations in dozens of stories, Ken Auletta wrote that Raines was overt about his desire that "the masthead" (the managing editor, his deputy, and the assistant managing editors) be more engaged in shaping stories and coordinating news coverage.

Dick Morris offers further evidence of the *New York Times*' increased bias. "Jack Shafer, the media critic for the on-line magazine *Slate,* described the new policy to *Newsweek* on December 9, 2002: '*The Times* has assumed the journalistic role as the party of opposition to the current Bush administration.'"

Not that anybody is counting, but so far we have one distorted Pew study, plus a stupid hummus joke that Franken cites to prove there is no liberal media bias. How much evidence has there been to the contrary?

A Franken Regular Refutes Claims That There Is No Liberal Bias in the Media

Another regular guest on Franken's radio program does not deserve to be associated with the weekly Bush bashers: *Newsweek*'s Howard Fineman. He is one of the more decent and honorable guests who visit with Franken on a weekly basis. He is a reasonable guy. On May 4, 2005, Franken said of Fineman, "He's the most sensible and insightful person I know." Hold on to that thought, Al. Franken's opinion of Fineman is only relevant, as far as I'm concerned, because he's a media personality who acknowledges the liberal media bias Franken claims doesn't exist.

The Media Research Center summarized one of Fineman's columns, posted on MSNBC.com on January 11, 2005:

> *Newsweek*'s chief political reporter, Howard Fineman, conceded in an online posting late Tuesday afternoon that the mainstream media have acted like a political party, and in the wake of the CBS scandal that party "is dying before our eyes." What he dubbed the American Mainstream Media Party (AMMP) "is being destroyed

> by the opposition (or worse, the casual disdain) of George Bush's Republican Party; by competition from other news outlets (led by the internet and Fox's canny Roger Ailes); and by its own fraying journalistic standards."

So let's do a little tally here. Franken says, "No liberal media bias." Daniel Okrent, Evan Thomas, Ken Auletta, Jack Shafer, and Howard Fineman admit there is a liberal media bias.

I think maybe it's time for Franken to pick "researchers" from another university.

11 "Quotable Notables": Liberal Media Bias as Reported by the MRC

In his book *Lies and the Lying Liars Who Tell Them,* Al Franken dedicates a little more than two chapters to refute the "myth" of liberal bias in the media. In contrast, in this chapter I am providing some more examples of *blatant* "liberal media bias" as compiled by the Media Research Center (MRC).

Remember how Franken's main piece of evidence to prove that there is no liberal bias was a single graph from the Pew Research Center and what he considered unfair media coverage of Al Gore's non-exaggeration exaggerations? What you are about to read is just a sampling of MRC's biweekly compilation from November 24, 2004.

> If Walter Cronkite was around today, I think John Kerry would be President.
>
> —*USA Today* founder Al Neuharth in a November 9 speech at Dakota Wesleyan University, as reported the next day by Harold Campbell in the Mitchell, South Dakota *Daily Republic*

> I'm going, "Oh, my God, are children going to grow up stupid?" And I don't say that to them, but when I hear some of their answers to questions, I'm like, "They still think that Saddam Hussein blew

up the World Trade Center!" And I'm telling you, I've been to cities [in the] Northeast, South, Midwest, far West, Pacific Northwest, I've been all over the country, and I'm like, "Oh, my God, how could they miss this?" And then I look at the election, and I'm going, "Well, of course our kids are not bright about these things because their parents aren't."

—FORMER *WORLD NEWS TONIGHT/SUNDAY* ANCHOR CAROLE SIMPSON, WHO NOW TRAVELS THE COUNTRY FOR ABC NEWS TO TALK TO HIGH SCHOOLERS ABOUT HOW TO CONSUME NEWS, AT A NATIONAL PRESS CLUB FORUM SHOWN ON C-SPAN, NOVEMBER 8

When you tell me, "Let the states decide," that scares me, okay? I've got a little map here of [the] pre–Civil War [United States], free versus slave states. I wish you could see it in color and large. But if you look at it, the red states are all down in the South, and you have the Nebraska Territories, the New Mexico Territories, and the Kansas Territories. But the Pacific Northwest and California were not slave states. The Northeast was not. It looks like the [Electoral College] map of 2004.

—CAROLE SIMPSON REACTING TO A COMMENT MADE BY MSNBC'S PAT BUCHANAN AT THE SAME FORUM

Most members of the establishment media live in Washington and New York. Most of them don't drive pickup trucks, most of them don't have guns, most of them don't go to NASCAR, and every day we're not out in areas that care about those things and deal with those things as part of their daily lives, we are out of touch with a lot of America and with a lot of America that supports George W. Bush.

—ABC NEWS POLITICAL DIRECTOR MARK HALPERIN DURING LIVE COVERAGE IMMEDIATELY BEFORE JOHN KERRY'S CONCESSION SPEECH ON NOVEMBER 3

Intimidation, harassment, fabrication, doctoring, spinning, decontextualizing and actual truth-telling have all been facets of the continuing firestorm over the probity of the elections on the Internet. The latest dueling weapons: scholarly analyses from researchers at major universities. One suggests that the actual statistical odds that the exit polling was wrong—that wrong—were 250 million to one."

—KEITH OLBERMANN ON THE NOVEMBER 12 *COUNTDOWN*

Okay, time to do morning papers. . . . *Stars and Stripes* starts it off: "U.S. Troops Control Most of Fallujah," the headline. "U.S. Officials Believe Most Insurgents Have Fled the City." Look at this picture here, if you can. "Troops' Bravery Honored in Iraq." These are all Purple Heart winners. Some day, one of them will run for president and someone will say they didn't earn the Purple Heart. Welcome to America."

—CNN's Aaron Brown on the November 10 *NewsNight* displaying a front-page photo of a line of U.S. troops in Iraq receiving their medals

I know a lot of you believe that most people in the news business are liberal. Let me tell you, I know a lot of them, and they were almost evenly divided this time. Half of them liked Senator Kerry; the other half hated President Bush.

—CBS's Andy Rooney on the November 7 *60 Minutes*

There's a definite sense this morning on the part of the Kerry voters that perhaps this is code, "moral values," is code for something else. It's code for taking a different position about gays in America, an exclusionary position, a code about abortion, code about imposing Christianity over other faiths.

—Diane Sawyer to Bush campaign adviser Joe Watkins on ABC's *Good Morning America,* November 4

There may not be any other man in history who better embodies the saying that one man's terrorist is another man's freedom fighter. . . . For most Israelis, many Jews, he was a bloody terrorist and nothing more. Yet elsewhere in the world, even among Arabs who questioned his leadership, he was treated as a hero, freedom fighter, revolutionary. A diminutive man who became a larger than life symbol of the Palestinian dream.

—ABC's Diane Sawyer reporting Yasser Arafat's death, *Good Morning America,* November 11

Matt Lauer: Let me talk about this idea that a ragtag group—not well fed, not well clothed, completely under-equipped as compared to this great British army and the Hessians—could accomplish this. And let me ask you to think about what is going on in Iraq today, where the insurgents—not well equipped, smaller in numbers—the greatest army in the world is their opposition. What's the lesson here?"

Lynne Cheney: Well, the difference of course is who's fighting on the side of freedom.

—EXCHANGE ON THE NOVEMBER 9 *TODAY* SHOW, WHERE MRS. CHENEY WAS PROMOTING HER NEW CHILDREN'S BOOK ON GENERAL GEORGE WASHINGTON'S CROSSING OF THE DELAWARE RIVER DURING THE REVOLUTIONARY WAR

Al Franken claims that conservatives keep whining about a mythical, nonexistent liberal bias as a tactic to get the networks to acquiesce to their demands to refrain from certain programming lest they be accused of "liberal media bias." So I have included two more quotes from well-respected members of the media establishment.

A CBS News veteran has acknowledged the liberal bias at the network division he once ran. In an op-ed in Thursday's *Los Angeles Times,* Van Gordon Sauter, the President of CBS News in the first half of the 1980s who also put in a stint as Executive Vice President of the CBS Broadcast Group, revealed that he "stopped watching" CBS News "some time ago" because "the unremitting liberal orientation finally became too much for me"

—AN EXCERPT FROM SAUTER'S JANUARY 13 OP-ED, "WHAT'S AILING CBS NEWS? LET'S MAKE A NOT-SO-LITTLE LIST." *THE LOS ANGELES TIMES*' SUBHEAD: "THE DIVISION'S EX-BOSS DECRIES A LEFTY BIAS AND LOST CREDIBILITY

Journalists are liberal because they are "liberated," better informed, and "more in touch," former Today and 20/20 cohost Hugh Downs contended Monday night on MSNBC's Scarborough Country. Downs denied liberal bias played any part in the CBS News scandal and argued that "people tend to be more liberated in their thought when they are closer to events and know a little more about the background of what's happening" and so "in that respect, there is a liberal, if you want to call it a bias" because "the press is a little more in touch with what's happening."

—MEDIA RESEARCH CENTER, JANUARY 14, 2005, DOWNS: REPORTERS LIBERAL BECAUSE THEY'RE "LIBERATED" & INFORMED

12 A College Conservative Experiences Liberal "Tolerance" and "Diversity"

Sure they throw pies, and hurl epithets. And sometimes they'll even throw the F-word at you, but they're just kids. And besides, college campuses are places of higher learning where students are encouraged to "expand their minds" and "seek out the truth."

One friend of mine, Donnie Phillips, a student at Brandeis University, has a different story to tell. He's a Republican student who didn't get the same kind of "love" from his fellow *tolerant* liberal peers that someone such as a Ward Churchill might receive on a college campus. Below is an article he wrote for his college newspaper:

> I supported President Bush's re-election because I hate women and all minorities. At least, that is what a Brandeis Democrat told me were my reasons. This unwarranted act of intolerance was one of many instances in which I, as a Brandeis Republican, felt threatened simply because of my ideology.
>
> Prior to Election Day I never discussed political issues with this student, nor my stance on equality. I thought it was extremely rude, disrespectful, and narrow-minded to project her views of the President onto me. If shoving her political positions down my throat was insufficient, as the evening progressed and the chances of a Kerry victory diminished, the frustrated student unnecessarily

branded me and my fellow Republicans "racists." Nevertheless, later in the evening I tried to engage her in a political conversation, attempting to express my real reasons for supporting Bush. When I explained the philosophical reasoning for tax cuts, her only response was yelling "F-CK YOU!" I was taken aback, hoping for a substantial answer from my opponent.

Incidents of this kind were in overabundance in the 24 hours surrounding Bush's re-election. For example, a gay Republican faced remarks like "Hope you don't want to get married someday," "Hope you two have fun not getting married together," and "Too bad you'll never get married." Another instance happened when an international student asked a Democrat why Democrats seem harsher than Republicans; she answered, "It is because Republicans are too weak and stupid to know how to defend themselves."

On a personal front, as I walked with two students towards the Shapiro Campus Center to join my classmates in watching the results as they were reported, I attempted to engage them in a political discussion. However, the moment I mentioned that I stood with Bush on his economic policy, in "fear" one student darted behind the other, exclaiming that I was evil and refused to talk to me. This immediately ended any chances of further intellectual debate. I looked for a hint of sarcasm or anything that would indicate that this student was not as close-minded as she purported to be but for the duration of the walk all she said was "I can't even talk to you."

After Bush was declared the winner, the reactions intensified. As I stood at the Sherman Cafeteria grill waiting for food, a student I did not know said, "Sad day, y'all, sad day." I countered with a statement of equal weight saying "I think today is a great day for America." Unnecessarily, the student loudly yelled "I'LL KILL YOU!" Though I did not really fear for my life, I ended the hostility with, "You won't touch me" and walked away. I understood that I was not going to change this person's mind but I also needed to stand my ground and defend my position. I was in a lose/lose situation. How else could have I reacted? More importantly how else should have I reacted?

Student intolerance of this kind bothers me, but it is more offensive when a professor pushes their own agenda. It is their job to teach me the course material from an objective point of view.

They should report the facts and it is up to the student to determine on which side of the fence s/he falls. Of my four professors, of which none of them teach politics, three of them made negative comments towards Bush and his administration. There are appropriate times and places for political debate, but classes on financial and economic theory are not them.

This article was not intended to discuss the issues of this year's election. Rather, the objective was to illustrate how members of the Brandeis community handled opposition. I admit that Tuesday night every time Bush won a state I clapped in his favor and understand that this may have upset some students. But I surely have a right to support my candidate, as there is a big difference between clapping and shouting "I'll kill you." Towards the end of the night, after Bush was the projected winner, three Democrats criticized me for gloating over the Republican victory. Whether they would have gloated had Kerry been the victor is of little relevance. However, it is also fair to believe that as a result of Kerry's loss, all support for Bush was received with more hostility than it was transmitted.

A year ago many people on campus believed that our attitude towards diversity was among the major issues that faced the Brandeis community. As the year progressed, many students and administrators stressed that the diversity ideal is more than skin deep. One such facet is intellectual diversity including having an open mind to an opinion to which one does not hold. But combining the Justice poll that claimed 90% of voters were voting for Kerry and the confrontations that I and others experienced as a result of this election, leads me to believe that Brandeis has a lot of progress to make in this standard we hold with such importance.

Donnie Phillips, at this writing, is a student in the BA/MA program in International Economics and Finance at Brandeis University. Donnie served two terms as a Student Union Senator and was recently awarded the Brandeis Achievement Award, a scholarship recognizing his dedication and commitment to the Brandeis community. This article originally appeared in an edited form in the November 9, 2004, edition of *The Justice,* the student weekly newspaper at Brandeis, and is reprinted with the permission of *The Justice* and the author.

13 How Liberals Love America

In chapter 5 of *Lies and the Lying Liars Who Tell Them,* Franken attempts to explain the difference between liberals and conservatives when it comes to loving America. He writes:

> They don't get it. We love America just as much as they do. But in a different way. You see, they love America the way a four year old loves her mommy. Liberals love America like "grown-ups." To a four year old, everything mommy does is wonderful and anyone who criticizes mommy is bad. Grown-up love means actually understanding what you love, taking the good with the bad, and helping your loved one grow.
>
> That's why we liberals want America to do the right thing. We know America is the hope of the world, and we love it and want it to do well. We also want it to do good.

News flash, Al! America is doing the right thing. We are the hope of the world, no thanks to you or your ilk, I might add. And as far as "We also want it to do good" goes, America not only does good—we do great.

So according to Franken, conservatives are irrational and immature children and liberals are rational, mature-thinking adults. Imagine the irony of Franken accusing others of being immature.

Let's take it point by point. I *do* love my country like a grown-up, just as I love my wife (and my mommy) like a grown-up. But if I have a problem with my wife, I do not take to the airwaves and announce to the world, "My wife is a liar! She told me she was only going to buy one pair of shoes." If everyone "loved" our spouses the Franken way, America would have a 100 percent divorce rate instead of the horrifying 50 percent it already has.

Is it really "grown-up love" or "helping America grow" when you tell foreign countries that our president is a liar for no reason other than to embarrass him and help get your guy elected? Was Rep. Jim McDermott (D-WA) "loving America like a grown-up" when he went to Iraq with fellow Michigan Democrat David Bonior and said Saddam Hussein was being cooperative and George Bush was lying? Is it grown-up love when liberals burn the American flag?

Was James Carville demonstrating "grown-up love" and sensitivity to the families whose children are fighting in Iraq by referring to the war in Iraq as "an idiotic war"? Is it "grown-up love" when Franken constantly invites guests onto his program to promote books about how we "bungled" the war in Iraq? Do the troops appreciate that?

It is conservatives, not liberals, who behave like adults. It is they who love their country like grown-ups while leftists like Tim Robbins, Martin Sheen, Barbra Streisand, Michael Moore, Janeane Garofalo, and Al Franken love their country like a six-year-old spoiled brat.

When a grown-up loves their mommy (as Franken puts it), even when that mommy makes mistakes, they work to correct it. They debate, discuss, adjust, and work to improve the situation. Six-year-old brats—the Franken liberals—love Mommy when she does what *they* want. Just like a spoiled brat, when they get what they want, they love you, but as soon as there is a challenge and the little brat doesn't get his way, it's, "I hate you! You're the meanest worstest mommy in the whole world!"

Just watch a liberal bash-America rally (Oops! I mean a love-America-like-a-grown-up rally). They love their freedom of speech. They love their right to assemble. They just hate what America stands for.

Nothing speaks to true patriotism as that expressed in song. Charlie Daniels, Lee Greenwood, and many other country music stars sing about what makes America great. But then you have Steve Earle, a singer who expresses his feelings for America in a different way, or as Franken would put it, in a "grown-up way."

Oh, you say you don't know who Steve Earle is? He's only the most famous radical leftist musician promoted by Al Franken on his highly rated radio show. Listening to his program, you can hear Franken play a brief clip of Earle's music from his CD called *The Revolution Starts Now* as a promo.

On Franken's link to the Air America Web site, you can even listen to a few of the songs prior to buying the CD. They offer three songs for preview: "F the FCC" (guess what "F" stands for?), "Rich Man's War," and "The Revolution Starts Now." Here are some of the lyrics to "F the FCC": "F__k the FCC. F__k the FBI, F__k the CIA. Living in the little mother f__ing USA." Sure sounds like some patriotic, grown-up America lovin' to me.

In "Rich Man's War" you have lyrics like "In Gaza throwing bottles and rocks when the tanks come. . . ." The "grown-up love" obviously extends to Israel, as well.

The "grown-up love" Franken so admires doesn't end with Steve Earle. On December 6, 2004, Franken played his own vile parody mocking our troops in Gitmo. The parody begins:

> **Franken:** We have a new correspondent, Pat Proft, who we sent to Guantánamo, an Air America radio correspondent. . . . According to the International Red Cross, the United States has subjected prisoners to physical and psychological abuse. . . . We have Pat Proft on the line.
>
> **Proft:** An army stenographer has taken down this confession here and has given it to me and I'll read it to you.
>
> **Franken:** So this is a confession taken from a prisoner . . . is that right?
>
> **Proft** (reading the confession): My name is Hakeem Bashtara. I joined the Taliban and WOO GOSH THAT'S HOT! . . . I joined the Taliban in OKAY, OKAY! in '99. I've renounced the teachings of the Taliban WHOA OW THAT'S HOT! and praise President Bush, the *glub glub, glub* [as if being forced headfirst under water] the savior of the world.

Franken apparently found this parody so funny that he's replayed it repeatedly.

On his June 7, 2005, program, replayed on the Sundance channel that night, Franken and his cohost, the adorable Katherine Lanpher, mocked Matt Drudge, who appeared on *Hannity & Colmes* to talk about how the Left takes a certain pleasure out of bad news in the war on terror. I think this parody is just but one example of 'certain people' capitalizing on the negative reporting.

This must be Franken's liberal, "grown-up way" of loving America and honoring our troops. And, oh yeah, how Democrats love to be funny.

Liberals vs. Left-Wingers

One of the most common tactics that Democrats use to demonize Republicans is to refer to them as the hard Right, the far Right, arch-conservatives, and ultra-conservatives. We in turn, refer to Democrats as liberals or the left wing, often blurring the two as if there is no distinction. I admit to sometimes mixing up the two, but there is a difference. It is important that we identify them properly.

A liberal can be someone who naively believes that rich people are the winners of life's lottery. Therefore, it is incumbent upon the rich to share their wealth with the less fortunate among us through high taxes. Some liberals believe that it is the role of government to make sure that every American is happy and has everything they want, even if they haven't worked to earn it themselves. Many liberals believe that it is the role of government to level the playing field for everybody. Nobody should have something that their less fortunate neighbor can't have or afford.

Some liberals even believe that America is a great country. Even the greatest country in the world. Sure, we aren't perfect, but who is? There are parts of our history that we are not proud of, but we have worked to repair them.

A leftist, though, takes a much harsher view of America. A leftist believes that we are no better than any other country, including the most brutal dictatorships known to mankind. A Leftist believes that Iraqis were better off under Saddam Hussein because they had free health care. A leftist believes that Fidel Castro's Cuba is better than America because they have free education for all. A leftist believes that America goes to war in order to dominate another people. A leftist believes that America goes to war to steal another country's resources. A leftist believes that George Bush is a greater threat to humanity than Saddam Hussein. A leftist will use our rights, such as freedom of speech and the right to assemble, in order to undermine our country and its institutions.

Here are some examples of liberals vs. leftists:

- Alan Colmes is a liberal, but Janeane Garofalo is a leftist.
- Rep. Gary Ackerman (D-NY) is a liberal, but Rep. James McDermott (D-WA) is a leftist.
- Steven Spielberg is a liberal, but Michael Moore is a leftist.
- Alan Dershowitz is a liberal, but Lynn Stewart and Ramsay Clark are leftists.
- Peter Beinart (editor of *The New Republic*) is a liberal, but Katrina Vanden Heuvel (editor of *The Nation*) is a leftist.

Al Franken is a liberal who is pushing the envelope and bordering on being a leftist. Every so often he crosses the line into "leftistism." When he writes that he loves this country but wants to see it "do good," what does that mean? When he writes that he wants to see America as "the hope of the world," I wonder when we lost that status. The fact is, America is a force for greatness and we *are* the hope of the world. I challenge Franken or any other liberal or left-winger to name another country that fits that billing.

On page 10 of *Lies and the Lying Liars Who Tell Them*, Franken writes, "Liberals don't hate America. We love America more than Ann Coulter. I love it enough to engage my readers honestly."

This is Franken's way of saying that Ann is a liar who has contempt for her readers. Furthermore, to extrapolate, since liars don't love their readers enough to engage them honestly, Ann doesn't love America.

I called this book . . . *Pants on Fire* because Al Franken lies and deceives his readers. Franken may be a liberal, but he lies like a leftist. He deceives his readers by misquoting or taking what conservatives have said out of context. He is a hypocrite for accusing conservatives of citing sources but lying about what they say, a tactic Franken uses repeatedly. Based on Franken's logic and reasoning on why liberals love America more than Ann Coulter, I believe it is fair for you and me to conclude that Al Franken must hate America and hate his readers—like a grown-up.

More Liberal "Grown-Up" Love

Following the free Iraqi elections, Franken became extremely defensive about the possibility that conservatives would accuse Democrats of having wanted the elections to fail, as many had predicted. So he and the adorable Katherine Lanpher repeatedly congratulated the Iraqi people and insincerely told his audience countless times how "We here at Air America are glad about the Iraqi election." He repeatedly praised the Iraqis during January 2005.

So how does Franken demonstrate his "gladness" about a free Iraq?

On March 17, 2005, he referenced an article from the *Wall Street Journal* that pointed out that "50 million people in Afghanistan and Iraq were enjoying freedom." Wanting to once again show their support for the Iraqi people, Franken and his cohost, the adorable Katherine, performed a skit with a "live hook-up" with a fictional BBC correspondent reporting from "free Iraq." As the "correspondent" was reporting of the "celebratory mood of the 50 million free Iraqis," gunfire, minefield eruptions, and explosions are heard in the background. Is this one of the "jokes" he tells on his USO tours?

In one of his segments with resident dittohead Mark Luther, Franken actually lashed out at Luther for statements made by conservatives, particularly Rush and the *New York Post*'s John Podhoretz, that "liberals, somehow, were disappointed in Iraq's first step toward freedom and independence because it meant ceding a victory to President Bush." While Luther did not back down in his defense of Rush's comments, he did tell Franken that he didn't believe Franken wanted the Iraqi election to fail. Maybe Luther was just being polite, but I don't doubt for a minute that Franken was extremely irritated whenever he thought about President Bush sticking to his guns and not letting the elite media deter him from his war against terrorists.

But the adorable Katherine herself chimed in, asking Luther, "Who isn't happy about good news coming out of Iraq?"

Well, Katherine, I'm glad you asked, because in a March 8, 2005, column titled "When Good News Strikes," *National Review* editor Rich Lowry cited a number of liberals who were just vomiting at seeing Arabs from Iraq to Lebanon to Egypt and Saudi Arabia to the Palestinian-occupied territories demanding the right to vote and have free elections—all because of Bush's "illegitimate and illegal" war against Saddam Hussein.

Lowry wrote:

> Liberal journalist Kurt Andersen has written in *New York* magazine of the guilty "pleasure liberals took in bad news from Iraq, which seemed sure to hurt the administration." According to Andersen, the successful Iraqi elections changed the mood. For Bush critics, this inspiring event was "unexpectedly unsettling," since they so "hat[ed] the idea of a victory presided over by the Bush team."
>
> Legendary liberal editor Charlie Peters confessed to his own attack of gluckschmerz: "*New York Post* columnist John Podhoretz asked liberals: 'Did you momentarily feel a rush of disappointment [at the news of the Jan. 30 Iraq election] because you knew, you just knew, that this was going to redound to the credit of George W. Bush?' I plead guilty . . ."
>
> On his March 1, 2005, show, comedian Jon Stewart—half-jokingly—expressed a feeling of dread at the changes in the Middle East and the credit President Bush will get for them. "Oh my God!" he said. "He's gonna be a great—pretty soon, Republicans are gonna be like, 'Reagan was nothing compared to this guy.'" . . . Stewart's guest that night was Democratic foreign-policy expert Nancy Soderberg. Soderberg tried to comfort Stewart, pointing out that the budding democratic revolution in the Middle East still might fail: "There's always hope that this might not work." Soderberg added: "There's still Iran and North Korea, don't forget. There's hope."

News alert! On June 17, 2005, for the first time since the U.S.-led coalition liberated Iraq, Al Franken announced positive news coming out of Iraq: the Shiite majority was going to allow the Sunni minority to play a larger role in the framing of Iraq's new constitution.

Great, Al, I'm proud of you, was my first thought. Then Franken blew it by revealing his true objectives. Following the news he said, "We try to report good news out of Iraq because there are people who say that we don't." So in order to prove his critics wrong, he'll report good news.

As I expected, his reporting good news was a one-shot deal. Just three days later he obviously didn't deem it newsworthy to report that the anti-Syrian slate in Lebanon's elections won in overwhelming fashion. The country was inching out of Syria's clutches, which had dominated Lebanon for close to thirty years. Was this story not important? Was Franken afraid that some might say this historic victory was a result of Bush's war on terror?

Even the *New York Times* reported the Lebanon story on its front pages. Franken, however, was too busy interviewing college girls who contended that "abstinence-only" sex education doesn't work.

Grown-Up Love from Air America

Whether it's Franken, the adorable Katherine, or other liberals with egg on their faces, there is no escaping the fact that when good things happen under George Bush's watch, the president will get the credit for it. Bill Clinton received credit for the great economy of the '90s, even though it happened in spite of him. That's just reality.

On one of my occasional visits to the Air America blog, I recently found some headlines that weren't exactly supportive of good things happening in the Middle East. Here is just a sampling of the "grown-up love" headlines Air America provided in February 2005 in support of the "good news coming out of the Middle East":

- "Anger in Italy, Bulgaria Over Latest U.S. Shootings.—The U.S. is trigger happy, Allies say. The U.S. Army unit that killed Italian agent had been accused of raping Iraqi women." <The headline doesn't say that our soldiers "accidentally" shot an Italian agent, or even use the term "shot," which is certainly less of an indictment and less inflammatory than "killing" an Italian agent.>
- "Dutch Keep Date, Leave Iraq." <It looks like Air America is happy that "another ally is abandoning the U.S.">

- “Pro-Syria Marchers Take to Streets.” <Who did Bush think he was kidding with those silly Lebanese who demanded Syria’s withdrawal and free elections? The true Lebanese are those who support the anti-American, pro-Syrian Lebanese members of our good friends Hezbollah.>
- “Ramadi Residents Fear a Fallujah-Style US Army Assault.” <That’s right, just like in *Fahrenheit 9/11,* the big bad Americans are just jacked up listening to heavy metal and licking their chops at the chance to crush more Iraqi towns and villages.>
- “Shia Alliance Leader: No Permanent US Bases.” <See? Even the people we helped liberate can’t stand us and want us out.>
- “Hopes Dim for Early Syrian Pullout.” <. . . and just as President Bush demanded a full and complete pullout.>

O’Reilly Exposes America Hater—Air America Embraces America Hater

Franken smear target Bill O’Reilly has spent much time exposing America hater Ward Churchill, who teaches at the University of Colorado. Franken, as I showed earlier, only takes on those issues he can use to attack President Bush, Rush, O’Reilly, and others. That is why Franken all but ignored the story except to use it to attack O’Reilly.

Air America didn’t ignore it, though. A headline from their Web site handled it this way under the headline “Free speech hits hurdles in America”:

> Since calling people who worked in the World Trade Centers “little Eichmanns,” Ward Churchill has become red meat for right-wingers, and the sudden icon of free speech for liberals. “This is not about me,” Churchill said at an academic freedom rally, “this is about the agenda to roll back the political discourse in the Academic Bill of Rights . . . (an agenda) approved by Dick Cheney, Newt Gingrich, and David Horowitz.” Academic institutions are intimidated by the controversy and are increasingly unwilling to embrace the contentious opinions of visiting professors. “What is happening in Boulder should frighten all scholars regardless of politics.”

They treated it as if the Churchill story is about free speech or even academia. Churchill isn't being denied his free speech, nor is he an academic. He is a fraud disguised as a professor.

Does Al Love America?

Asking whether Al Franken loves America or our troops is like asking whether Al Qaeda uses too much oil in their hummus. The problem with Al Qaeda is that they want to kill us.

Franken attacks and is very resentful of accusations that the Left takes "a certain pleasure" when bad news comes out of Iraq or our war on terror. He has attacked Rush Limbaugh, John Podhoretz, and Matt Drudge for making these claims. Here is his own record on the subject:

- His parody with Gitmo correspondent Pat Proft mentioned earlier in this chapter
- His parody from the *Best of the O'Franken Factor* mocking U.S. prison guards (see chapter 23)
- His skit with a fictional BBC correspondent reporting from a "free Iraq" with explosives and bombs going off in the background
- His embrace of Michael Moore's *Fahrenheit 9/11,* which depicted our troops as crazed, sadistic heavy metal rock 'n' roll killers.

I don't believe that every liberal, or even most liberals, takes pleasure from the bad news out of Iraq, but I *do* believe that most leftists do. Draw your own conclusions.

"We Are 100 Percent Behind Our Troops"

How many times have we heard Nancy Pelosi or other liberals make this claim? And how many times have conservatives or Republicans been criticized for questioning the patriotism of Democrats? How many times have we been told that questioning the war in Iraq is the most patriotic thing Americans can do? And how many times have we been asked, "Do you want fries with that shake?"

Sorry, comrades, but supporting an early pullout of our troops is *not* supporting our troops. The brave men and women who enlisted in the military, with few exceptions, did so out of a love and appreciation for this country. Many liberals just can't or don't want to comprehend that.

It makes me laugh to hear Franken explain how liberals love America like grown-ups, as if that's supposed to mean something profound. It sounds a lot like, "I maintain impossibly high standards when it comes to telling the truth."

Loving America is not like wearing a mood ring. One day I feel one way, the next day I feel a different way. Sure, a person can criticize the government. That's the democratic way, but it's not to be confused with the patriotic way.

On June 9, 2005, *Ring of Fire* hosts Robert Kennedy Jr. (a frequent Hannity guest) and Mike Papantonio prepped the Franken audience for their upcoming weekend show on the military's plan for recruitment. Here was that promo:

> Are you a dropout or drug addict? Well the U.S. military may want you and they'll do just about anything to enlist you. . . . Join us this week on *Ring of Fire* as we talk to a "counter recruiter" who is telling teenagers the truth about military life in war time.

On June 17, 2005, Franken himself included a long segment on his radio and television show exposing military recruitment practices. What a way to support our guys!

Let me be clear: I would not want recruiters to lie to teenagers or anybody else about reality in the military. Nobody should be told that life in the military is like Cub Med. But look at the opening of the show prep: "Are you a dropout or drug addict?" Is that how these "troop-supporting" liberals see our recruiters? As nothing more than sneaky lowlifes?

I would not be surprised to learn that *some* recruiters have employed techniques that are unacceptable at any level, but there is no way that this is emblematic of the institution itself. From what I have seen and heard on Air America, there have been no positive stories about new enlistees.

Let's see. Among the lying allegations of the Left is the accusation that only poor people enlist and the sons and daughters of the privileged get to sip piña coladas as their chickenhawk parents support sending off the children of the poor to fight our wars. Does the name Deryk Andrew Schlessinger mean anything to you? He's the son of renowned conservative talk-show host Dr. Laura Schlessinger.

He enlisted with the U.S. Special Forces in 2004. I wonder if Al Franken will interview this kid and ask him why he, the son of a famous and fabulously wealthy person, would want to risk his life for his country when there are so many poor schlubs out there who can do it for him.

Anyway, I visited the *Ring of Fire* Web site to see if they had posted any more information about their upcoming show and their "counter recruiter" guest. There I found that the "guest" would be Liz Rivera Goldstein, founder of a group called the Teen Peace Project. Next I went to *their* Web site.

I found some very interesting information about their mission and goals. Oddly, there was nothing about protecting teenagers who are dropouts or drug addicts. Rather, it is an anti-military and anti-war organization. Here are just a few of their goals:

- Educate young people about the history of nonviolence.
- Document conscientious objector status in case a draft is reinstated. (In this section they discuss and teach students how to deceive recruiters to prove that they are indeed conscientious objectors.)
- Identify actions to work for peace and justice.
- Build community support for conscientious objectors.
- Oppose school recruiting.
- Educate students about the draft and military service.

In case you are wondering who the intended students of this brainwashing propaganda are, they are kids under twelve years old. I guess the Teen Peace Project wants to recruit them when they're young and impressionable.

That's right. All this is from the very people who have been screaming for the last few years how patriotic they are and how much they love our troops and how dare we impugn their patriotism.

You would think that Air America, the leading progressive, liberal radio network, would do everything in its power to avoid groups who do nothing more than confirm what so many in this country already suspect is the prevailing attitude of liberals toward our military.

14 When Is a Lie a Joke? (When You're Al Franken and You Get Caught)

In chapter 33 of *Lies and the Lying Liars Who Tell Them,* Franken attacks President Bush's position on abstinence-only sex education. Now there's a real shocker! For roughly a page and a half Franken writes very solemnly about how "abstinence-only education does not work." As evidence Franken cites a multitude of sources, including: the (liberal) Alan Guttmacher Institute, the American Medical Association, the Centers for Disease Control (CDC), and Brian Wilcox of the University of Nebraska.

After such ponderous prose, Franken then writes, at the bottom of page 284, "There's one way to make these abstinence-only programs work. We need to change the whole culture. . . . And that it's cool to be a virgin. And that's why I have sent the following letter to twenty-seven of our nation's most respected public figures." He actually sent only one letter (that we can confirm), and that was to Attorney General John Ashcroft.

In the letter Franken pretended to be a fellow at Harvard's Kennedy School of Government and to be writing a book about abstinence programs. He claimed that he planned to include a chapter in the book that would provide young people with role models of leaders who "walked the walk instead of just talking the talk" and refrained from having sex until they were married. In it he falsely claimed that he already had received "wonderful testimonies" from numerous high-profile public officials, and solicited Mr. Ashcroft for his own story.

Franken first got into trouble when it was discovered that this letter was written on Harvard University letterhead without the university's knowledge or permission, which Franken 'fessed up to once he was caught. This is probably the only chapter that caused Franken some angst with the media regarding his "truth-telling." As minor as the points that they caught him on were, his responses were not all that convincing.

Here's what he said in a September 7, 2003, interview with Howard Kurtz on CNN's *Reliable Sources:*

Kurtz: Let's talk about John Ashcroft. You apologized to the attorney general for sending him a letter on the stationery of the Harvard Shorenstein Center. . . .
Franken: Which I regret. Yes, yes.
Kurtz: (unintelligible) and which knew nothing about this.
Franken: Right.
Kurtz: Asking him to tell his personal story about remaining abstinent before marriage.
Franken: Right.
Kurtz: You said that you had many other accounts from people about abstinence.
Franken: Right.
Kurtz: Here's the book, *Lying Liars.* . . . How could you engage in that kind of deception?
Franken: This is called a prank. I'm not misleading my readers.
Kurtz: But you're misleading Ashcroft.
Franken: Yes, but it would be like saying, you know who are the most dishonest people in the world? The producers of *Candid Camera.* It's like what I did was—this administration promotes abstinence-only sex education, which has been—the mounting evidence show's that it's been—that's not intended as a pun—that shows that it does not work.

And that's why the NIH and the Centers for Disease Control and the American Medical Association and every mainstream and

> distinguished scientific and medical institution backs comprehensive sex ed.
> **Kurtz:** I understand. You were trying to make a political point.
> **Franken:** So I . . .
> (Crosstalk)
> **Franken:** So I sent a letter to him—it's not dishonest. It's a joke. . . . And, yes, if you read the letter in the context of the book, there's no way not to interpret it as a joke.

So Franken began his interview by "regretting" the letter, and then later suggested that "we need to get a life," since no one ever beat up on *Candid Camera.* Franken then wrote another apology, this time directly to Attorney General Ashcroft, in which he expressed his "sincere" and "deeply felt contrition" for any offense he may have taken over his little joke at his expense.

After reading what appeared to be Franken's sincere and deeply felt contrition to Attorney General John Ashcroft, as well as his deeply felt regrets in his interview with Howard Kurtz, you can only imagine my shock at reading Franken's true feelings about this whole event with a left-wing publication.

It seems that when speaking with CNN or trying to get Harvard off his back, Franken regrets the incident, but when speaking with *Salon* magazine, as he did on August 27, 2003, his attitude is, what's all the fuss about? It's not like I told a real lie.

Less than halfway through this book, Franken, whose numerous quotes about the "importance of truth," is already qualifying what a "material" or "real" lie is, and what isn't.

AL'S RESPONSE TO HARVARD LETTER TO JOHN ASHCROFT

Here is an excerpt from the *Salon* magazine interview:

> I don't know why, but people have been trying to put this in the same category as the other kinds of lies. <Reminder: "I hold myself to an impossibly high standard when it comes to telling the truth."> No one who reads the book thinks I'm writing a book called *Savin' It.* <Nobody would have ever believed that you would write a book titled *Lies and the Lying Liars Who Tell Them*, which, by the way, is a lot less believable than *Savin' It.*> I think even in

> the context of receiving it it's clear what it is, which is a prank to these 27 people, but it's not like announcing to the public that I won something I didn't win, or that I'm going to fund education for people that I'm not going to fund, or that the vast majority of my tax cuts are going to the bottom, or that I was vigilant before 9/11, or that Iraq tried to obtain uranium from Niger. Those are really lies; this is a totally different thing. It's a chapter in a satirical book which makes a satirical point. <Look at how blatantly he defends being untruthful by suggesting that his lies are not as bad as other people's lies.> But it's something the media can bring up, and I think it's their way of going like, "We're going to give a fair and balanced news report." (source: http://www.alfranken-web.com/smear2.html#harvard)

When Franken told Howard Kurtz that the CDC's stated position on abstinence-only education is that it doesn't work, he was wrong on several accounts. He was lying. In fact, they reported that abstinence-only education is working. Fewer teens are having sex, and the age at which young people begin having sex is on the rise. Teen pregnancy rates are also going down.

The report "Teenagers in the United States: Sexual Activity, Contraceptive Use, and Childbearing, 2002" stated that among males 15–19, the declines were particularly large. In 1995, 55 percent of teenage boys in that age range said they were sexually active; only 46 percent said they were in 2002 (Bill Clinton was president in 1995, George Bush in 2002). Compared to a similar review in 1995, teenagers are putting off having sex, and the average age of the first time has risen.

The report declares that abstinence education has been so successful that the number of teens abstaining from sex before marriage has almost achieved the goals set for 2010.*

Let's see how many lies Franken has told up to this point about this incident:

Lie #1: Franken says "this was a prank . . . not misleading his readers."

*Source: New CDC Report Shows Abstinence Education Works, Pregnancy Rates Lower. Steven Ertlet, LifeNews.com, December 13, 2004.

The Truth: It was not a prank. The first part of this brief chapter in Franken's book cites a number of studies showing that abstinence-only programs don't work. He then jumps right in with his letter to Ashcroft. The word *prank* doesn't even appear in his chapter. The proof that this chapter is not a joke, a prank, or just a piece of satire is that when he is pulling a prank, he tells us in the book. A good example of this occurs in chapter 31, "I'm a Bad Liar." Franken writes:

> I never lie. That is, unless it's absolutely necessary. So the story I'm about to tell you is a little embarrassing. . . . My son, Joe, a junior in a very high-powered, expensive New York City private high school, was beginning his college search. We started to put together a list of schools to visit during spring break. . . .
>
> My wife, who, I have to tell you, is not usually funny, had a hilarious idea. Why don't I take Joe down to Bob Jones University as a prospective student (which technically, he was) and have fun at their expense?

You see, *that* was a prank. And Franken made sure to let you, the reader, know it.

Lie (or deception) # 2: He compares what he did with *Candid Camera.*

The Truth: This is really insulting people's intelligence. *Candid Camera* was a show whose very premise was about catching people off guard, in awkward moments, or in embarrassing situations, like grown men picking their noses or little boys urinating on a police car. That is why it was called *Candid Camera.* Franken's book, on the other hand, was a smear job written under the guise of "exposing the Lying Liar conservatives." If Franken's claims in his book about the failure of "abstinence-only" education were jokes or pranks, does this mean that all the other allegations and smears against O'Reilly, Hannity, Coulter, Fox News, etc., are also jokes or pranks that shouldn't be taken seriously?

Lie #3: "Abstinence-Based Education Doesn't Work."
The Truth: Franken cites scientific evidence, including the Centers for Disease Control (CDC), that "abstinence-only" education does not work. But the 2004 CDC Report says the exact opposite of what Franken claims it says. Looks like another Frankenism!

Howard Kurtz was not the only CNN commentator to challenge Franken. Paula Zahn also had some questions to ask Super Truth Dude (STD). In an interview broadcast August 25, 2003, she asked Franken about his deceptive letter to Ashcroft and his comments on abstinence-only education.

> **Zahn:** So the folks who are saying out there, what credibility does Al Franken have when it comes to the issue of lying? He just got caught with his finger in the cookie jar.
> **Franken:** I think if you look at it in the context of the book, it was—I'm a satirist. And it was satirical. And I think that if you read the letter, you saw what the purpose of the letter was, which is, that these people who push—abstinence-only sex ed doesn't work.

So which is it, Al? Are you just making jokes, or are you seriously trying to prove that "abstinence-only sex education" doesn't work?

The Family Research Council replied with an August 27, 2003, press release that showed Franken is either completely ignorant or a liar, or just didn't take this issue very seriously beyond his desire to attack John Ashcroft and other conservatives. Here is a part of that release, which appropriately was titled "Al Franken 'Lying' about Abstinence Education":

> **AUTHOR OF *LIES AND THE LYING LIARS WHO TELL THEM* SHOULD WRITE A BOOK ABOUT HIS OWN PROBLEMS WITH THE TRUTH**
>
> Mr. Franken then proceeded to tell a lie of his own, saying that abstinence education "doesn't work" and that the decrease in teen pregnancy in the 1990s was a result of condom-based sex education. . . .
>
> In fact, many abstinence education programs have proven to be effective in helping teens remain abstinent. At the end of the 1990s, the National Center to Prevent Teen Pregnancy released a

comprehensive study which showed that abstinence was on the rise, condom use was sharply down, and public support for abstinence was growing. Also, a 2003 study from the journal *Adolescent and Family Health* found that the decrease in teen birth rates was due to an increase in the number of abstinent teens, not increased condom use.

More Evidence That Franken Wasn't "Joking"

On his radio program broadcast from the Republican convention on August 30, 2004, Franken managed to snag an interview with former Republican Majority Leader of the House Dick Armey. Just as the interview came to a close and Armey had gone onto another interview, Franken lamented to his cohost, the adorable Katherine, "I didn't get to ask him about his abstinence story."

> You know this administration has, you know, spent millions of dollars on abstinence-only education. . . . That's what they want and it doesn't work. . . . In my book I sent a letter to the Attorney General and some other people asking for their abstinence stories. . . . I felt kids needed abstinence heroes. . . . People like Bill Bennett, Dick Armey . . . and you know give funny stories.

You see? He didn't say, "You know in my book I wrote this satirical chapter about abstinence, which was so funny that Team Franken and I couldn't stop laughing for a week . . . and I was hoping to 'prank' Dick Armey before he left."

Franken's chapter, like many others in his book, was deceptive and dishonest. Unfortunately, it was the *only* chapter the media even came close to exposing as fraudulent.

Abortions—Up or Down?

I cannot think of a more appropriate falsehood to debunk after "Abstinence only education doesn't work," than "Under Bill Clinton, abortions went down, but increased under Bush." On the surface of it, it is laughable. Just what bill or pronouncement from the "Do it if it feels good" president caused pregnant women to pause and re-think if maybe they shouldn't abort their unborn children? Was it his vetoing a ban on partial-birth abortion? Was it his close relationship with Planned Parenthood, NARAL, and every other pro-abortion organization?

Well, whatever it was, he's got Franken parroting that line. He repeats it on his show whenever the subject comes up.

Best of all, the study that shows abortions actually *decreased* under President Bush isn't from some right-wing wacko extremist woman-hating organization. It comes from the Alan Guttmacher Institute (an institute Franken was all too glad to cite to prove that abstinence-only education doesn't work), which shows both the abortion numbers and the abortion rate on the decline both from 2000 to 2001 and from 2001 to 2002.

During the first two years of Bush's term in office, the number of abortions declined. The rate of abortion also declined, from 21.3 procedures per 1,000 women ages fifteen to forty-four in 2000 to 21.1 in 2001 and 20.9 in 2002. Guttmacher's abortion ratio, the number of abortions per 100 pregnancies ending in abortion or live birth, dropped from 24.5 in 2000 to 24.2 in 2002, the lowest abortion ratio Guttmacher has reported since 1974. (source: http://www.guttmacher.org/pubs/2005/05/18/ab_incidence.pdf)

15 Hannity vs. the Center for American Progress

Among the left-wing attack dogs supporting the Franken and Moore machines is the Center for American Progress (CAP), founded by Clinton chief of staff John Podesta and lavishly funded by George Soros and other liberal multimillionaires. The CAP launched months before Air America, but it increased its activism and profile after Franken took to the airwaves.

On June 16, 2004, CAP put out a paper called "The Document Sean Hannity Doesn't Want You to Read." (One of the ways left-wing groups call attention to themselves is by invoking the names of conservatives who are more popular and more successful than they are. Sean Hannity's name no doubt serves that purpose.) The press release begins as follows:

> Speaking at the Take Back America conference on June 3, 2004, Center for American Progress CEO John Podesta said, "I think you get so distant from the facts as—as guys like Limbaugh and Sean Hannity do, yeah, I think that tends to—it kind of—it tends to corrupt the dialogue." Apparently he struck a nerve with Fox News' Sean Hannity. Hannity challenged Podesta to "defend and explain one example where I—where I said something that was so false." Since choosing just one of Hannity's distortions is too difficult, here are fifteen examples."

With this release the CAP shows that it is no more reliable or responsible than Al Franken, whose show they appear on daily, or David Brock's MMFA. Here are a few extracts fom the CAP report along with my responses:

WMDS

> **Hannity:** "You're not listening, Susan . . . He had weapons of mass destruction. He promised to disclose them. And he didn't do it. You would have let him go free; we decided to hold him accountable." (April 13, 2004)
>
> **CAP:** "Hannity's assertion comes more than six months after Bush administration weapons inspector David Kay testified his inspection team had 'not uncovered evidence that Iraq undertook significant post-1998 steps to actually build nuclear weapons or produce fissile material and had not discovered any chemical or biological weapons."

Truth: Many high-ranking members of the Clinton administration, including President Clinton himself, stated that Saddam Hussein had WMDs. That David Kay testified his team could not uncover Hussein's weapons programs does not refute what Hannity said any more than it refutes what Clinton believed. Further, look closely at what Sean actually said: "He promised to disclose them (WMDs)." Regardless of Kay's testimony, Saddam Hussein never disclosed where his weapons were.

A story that was not widely reported in the United States was published on March 12, 2005, in Britain's *Daily Telegraph*. The paper reported that Hussein's foreign minister, Tariq Aziz, tried to bribe the United Nations chief weapons inspector Rolf Ekeus (1991–97) to doctor his reports on the search for weapons of mass destruction. According to Erebus's report, Aziz offered him $2 million for a "clean report." That's a pretty hefty bribe for weapons that "didn't exist."

On July 18, 2004, Howard Kurtz of CNN's *Reliable Sources* had the following exchange with ABCs Ted Koppel regarding WMDs:

> **Kurtz:** With the luxury of hindsight, were the media—were all the journalists who were covering this, were they skeptical enough?

Were they aggressive enough about the claims of weapons and related support for terrorism that Dick Cheney and George Bush were making in the run-up to war? Did the media do their job?

Koppel: I think we were probably a little bit too timid across the board. But looking back on it now, Howie, I don't know of anyone back then, not the French, not the Germans, not the Russians, certainly not the British, not American intelligence—I know of no one who did not believe that Saddam had weapons of mass destruction.

And in fact, the last time that international folks were in there, back in 1998, it was quite clear that Saddam still had WMDs. And it didn't make sense. Why, if the man could avoid an invasion by the United States simply by letting folks come in and see that he didn't have any weapons of mass destruction, why not do it? I don't quite understand that one to this day.

RECESSION

CAP cites twenty different instances where Sean Hannity said or suggested that George W. Bush inherited a recession. According to CAP, that is a lie. Here are a few examples of Hannity's "lies":

- "The President inherited a recession." (July 10, 2003)
- "First of all, we've got to put it into perspective, is that the president inherited a recession." (March 26, 2004)

CAP: "The recession officially began in March of 2001—two months after Bush was sworn in—according to the universally acknowledged arbiter of such things, the National Bureau of Economic Research (NBER). And the President, at other times, has said so himself."

Truth: David Brock has been on the same "Bush recession" bandwagon that CAP is attempting to claim here. According to Brock's group, the NBER has determined that a peak in business activity occurred in the U.S. economy in March 2001. Other Bush bashers have repeated these same findings, including guests on Franken's show.

I called NBER myself to get a clarification of their findings. I told them that I had read about their studies on a liberal Web site and wanted to know if it was in any way possible for a president, regardless of party affiliation or policy, to affect the economy—positively or negatively—just two months after being sworn in. The woman I spoke to said that it was *not* possible for the president to change the economy in two months, but that political spinners will use this study to suit their own objectives.

She obviously knew what she was talking about.

THE HISPANIC VOTE

> **Hannity:** "The Hispanic community got to know him in Texas. They went almost overwhelming for him. He more than quadrupled the Hispanic vote that he got in that state." (September 16, 2003)
> **CAP:** Exit polls varied in the 1998 governor's race, but under the best scenario Bush increased his Hispanic vote from 24 to 49 percent, a doubling not a quadrupling.

Truth: CAP's math may well be correct, but does Hannity's miscalculation constitute a corrupting of the dialogue, as alleged by the CAP report? Hannity's point remains the same: George Bush, a Republican, did very well within the Hispanic community.

WHITE HOUSE VANDALISM

> **Hannity:** "Look, we've had these reports, very disturbing reports—and I have actually spoken to people that have confirmed a lot of the reports—about the trashing of the White House. Pornographic materials left in the printers. They cut the phone lines. Lewd and crude messages on phone machines. Stripping of anything that was not bolted down on Air Force One. $200,000 in furniture taken out." (January 26, 2001)
> **CAP:** According to statements from the General Services Administration (GSA) that were reported on May 17, 2001, little, if anything, out of the ordinary occurred during the transition. They [CAP] quote Fairness and Accuracy in Reporting (FAIR), an extremely left-wing media research organization, as stating that "the condition of the real property was consistent with what we would expect to encounter when tenants vacate office space after an extended occupancy."

Truth: Al Franken has also lied or not engaged his readers honestly on this topic of post–Clinton White House vandalism (or as Franken likes to call it, a "prank"). In chapter 22 of *Lies and the Lying Liars Who Tell Them,* Franken writes, "Of course, none of this horrible vandalism actually occurred. . . . Fourteen months later, this, the final investigation of the Clinton administration, yielded a 217-page report that found no damage to the White House nor to the Executive Building" during the presidential transition. Franken and CAP both cite the Government Accountability Office (GAO), as their source.

Here is what the GAO *actually* wrote in their June 2002 report, "The White House, Allegations of Damage During the 2001 Presidential Transition":

- Page 9: "Damage, theft, vandalism, and pranks did occur in the White House complex during the 2001 presidential transition."
- Page 10: "Incidents such as the removal of keys from computer keyboards; the theft of various items; the leaving of certain voice mail messages, signs, and written messages; and the placing of glue on desk drawers, clearly were done intentionally. . . . Some documentation corroborating a number of the observations existed. EOP [Executive Office of the President] facilities, computer, and telephone officials said that much repair and replacement work was done during the transition without documentation being prepared because of the need to complete the work quickly."
- Page 11: "Twenty nine EOP staff said they observed about two dozen prank signs, printed materials, stickers, or written messages that were affixed to walls or desk; placed in copiers, desks, and cabinets; or placed on the floor."

This report can be reviewed at www.gao.gov/news.items/d02360.pdf. It's easy to read there about the "reported damage" that Franken and his fourteen Harvard student researchers couldn't find.

KERRY TAX PLAN

Hannity: "The Kerry campaign wants to cut taxes on people who make two hundred thousand dollars. She [Teresa Heinz Kerry] only paid 14.7 percent of her income in taxes, because their plan doesn't

> go to dividends, only income. So they don't want to tax themselves." (May 12, 2004)
>
> **CAP:** They [CAP] quote a press release the Kerry campaign issued on April 7, 2004, that said that Kerry wanted to "restore the capital gains and dividend rates for families making over $200,000 on income earned above $200,000 to their levels under President Clinton."

Truth: The *Wall Street Journal* reported in October 2004 that "from Teresa Heinz Kerry's 2003 returns, on her remaining taxable income of $2.29 million, Mrs. Kerry paid $627,150 in taxes . . . a rate of 12.4 percent on her $5.07 million overall income. This puts her tax rate at well below that of other filers in her 'super rich' neighborhood."

Maybe the CAP report should be renamed, "The Documents the Left Doesn't Want You to See About the Documents Sean Hannity Does Want You to See."

16 Franken Defends Clinton's Record in the "War on Terror"

(THE MOST DESPICABLE FORM OF DECEPTION BY FRANKEN AND TEAM FRANKEN)

I confess: I have never blamed Bill Clinton for the 9/11 attacks, although I believe his approach to fighting terror was inept. Maybe he just didn't want to "tease the hornet's nest," at least not while he was busy teasing other things. But I just can't believe that any president would knowingly ignore evidence that our country was going to be attacked the way we were on 9/11.

My second confession is that with every new lie I discover on Franken, I ask myself, "How much lower can this guy go?" Sure, he lied about media bias and the Pew polling data, but did anybody really take him seriously when he said that ABC, CBS, *New York Times*—at least they "try to be fair"? Sure, he lied about Bill O'Reilly claiming to have won a Peabody Award, and it was really a hoot when he cited the *Newsday* article to prove that O'Reilly was a pathological liar, only to acknowledge that he never actually read the article.

These inconsequential lies merely prove that Franken is more a nuisance than someone who should be taken seriously. However, lying and distorting research about the war on terror performed for the *Washington Post*, whose integrity means a lot to them, is something to be taken much more seriously.

Much of what follows about the Clinton administration's handling of terrorism is shocking and disgusting. The only reason it appears here is to expose, once and for all, Franken's disgusting, outright despicable, and deceptive methods for misleading his readers and supporters and the obvious lengths he will go to protect his party over our country.

• • •

In chapter 15 of *Lies and the Lying Liars Who Tell Them,* Franken writes, "Clinton, as I will demonstrate below, focused more on terrorism than any previous administration." This is absolute bunk.

He cites a passage by the *Washington Post*'s Barton Gellman from a report published on December 20, 2001: "By any measure available, Clinton left office having given greater priority to terrorism than any President before him."

"Clinton," he [Gellman] wrote, "was the first administration to undertake a systematic anti-terrorist effort."* Well, there you go. Clinton was vigilant in his war on terror, and we know that because Al Franken brought us the quote to prove it.

Franken's quote from Gellman's article about Clinton having "given greater priority to terrorism than any president before him" is accurate. The way he uses the vast majority of the report is incredibly low and deceitful. To put things into perspective, Gellman's report was more than five thousand words, which is the equivalent of fourteen to sixteen book pages. Franken cites just one sentence while ignoring the weight of the report.

Most of Gellman's article was a lengthy and detailed criticism of the way Clinton fought terrorism. Because it contains so much criticism of the Clinton administration, I will only include the points that show what the Clinton administration did *not* do to fight terrorism, contrary to Franken's repeated defense of the Clinton administration's efforts:

- "But neither Clinton nor his administration treated terrorism as their top concern, because it was not. Without the overriding impetus provided by September 11, the war on terror in the

*This was a statement made by Sandy Berger to Barton Gellman. It was not, as Franken wrote in his book, an evaluation from Gellman.

1990s lost as many struggles inside government as it won." <This point directly follows the statement Franken quoted about Clinton's efforts.>

- "The Treasury Department declined to monitor money transfers outside the formal banking system, such as the *hawala* network used by Bin Laden's operatives, and opposed funding for a White House–sponsored National Terrorist Asset Tracking Center. The department strongly cautioned against proposals for covert action against Bin Laden's financial accounts, arguing that the United States should be the foremost defender of the norm that cyber-attacks on banks are themselves acts of terror."
- "FBI investigators, who knew as much then as they do now about some domestic fundraising sources for foreign terror, were prevented from opening criminal or national security cases for fear that they would be seen as 'profiling' Islamic charities."
- "In two of the countries of central concern—Pakistan and Saudi Arabia—terrorism seldom rose higher than third place on the agenda when Clinton and his Cabinet secretaries sat down with their counterparts." <Michael Moore and other leftists have repeatedly accused President Bush of ignoring Saudi Arabia's role in funding terrorist groups.>
- "Even in Afghanistan, a country that otherwise held no strategic interest for the United States, the Clinton administration chose not to exhaust its available carrots and sticks with the Taliban regime that sheltered Bin Laden from 1996. To induce the Taliban to hand over Bin Laden, Clinton offered neither the incentive of normal relations nor the threat that he would back armed opponents of consolidated Taliban rule."
- "Beneath every trade-off lurked the incontestable fact that terrorism on the grand scale remained a 'hypothetical' danger through Clinton's final day in office. In the 1980s and 1990s, 871 Americans died in terrorist attacks at home and overseas, an average of not quite 44 a year. In actuarial terms, chicken bones were deadlier. Colleagues told Paul R. Pillar at the CIA's counterterrorism center, he wrote later, that 'fewer Americans die from it than drown in bathtubs.'" <In his book, Franken

writes that Sandy Berger warned Condi Rice that the Bush administration will spend more time on terrorism than any other subject.>

- "Presidential Decision Directive 35, which remains classified, set out the Clinton administration's intelligence collection priorities on March 2, 1995. Terrorism came in the third tier, after support for ongoing military operations and analysis of potential enemies in Russia, China, Iraq, and Iran."
- "'Terrorism is the enemy of our generation, and we must prevail,' Clinton told an August 5, 1996, audience at George Washington University. But he added a proviso: 'While we can defeat terrorists, it will be a long time before we defeat terrorism.' Clinton did not foresee decisive victory. The task was to manage terrorism as an unavoidable feature of the global landscape." <In 2004 both Al Franken and John Kerry argued that "we can reduce terrorism to a nuisance level.">
- "'In light of September 11th, we ought to do some soul searching,' said Michael A. Sheehan, who served as Clinton's last assistant secretary for counterterrorism. 'That's what I'm doing. But it has to be said that it was the collective judgment of the American people, not just the Clinton administration, that the impact of terrorism was at a level that was acceptable.'" <Was there any time during the Clinton years that "it was the judgment of the American people that the impact of terrorism was at a level that was acceptable"?>
- "'No issue frustrated (Richard) Clarke more than his inability to open an effective financial front in the war on terror, according to regular participants in his Counterterrorism Strategy Group. . . . 'He wanted to identify assets and freeze them,' a colleague said. 'He couldn't get the interagency process to move.'" <Clarke later wrote a book blaming 9/11 on President Bush, making him a hero to the Left.>
- "A central irritant was the government's antiquated approach to tracking money. On the day of his 1995 U.N. speech, Clinton had directed Treasury to lead an initiative to disrupt new techniques of illicit financial transfer. Three years later, there had been no progress."
- "The principal concern was a type of channel originating in the

Middle East and South Asia called *Hawala,* from the Arabic word for 'change' and the Hindi word for 'trust.'" Hawala offered a method of transferring money across international borders without physically moving it, relying on trusted partners on each side. To send money to Pakistan, for example, a person could hand cash dollars to a tea shop owner in Brooklyn. The shop owner would call a relative in Pakistan with instructions, and the relative would pay out the sum in rupees at the other end."

- "Hawala appeared to create a vulnerable point of entry for Al Qaeda operational funds into the United States. White House officials could find no government agency willing to police it." <According to the article, the Bush administration shut down two hawala operators in the United States as part of a crackdown on Al Qaeda financial assets on November 8.>
- "One member of the Counterterrorism Strategy Group remembers Clarke 'pounding on the tables and railing about the Holy Land Foundation,' a Texas-based charity whose accounts were seized this month after years of government debate. FBI eavesdropping at a Marriott Courtyard Hotel in Philadelphia as long ago as 1993 linked the foundation to Hamas, the most active Palestinian terrorist group against Israel." <President Bush shut down the Holy Land Foundation.>
- "But investigators at the bureau felt handcuffed. After preparing the case, one of them said, they were refused permission to take the next steps. The Texas charity, like the Hamas political leadership, maintained it concerned itself only with social services. "'There was a lack of political will to follow through and allow investigators to proceed on the case, despite the fact that all of the *I*'s were dotted and the *T*'s crossed,' said a government analyst who reviewed it. You have a front organization that you know is contributing to terrorists, with extremely solid intelligence information, but it is also making charitable contributions, and that is its ostensible purpose. When I say political, I mean we can't have the public come out and say we're bashing Muslims.'"
- "In meetings of Clinton's Cabinet-ranking national security officials, Defense Secretary Cohen and Gen. Henry Shelton,

Chairman of the Joint Chiefs of Staff, complained repeatedly that the government was not bringing its financial leverage to bear on Bin Laden's network. 'We knew where the front organizations were,' Shelton said in an interview. 'We know today. If we allowed the money to continue to pour in, that was something we were giving them as a freebie.'"

- "The government was capable of manufacturing 'all the indices of authentication' needed to make a validated withdrawal from a terrorist account, said one person who participated in the internal debates. It was also capable, some advocates believed, of raining electronic havoc on a business or financial institution as a whole."
- "But Treasury Secretary Robert Rubin took a strong stand against the idea [of attacking terrorist financial networks] in principle. 'As the world's preeminent financial center,' he said, 'the United States had the strongest interest in maintaining a global norm that cyber attacks on banking systems are acts of war. The United States could not defend that principle if it engaged in such attacks, and its own vulnerabilities would be substantial.'"
- "Terrorists could not operate without sanctuary and state support. To remove them, Sheehan, the State Department's counterterrorism coordinator wrote, would require substantial changes of behavior by five key states: Afghanistan, Pakistan, Saudi Arabia, The United Arab Emirates, and Yemen. Only the top leaders of those countries could make the necessary political decisions, he wrote, and only the highest-ranking American leaders could engage them. What Sheehan proposed in effect was to place terrorism at or near the top of the agenda whenever Clinton, Albright, or Cohen spoke to their counterparts. That is what happened under Bush after September 11. But for Clinton, in the times in which he governed, the proposal was out of the question."
- "After the Gulf War and the collapse of the Soviet Union, there was a very real sense of a window of opportunity to achieve a comprehensive peace in the Middle East. . . . The assumption was that if you could achieve that kind of breakthrough, it would have a transforming effect on the whole region. That, in

turn, would deal a blow to those who opposed the peace process, particularly using terrorism to do so." <Note that the Democrats, who blame President Bush for miscalculating in Iraq, allowed terror cells to flourish when they were in charge under the misguided belief that a peace between Israel and the Palestinians, which will never happen, is all that it would take to win the war on terror.>

In his book *Off with Their Heads*, Dick Morris, who was as close to Bill Clinton as anyone, wrote extensively on Clinton's lack of interest in fighting terrorists. In a sixty-page chapter titled "*Après Moi, Le Deluge*—How Clinton Left Ticking Terror Bombs for Bush to Discover," Morris writes, "If history is just, President Bill Clinton will be blamed for leaving George W. Bush a nation unaware of, and unprotected from, the deadly peril that hit seven months later."

Morris continues:

> How much did he [Clinton] know? Everything he needed to. Al Qaeda had struck the United States repeatedly on his watch, bombing the World Trade Center, the U.S.S. Cole, two U.S. military barracks in Saudi Arabia, and our embassies in Africa. Iraq had kicked out U.N. weapons inspectors, and it was diverting most of the $2 billion per year it was getting in oil money to buy and develop arms. And American intelligence had found that North Korea was secretly building nuclear weapons in vast, underground caverns, violating a commitment it made to Clinton in 1994. Clinton knew where all three time bombs lay.

In *his* book *Let Freedom Ring,* Sean Hannity writes that "the *New York Times* even quoted former Clinton advisor George Stephanopoulos admitting that the Clinton-Gore administration never gave much attention to protecting the American people from Bin Laden."

I believe the point has been made.

• • •

Bill Clinton did not take the war on terror seriously, despite anything that Al Franken or other Air America hosts say to the contrary.

Franken took the work of an honest reporter and distorted its findings. He has lied to his readers and, to this day, lies to his listeners. Perhaps had Clinton taken the warning signs more seriously, 9/11 may not have occurred and we would not be at war right now.

As Dick Morris argues, fair-minded historians will judge Bill Clinton for his failure to take all measures necessary to make sure 9/11 couldn't happen. Had he been a tough and serious commander in chief, it is likely that our enemies may have thought twice about attacking us. We know that Qaddafi has had a change of heart about sponsoring terrorism after witnessing President Bush's resolve.

This chapter shows that Franken lied about Clinton's war on terror; he lied about the main thrust of the *Washington Post* article by Barton Gellman; and he lied about what the Bush administration knew about the terrorist threat following the transition into office in 2001.

Unlike the "abstinence letter" lie, this was serious.

Clinton Admits He Rejected Bin Laden

It's bad enough when Franken distorts other people's work and research to satisfy his own duplicitous ways. But what do you say when you have Bill Clinton, in his own words, admitting something Franken claims he never said.

Huh?

On page 113 of *Lies and the Lying Liars Who Tell Them*, Franken once again demonstrates his willingness to mislead his readers with reckless and intentional charges of conservatives telling a lie. Franken writes, "In *Let Freedom Ring,* Hannity outlines a charge that he frequently makes both on television and on the radio: that Clinton let Bin Laden slip from his grasp. . . . But knowing what we already know about Sean Hannity and the standards to which he holds himself, what are the chances that this whole charge is just baloney?"

In the next paragraph Franken asserts that Hannity's sole source was Mansoor Ijaz (now a Fox News analyst), a man Sandy Berger claims has "no credibility." Never mind that Franken himself is relying on Berger, who himself lacks credibility due to his statement, "I accidentally stuffed classified documents in my socks and pants" to explain how he removed classified documents from the National Archives.

Ijaz was *not* the sole source of the Sudan-Bin Laden story. Bill Clinton himself acknowledged it while addressing the Long Island Association's Annual Luncheon at Crest Hollow Country Club in Woodbury, New York, on February 15, 2002. In contrast, Al Franken denies (on August 11, 2004, and on other radio programs) that Bill Clinton ever had this opportunity. You'd think Franken would call Clinton, as he called O'Reilly, to get his story straight.

The following is Bill Clinton, in his own words, in answer to a question from LIA President Matthew Crosson:

> **Crosson:** In hindsight, would you have handled the issue of terrorism, and al-Qaida specifically, in a different way during your administration?
>
> **Clinton:** Well, it's interesting now, you know, that I would be asked that question because, at the time, a lot of people thought I was too obsessed with Osama bin Laden and al-Qaida. And when I bombed his training camp and tried to kill him and his high command in 1998 after the African Embassy bombings, some people criticized me for doing it. We just barely missed him by a couple of hours. I think whoever told us he was going to be there told somebody who told him that our missiles might be there. I think we were ratted out. . . .
>
> So we tried to be quite aggressive with them. We got—uh—well, Mr. Bin Laden used to live in Sudan. He was expelled from Saudi Arabia in 1991, then he went to Sudan. And we'd been hearing that the Sudanese wanted America to start dealing with them again. They released him. At the time, 1996, he had committed no crime against America so I did not bring him here because we had no basis on which to hold him, though we knew he wanted to commit crimes against America. <This statement, you will agree, is the smoking gun. Acknowledging that he didn't want to bring him here means, "I could have if I wanted to.">
>
> So I pleaded with the Saudis to take him, 'cause they could have. But they thought it was a hot potato and they didn't and that's how he wound up in Afghanistan.
>
> We then put a lot of sanctions on the Afghan government and—but they inter-married, Mullah Omar and Bin Laden, so that essentially the Taliban didn't care what we did to them. . . .

> Now, after he murdered 3,100 of our people and others who came to our country seeking their livelihood, you may say, "Well, Mr. President, you should have killed those 200 women and children." But at the time we didn't think he had the capacity to do that. And no one thought that I should do that. Although I take full responsibility for it. You need to know that those are the two options I had. And there was less than a 50/50 chance that the intelligence was right that on this particular night he was in Afghanistan. . . .

When Hillary Clinton was asked about her husband's comments on rejecting Bin Laden, she answered:

> That's not my understanding of the facts. But as I understood the facts there was never a full and thorough offer. <Question: does this mean that there was an offer, just not as full and thorough as she would have liked? One has to parse Bill's and her statements very, very carefully.> But remember, when we were looking to try to deal with Bin Laden, there wasn't any, at that point, any absolute linkage as later became with both the bombings in Africa and the USS *Cole*. And it was also the fact that I think it's hard for us to remember that the United States at that point and time as well as our allies had a very different mindset about the best way to deal with these potential problems around the world. We didn't have the support of many of the countries and intelligence agencies that we were able to attain after 9/11.

Hillary's response, of course, raises more eyebrows than it answers questions.

Did we or did we not have the opportunity to arrest Bin Laden? What do you mean we didn't have the same "mindset" then that we have after 9/11? Was terrorism regarded as a real threat before 9/11 or was it not?

Franken frequently complains that the incoming Bush administration ignored Sandy Berger's warnings that they would spend more time on Bin Laden than any other issue. So if Berger knew Bin Laden was a grave threat, what did Hillary mean when she said, "It wasn't the mindset of our allies"?

John Kerry said 9/11 hadn't "changed him much," because according to Richard Clarke and Al Franken, he already "got it." So if *he* "got it," how come the rest of the Clinton administration didn't "get it"?

Why was the "mindset" of our allies important in capturing Bin Laden? Didn't John Kerry say, which was often repeated by Franken, that he would never surrender our security to other nations?

Al Franken isn't the only one who defended Bill Clinton's inaction against terrorism and Bin Laden. According to the Gellman report, Dick Clarke was also very frustrated by the dismissal of his suggestions by the Clinton administration. All that changed when Clarke realized he could trade his anger and frustration at Clinton into big bucks by attacking George Bush.

Clarke's book, *Against All Enemies,* contradicts what he had said earlier when it was "praise Bush" and "blame Clinton" time.

In its March 20, 2004, issue, *Newsmax* exposed Clarke's double speak:

> Just a year ago Clarke was singing a different tune, telling reporter Richard Miniter, author of the book *Losing bin Laden,* that it was the Clinton administration—not team Bush—that had dropped the ball on bin Laden. Clarke, who was a primary source for Miniter's book, detailed a meeting of top Clinton officials in the wake of al-Qaida's attack on the *U.S.S. Cole* in Yemen. He urged them to take immediate military action. But his advice found no takers.

Yet, on page 114 of *Lies and the Lying Liars Who Tell Them,* Franken wrote of Clarke's aggressive plan, presented to Clinton security adviser Sandy Berger to combat terrorism.

Franken Ignores Testimony for "Operation Ignore"

In chapter 16 of *Lies and the Lying Liars Who Tell Them,* "Operation Ignore," Franken writes at length about how the Bush administration ignored everything passed on to them from the outgoing Clinton administration on how to deal with the Al Qaeda/Bin Laden threat. He claims they did so out of spite and contempt for the Clintons. He cites Richard Clarke, who later went on to write a book blaming President Bush for ignoring the signs that might have prevented 9/11.

However, in what looks like yet another example of Clarke's amnesia and Franken's own "operation ignore," Clarke *praised* President Bush and his anti-terror objectives in a White House briefing in early August 2002 while he was still President Bush's counterterrorism coordinator. The transcript from Fox News, dated March 24, 2004, reports that Clarke made seven important points.

1. There was no plan on Al Qaeda that was passed from the Clinton administration to the Bush administration.
2. The Clinton administration had a strategy as early as 1998, and it remained the same until they left office.
3. In January 2001, the Bush administration decided to vigorously pursue the existing policy.
4. In early February they decided to look at whether or not to continue the previous policies.
5. The administration decided to add to the Clinton strategy by increasing CIA resources five-fold to go after Al Qaeda.
6. The newly appointed deputies, whose appointments had been held up until late March and early April, began to develop the details of the new strategy.
7. At the end of the summer they increased the funding fivefold, effectively changing the policy on Al Qaeda from one of rollback to one that called for its rapid elimination.

A question-and-answer period followed Clarke's statement. One exchange of questions and answers proves to be quite revealing.

> **Question:** What is your response to the suggestion in the [August 12, 2002] *Time* [magazine] article that the Bush administration was unwilling to take on board the suggestions made in the Clinton administration because of animus against the—general animus against the foreign policy? <This is Franken's frequent charge.>
> **Clarke:** I think if there was a general animus that clouded their vision, they might not have kept the same guy dealing with the terrorism issue. This is the one issue where the National Security

> Council leadership decided continuity was important and kept the same guy around, the same team in place. That doesn't sound like animus against, uh, the previous team to me. <In chapter 16 of *Lies and the Lying Liars Who Tell Them,* Franken writes in detail how the Bush administration ignored the terror warnings from the Clinton administration because, "Clinton-hating was to the Bush White House what terrorism-fighting was to the Clinton White House." In English: animus, which according to Clarke did not exist.>
>
> **Jim Angle:** You're saying that the Bush administration did not stop anything that the Clinton administration was doing while it was making these decisions, and by the end of the summer had increased money for covert action fivefold. Is that correct?
>
> **Clarke:** All of that's correct.

Even with fourteen Harvard researchers and Richard Clarke on his side, Franken can't seem to get his story straight.

- He lied about Clinton's war on terror.
- He lied about the Gellman report.
- He lied about Richard Clarke's testimony and version of events.
- He lied about what Sandy Berger passed onto Condi Rice.
- He lied about President Bush ignoring Clinton administration intelligence out of spite and animus.

Maybe he ought to leave reporting on the war on terror to those with expertise and go back to harassing the Peabody lady.

Paul Gigot Tells Franken to Get Lost!

In chapter 24 of *Lies and the Lying Liars Who Tell Them,* ("Paul Gigot is Unable to Defend an Incredibly Stupid *Wall Street Journal* Editorial"), Franken took exception to a February 2003 *Journal* editorial that was critical of Bill Clinton's war on crime in the '90s, saying he did nothing that contributed to the reduction of gun violence and crime. As Franken has declared war on those who criticized Bill Clinton's war on terror, he decided to go after Gigot for criticizing Clinton's war on crime. In his book, he writes that when he called Paul Gigot, Gigot basically told him to get lost.

While Franken was able to distort Barton Gellman's report in defending Clinton's war on terror, when it came to Clinton's war on crime he had to make up his own stuff. Here are some examples:

He cites Bill Clinton's signing of the Brady Bill, the "100,000 new cops program," and having aggressively enforced the Community Reinvestment Act (which requires banks to lend money to small businesses and homeowners in poorer communities) as the primary reasons gun violence and crime went down during the early Clinton years, particularly in 1993. But here are the facts he left out:

- In 1993 New York City had a mayor and a police commissioner (Rudy Giuliani and Bill Bratton) who together cleaned up and reduced the crime level in NYC to historic lows. It had nothing to do with Bill Clinton.
- The Brady Bill didn't take effect until November 30, 1993, which would mean Al Franken actually believes that in just a one-month period—December—crime across the United States dropped by 3 percent for the entire year.
- As far as the 100,000 new police officers Bill Clinton pledged, we're still waiting for that to happen.
- The Community Reinvestment Act Franken spoke of didn't get signed into law until 1999.

Now we know. When Bill Clinton lies, it's "just about sex." What is it about when Al Franken lies about Bill Clinton?

17 It Depends on the Meaning of *Meant*

A wise man once said, "Those of you who think you know it all are really annoying to those of us who do." I'm not claiming to be either one of those characters, but I know what I know and research what I don't know.

Al Franken, on the other hand, knows it all. He knows Social Security; he knows minimum wages; he knows about fighting terrorism; he knows about liberal media bias; he knows his researchers will cover his back when he gets caught; but most of all he knows what John Kerry means, even when Kerry himself says something different than Franken claims he says.

What Franken does regularly, whether in his books, on his radio show, or at public appearances, is attack Republicans for what they said, not what they meant. But he will defend a liberal to the hilt for what they could or should have meant, not what they actually said.

For instance, Franken frequently made the claim during the 2004 presidential campaign that "the Bush campaign lies and puts out attack ads on John Kerry by taking his words out of context." Consider what happened on the *Al Franken Show* on October 20, 2004.

First, Franken played a clip of Bush addressing supporters, and "quoting out of context," according to Franken, Kerry's statements to *New York Times* reporter Matt Bai, whom Kerry told, "9/11—it didn't change me much at all." This was also the same Kerry interview in which he said that if elected president, he "hoped to reduce terrorism to the level of being a nuisance." The Bush team jumped all over it. According to Franken this is an example of how these "disgusting Bush people just lie and lie . . . and take things out of context."

First, here's what Franken said Kerry *meant*: "Kerry was saying, '9/11 didn't change me much at all,' and that's because Bush had the wrong attitude about terrorism before 9/11, and it's actually the same one they cling to today." I have no idea what that even means.

Franken continued, "As Richard Clarke said in the Matt Bai article, Kerry already 'got it' in 1993 and so didn't need to be changed by 9/11. It is not only about the nations you can bomb, it is about these global 'non-state actors' that can move around. It's about financing." (*Note:* According to the Gellman report, the Clinton administration had many opportunities to shut down financial institutions supporting terrorism abroad, but chose not to.) "It's not about bombing a nation, and Kerry understood that. And it's about this globalization, and Kerry understood this from his investigations from BCCI and his investigation of Iran-Contra." (So . . . investigating banking scandals is just like investigating terror threats.) "So this is something that Kerry understood before. And Cheney, and Wolfowitz, and Bush still don't understand it today. That's why we're at war in Iraq."

Before getting to what Kerry *meant* (without Franken's interpretation), or what Matt Bai actually wrote, or what Kerry actually said, it's interesting to note what Richard Clarke, whom Franken once again misquotes, actually said in the article:

> Richard A. Clarke, who coordinated security and counter terrorism policy for George W. Bush and Bill Clinton, credits Kerry with having seen beyond the national-security tableau on which most of his colleagues were focused . . . that there was a new "non-state actor" threat, and that "non-state actor" threat was a blended threat that didn't fit neatly into the box of organized criminal, or neatly into the box of terrorism. <Okay, so far so good.>

> Kerry came to believe, however, that Americans were in greater danger from the more shadowy groups he had been investigating—"non-state actors" armed with cell phones and laptops—who might detonate suitcase bombs or release lethal chemicals into the subway just to make a point. They lived in remote regions and exploited weak governments. Their goal wasn't to govern states, but to destabilize them.

Unfortunately for both Franken and Kerry, *who already got it before 9/11,* hijacked planes, not cell phones or laptops took down the Twin Towers.

It's interesting to note the portions of what Kerry actually said that Franken chose not to quote.

> I mean, it didn't change me at all. It just sort of accelerated, confirmed in me, the urgency of doing the things we needed to be doing. I mean, to me, it wasn't as transformational as it was a kind of anger, a frustration, and an urgency that we weren't doing the kinds of things necessary to prevent it and to deal with it.

When I read the complete quote, I knew that Franken had given me another chapter for my book. Once again, he had put his own spin on things that other people said. It was obvious that not only was Kerry caught in another one of his "inarticulate moments," but Franken once again showed himself to be truth-challenged.

Jonah Goldberg, the brilliant and esteemed editor at large for *National Review Online,* wrote an article on Kerry's comment that appeared on October 26, 2004. Goldberg understood Kerry's statements in this way: "Kerry believes he had all—or at least most—of the answers for what America needs to do to protect itself in the post 9/11 world before 9/11. It sounds to me like he's saying, 'If only they'd listened to me beforehand.'"

Goldberg's article refutes Kerry's and Franken's suggestions that Kerry "didn't have to be changed by 9/11, because he *already* got it." Searching Nexis from 1992 until September 10, 2001, he found that "John Kerry" and "Bin Laden" appeared in the same paragraph only three times. When he searched using "John Kerry," "terrorism," and "editorial," he did not find a single piece Kerry had written that deals substantively with terrorism as we understand it today. Nor are there any references to legislation Kerry ever drafted for fighting terrorists.

Goldberg also cited Kerry's book, *The New War*, which the Kerry campaign claimed foresaw the war on terror. But the book actually shows how Kerry had no idea what the war on terror would actually be like. This part of Goldberg's article was very revealing:

> However, in the wake of the *Cole* attack—four years ago this month—Senator Kerry defended the Clinton administration on CBS's *Face the Nation*. In response to an attack that killed 17 U.S. servicemen, then VP candidate Cheney questioned whether the attack could be attributed to a lack of military readiness. Kerry's response was, "While there are legitimate questions always about military readiness in the context of a campaign, Yemen and what happened to the *USS Cole* is not one of them. . . . I mean, really, any terrorist can attack anywhere in the world at any time."

Gee, Al, what do you think Kerry "meant" by that?

Terror as a "Nuisance"

When John Kerry said, "We have to get back to the place we were, where terrorists are not the focus of our lives, but they're a nuisance," he gave another gift to President Bush's team. Franken claims that this is just another example of the president "lying and distorting Kerry's words."

Here, though, is the *entire* Kerry statement:

> We have to get back to the place we were, where terrorists are not the focus of our lives, but they're a nuisance. As a former law-enforcement person, I know we're never going to end prostitution. We're never going to end illegal gambling. But we're going to reduce it, organized crime, to a level where it isn't on the rise. It isn't threatening people's lives every day.

Richard Holbrooke, who was frequently mentioned as a potential secretary of state in a Kerry administration, said, "We're not in a war on terror, in the literal sense. The war on terror is like saying 'the war on poverty.' It's just a metaphor."

So now Holbrooke suggests that the war on terror, and perhaps terrorists themselves, like the war on poverty, is just symbolic. This has to be the first time in U.S. history that rivers of American blood were spilled by symbolism. I wonder what symbol those planes crashing into the World Trade Center represented?

Terrorism at any level is never a nuisance, and a 9/11 type of attack every ten years is far more than a nuisance. Preventing terrorists from destroying our country is a far more demanding task than rounding up prostitutes. I do not think the British would consider the bomb blasts in London of July 7 to be a "nuisance" either. Nevada has had legalized prostitution and gambling for years; New York City had 9/11 once. Which do you think served a bigger blow to our national psyche and spirit, or a bigger nuisance?

Not allowing terrorism to dominate our lives is a matter of psychology and inner strength. The question we must all ask ourselves is, "Do we let them win?" In Spain, where voters elected a Socialist prime minister following the terror blast in Madrid, the answer was a resounding "Yes!" Throughout most of Europe, where pandering to Arab tyrants and dictators is routine, the answer is yes.

Israelis, who have been victimized by terror attacks more than any other peoples, do not let terrorism dictate their lives; but it *is* a part of their daily lives. Although prostitution and gambling in Israel exist as well, nobody would be insane enough to suggest that controlling those vices is in any way like protecting citizens against homicide bombers.

18 Al Franken's Secret Crush on Ann Coulter

I'm not just trying to taunt Franken. I'm really not. Though I'm not a psychiatrist, I know the classic symptoms when I see them.

Have you noticed that the only female on the cover of Franken's book is Ann Coulter? While there are a number of provocative, intelligent, and beautiful Republican women on the cable news shows, Franken singles out Ann. If you look closer at the four pictures on his book cover, the three men are wearing very visible dark suits, while Ann is the only one whose shoulders are bare. And if you look *very* closely, while the guys all look very grim, Franken chose a picture of Coulter whose eyes are glancing over his way with a "come hither" look.

On March 8, 2005, Franken interviewed the respected editor of the *New Republic*, Peter Beinart, and offered him advice on how to debate Coulter, including asking leading questions about her sexual activity. Beinart seemed slightly taken aback by the sheer viciousness of his suggestions, but Franken—is he a pervert?—thought they were "fair game."

Well, how would *you* read Franken's awkward and boorish behavior toward Ann? If he doesn't have a secret crush on her, then why does he do it?

His obsession with Coulter doesn't end with his book. He spent two days on his program (April 18 and 19, 2005) complaining about her being on the cover of *Time* magazine. He actually spent more time talking about the *Time* cover then he did about Sandy Berger's pleading guilty to stealing and destroying classified documents, ostensibly to cover up evidence that would have revealed how little the Clinton administration did to fight terrorism. Franken even spent more time on the Coulter cover than he did on little Jessica Lunsford, who was murdered by a sex offender in Florida. You gotta hand it to Al. He really has his finger on the pulse of the hottest issues of the day!

Look at what Franken calls his chapter on Coulter in *Lies and the Lying Liars Who Tell Them:* "Ann Coulter: Nutcase." I am sorry, but Franken's lashing out in this manner is typical of a man who has lust in his heart for the forbidden fruit.

In his opening against Coulter, he charges her with—you guessed it!—"a big lie." What was the lie? Apparently she ran into him after a *Saturday Night Live* gig, walked over to him, and said hello. He responded cordially, which he later stated he regretted. Then in an interview with the *New York Observer,* she said she was friendly with a few well-known liberals, including Franken. This was news to Franken because he says that he hates her, blah, blah, blah. This incident made Coulter a "lying liar" and put her on the front cover of Franken's book.

According to Franken, she said they were friendly because "she wanted to establish her bona fides as just a lovable gal about town." But maybe Franken made a big deal out of this because he wants to establish *his* bona fides as a lovable guy—or something—about town.

Really, which of these two—Franken or Coulter—has used the other to gain fame and notoriety? If Coulter's friendliness really bothered him so much, why did he bring it up? Is he trying to make other liberals jealous because Coulter notices *him*? And, you know, it's funny, isn't it, how the other liberals Ann mentioned she was friendly with didn't attack her?

Franken contends that Coulter was using his name to advance her career—Right! As if she, who already has a strong following and fan base, thinks she will get more listeners or fans by "dropping" Franken's name. Would they be "Franken droppings"?

In typical Franken slash-and-burn fashion, he attacks her by citing some seemingly harsh comments without citing the source or context of her comments. As he frequently does when writing about conservatives, his objective is to make the Coulter quotes sound a lot worse than they would be if Franken had the integrity to cite their actual context.

Wait a minute! I thought Franken was disgusted when he sees people take the words of others out of context? Hmmm, Al?

Here are some of Ann's statements that Franken quotes:

- "Liberals hate America."
- "Liberals hate all religions except Islam." <Coulter actually said, ". . . except Islam post 9/11.">
- "Liberals hate society."
- "Liberals seek to destroy sexual differentiation in order to destroy morality."

As usual, Franken did not cite the source, book page, or context for any of these harsh statements. When I did a Google search of "Ann Coulter" and "liberals hate society," I found an article from the *New York Observer* called "Coultergeist," which appeared in its August 26, 2002, issue. It included some of the quotes mentioned above.

First, with reference to all the accusations that begin with "Ann says liberals are . . .": Ann Coulter herself has made it abundantly clear on several occasions that she does not mean *all* liberals. In her latest best seller, *How to Talk to a Liberal (If You Must)*, she makes it clear that she is talking about the *liberal power elite*. If Franken doesn't understand that, then perhaps he has a problem with intellectual honesty as well.

"Liberals Hate America"

This quote, too, came from the *New York Observer* article, and here is the context. It was toward the end of the interview, and anybody who read it could see that it was a very casual and enjoyable exchange. She said some provocative things, but most of it was in jest to annoy her liberal detractors, including Al Franken.

She was asked, "What happens if everybody finally converts to conservatism, then will the liberals give in?" Ask yourself, was the interviewer being serious or jocular? If you answered that he was being serious, then stop reading this book because you're not going to get the rest of it either. But if you agree that he was being comical (another word for "jocular"), doesn't it seem reasonable to believe Al Franken knew that the question was being asked whimsically?

Regardless, her joking answer was, "No, liberals are too stupid; they will never give in. They are implacable. They don't read. They hate America."

You would think that Mr. Comedy would get it. She was joking, Al!

And this from the guy who constantly complains that conservatives don't have a sense of humor!

But maybe Ann was on to something. I know that Ann does not mean that all liberals hate America, though Franken would like to depict her in this way. In *How to Talk to a Liberal (If You Must)* she writes on page 16, "[T]he vast majority of liberals are not intentionally sabotaging the nation."

So who might some of these anti-America liberals be? They don't have "I hate America" bumper stickers—that would be too obvious—but some of them have "No blood for oil" stickers, which borders on anti-Americanism. Their accusation, in essence, is, "We Americans are willing to send and risk the lives of our young men and women just to control the flow of oil." That's pretty vicious "I hate America" rhetoric in my book.

During the lead-up to the Iraq war, many of us watched anti-American demonstrators on C-Span pretend they were patriots who were just anti-war. Their posters and placards condemned our country as racist and imperialistic. That's not patriotism or even dissent. It's a call to revolution.

Rather than honest debates, they attack and demonize President Bush and the United States as imperialist bullies. Hating America doesn't always have to be overt. Saying that America got what it deserved on 9/11 suffices as well.

They denounce America because we don't have a socialist system that provides free health care for every American as they do in Iraq. That's right—Iraq. In a debate in which I participated at Pace University in New York City, on October 31, 2002, a co-panelist from the anti-America group ANSWER actually argued that Saddam provided free health insurance for all Iraqis, while millions of Americans lack health insurance. [Excuse me! Health *insurance* in Iraq?] But I guess that's only fair. After all, if Saddam's secret police are going to pull out your tongue, chop off your arms, rape your woman, throw you off a building while blindfolded, and make you walk barefoot in hot tar, well, the least these torturers can do is foot the hospital bill.

Watch the anarchists who violently disrupt G-8 economic summits. Are they really fighting for justice, or are they trying to undermine our way of life? Listen to other liberal intellectuals who say that U.S. troops should be put on trial before an international tribunal for war crimes. (To be fair, Franken probably wouldn't support such show trials, as he "loves the troops, and even performs for and entertains them.")

"Liberals Hate All Religions Except Islam"

Franken *did* lie with this misquote. Ann's statement quote was, "Liberals hate all religions except Islam—post 9/11."

How many examples do I need to give?

Christian students can't have a moment of silence in the public school classroom to reflect on their Lord. Christians can't have Christmas decorations in a public park. Christian teachers can't wear a cross necklace in the classroom. After the Bush reelection victory in 2004, Michael Moore derided the red (Bush) states as "Jesus Land."

In his book *Persecution*, David Limbaugh writes how practicing Christians are frequently demonized by the Left, and their friends in the media, as "radical right-wing extremists, Bible thumpers." He wrote of a recent incident in California where young students in California were graded on how well they pretended to be Muslims during a school activity. They were instructed to take Muslim names, chant prayers, simulate a pilgrimage to Mecca, and be observant of the Five Pillars of Islam. "We're not talking about learning about a religion, which is permissible under the Constitution—we're talking about becoming part of that religion in a worship exercise, simulated or not," according to Limbaugh.

Limbaugh also writes of a school in Edison, New Jersey, that reportedly rebuked a substitute teacher for leaving religious literature in the faculty lounge because of its potentially offensive content. Yet the school had allowed other teachers to leave literature trashing the religious right.

In 2004 the University of North Carolina made the Koran required reading for all incoming freshmen. Try making the New or Old Testament required reading in a public university, and see how quickly the ACLU sues you.

On December 20, 2004, *Washington Times* columnist Diana West penned how Christmas is under assault in Italy:

> Then there's the elementary school in the northern Italian city of Treviso that has decided to nix its traditional Christmas pageant depicting the birth of Christ in order to present a dramatic, um, *Virtumas* presentation of the adventures of Little Red Riding Hood.
>
> Substituting Li'l Red's fairy-tale trip to Grandma's house for Mary and Joseph's biblical trip to Bethlehem may sound like something that happens down the rabbit hole, but Reuters reports that things are on the level: "The teachers said the famous tale was a fitting representation of good and evil and would not offend Muslim children." And Muslim children, it turns out, are the only "non-Christians" in the Reuters story.

In his December 29, 2004, column, economist Walter Williams writes: "According to an Associated Press story (November 26, 2004), 'A public school teacher is suing his district and principal for barring him from using excerpts from historical documents in his classroom because they contain references to God and Christianity.' The historical documents in question are: the Declaration of Independence and *The Rights of the Colonists* by John Adams."

I think these stories make Ann's point quite well.

"Liberals Seek to Destroy Sexual Differentiation in Order to Destroy Morality"

Yes, on page 28 of *Slander,* Coulter writes, "*The Vagina Monologues* is the apotheosis of the Left's desire to treat women's sexuality like some bovine utilitarian device, stripped of any mystery or eroticism.

"Another way liberals think women should be like men is in the relentless pursuit of casual sex."

On page 142 of *How to Talk to a Liberal (If You Must),* Ann refers to a January 2000 article she wrote, "Chicks with D****." Her point was that the characters on HBO's *Sex and the City* portrayed women as horny girls constantly on the make, just like typical guys—not typical women.

With all this salacious material out there for Franken to salivate over, how can it be that all he does is cite her quote?

"Liberals Hate Society"

On page 27 of *Slander,* Coulter writes, "Every pernicious idea to come down the pike is instantly embraced by liberals to prove how powerful they are. Liberals hate society and want to bring it down to reinforce their sense of invincibility. Secure in the knowledge that their beachfront haciendas will still be standing when the smoke clears, they giddily fiddle with the little people's rules and morals.

"While the rich are insulated by their wealth from the societal disintegration they promote, the rest of us are protected from these Dionysian revolutionaries and their pet intellectual disenchantment only by our abiding belief in G-d."

In chapter 24 I provide what I believe is the reason Franken merely cited her quotes, rather than detail their context as I did. It appears that Franken got these quotes not from researching Ann's work, but ripping them off from another liberal author who also chose not to cite the context of her statements.

"We Should Invade Their Countries, Kill Their Leaders, and Convert Them to Christianity"

Ann Coulter is a very passionate person with very strong beliefs. One of her best friends, Barbara Olson, wife of Solicitor General Ted Olson, was killed in one of the hijacked planes on 9/11. Imagine what you'd feel if you heard a liberal say something like "We have to try to understand why the terrorists did this . . ." when one of your closest friends was killed by a hijacker obeying Osama bin Laden's commands.

You would think Franken, who always seems to "fight back tears" when talking about the untimely passing of his friend, the late Senator Paul Wellstone (D-MN), would respect Coulter's anger toward terrorists.

On February 7, 2003, I e-mailed Franken to ask whether it was appropriate for speakers at Senator Paul Wellstone's funeral to indulge in long denunciations of the Bush administration, Republicans, and other political speak. His response: "Unusual? Yes. Inappropriate? No. Except for Rick Kahn's remarks. But remember, he had just lost his two best friends. . . . He should have been cut some slack."

Franken sent another e-mail later that evening, "Do you really blame Mark Wellstone for ending his speech the way he did? My G-D! His father, mother, and sister died a few days before."

This is typical hypocrisy from Franken. He expects sympathy and understanding when *his* friends say something out of character or inappropriate, but he is ready to lambaste conservatives when he catches them in an understandably vulnerable moment.

But to get a better understanding of Ann's point when she wrote, "We should invade their countries, kill their leaders, and convert them to Christianity," one need only look at some of her columns where, unlike Franken, she provides a context. In her column "My Name Is Adolf" (September 12, 2002), she writes, "The Koran does not strictly inveigh against killing *someone else* for Allah. . . . Christian convert authors Ergun Mehmet Caner and Emir Fethi Caner say the Koran 'promises paradise to those who die in battle for Islam more certainly than it promises salvation to anyone else.'"

Continuing on in the article, she writes of hero Todd Beamer, who led ordinary, yet brave, Americans on United Airlines flight 93 to retake the plane from the terrorists. "Unlike the hijackers, whose battle cry was Allahu Akbar, in advance of slaughtering as many innocent civilians as possible, the Christian Beamer recited, 'The Lord is my Shepherd, . . . He leadeth me in the paths of righteousness for His name's sake, . . . I will fear no evil: for Thou art with me.'"

Yeah, Ann Coulter's comments were really out of line or unreasonable.

Ann Can Fend for Herself

On page 5 of *Lies and the Lying Liars Who Tell Them,* Franken writes, "Coulter has appeared on shows like *Good Morning America, Hardball, Larry King Live* . . . to complain, among other things, that conservatives don't get on TV enough." When she was asked about the Franken charges during an interview, she ably responded to each one. Here are just a few of her rebuttals:

> Franken claims I complain that conservatives don't get on television enough. Inasmuch as I am on television a lot, this would be a hilarious point. Too bad I never said it. My book, *Slander*—which Franken seems to have gone over with a fine-toothed comb—would have been a good place to make that point if I wanted to make it. *Slander* contains an entire chapter on the media, and yet I never claim that conservatives are not on television enough. What I say is: "Democrats in the media are editors, national correspondents, news anchors and reporters. Republicans are 'from the right' polemicists grudgingly tolerated within the liberal behemoth."
>
> By the way, I also say: "The distinction between opinion journalism and objective news coverage is seemingly impossible for liberals to grasp." Franken's absurd description of my point proves it.

On pages 9 and 10 of *Lies and the Lying Liars Who Tell Them.* Franken writes: "Take, for example, this gem from page 68 (of *Slander)*. To support her claim that the mainstream media is in the hands of Lefties, Coulter makes the point that *Newsweek* bureau chief Evan Thomas 'is the son of Norman Thomas, a four-time Socialist candidate for President.' Actually, Norman Thomas was the Socialist candidate *six* times." He continues that Norman Thomas was not even the father of Evan, more Franken evidence that Ann Coulter makes things up. He includes part of a phone call to Evan in this chapter:

> **Franken:** Evan, thank you for taking my call.
> **Evan:** No problem, Al. What's up? <How did he know it was Al?>
> **Franken:** Was Norman Thomas your father?
> **Evan:** No.

Ann Coulter's response?

> I claim Evan Thomas's father was the Socialist Party presidential candidate Norman Thomas. Franken drones on and on for a page

and a half about how Norman Thomas was not Evan Thomas's father—without saying that he was Evan's grandfather. This was one of about five inconsequential errors quickly corrected in *Slander*—and cited 1 million times by liberals as a "lie." Confusing father with grandfather is a mistake. Franken's deliberate implication that there was no relationship whatsoever between Norman and Evan Thomas is intentional dishonesty.

19 Bill O'Reilly Takes Down "Punk Boy" Jeremy Glick

The February 4, 2003, episode of *The O'Reilly Factor* belongs in the Hall of Fame. It had everything you could hope for in a good vs. evil verbal takedown.

In this episode, Bill O'Reilly had as his guest Jeremy Glick, a young man whose father was killed in the World Trade Center on 9/11 and who signed an anti-America/anti-Israel ad in the *New York Times* as part of a group called Not in Our Name. The opening of the ad was, "A Statement of Conscience," which began with the words, "Let it not be said that the people of the United States did nothing when their government declared a war without limit and instituted stark new measures of repression."

This interview was so explosive that after I saw the 8:00 p.m. broadcast, I made sure to watch the repeat at 11:00 p.m.

O'Reilly was curious about how someone who had so recently lost his father in the World Trade Center would align himself with such a hard-core left-wing group. If O'Reilly had done a little more research into Glick's background, he wouldn't have been so surprised. According to Glick's biography, he sits on the editorial board of the newspaper *Unity and Struggle* with his friend and comrade (his choice of words, not mine) Amiri Baraka.

Who is Amiri Baraka? He is the former disgraced Poet Laureate from New Jersey who wrote, among other anti-America tripe, a poem claiming that Israel was in on the 9/11 attacks titled "Somebody Blew up America."

Did Franken know that Glick, whom he portrayed as a poor boy victimized by O'Reilly's bullying, was really a dyed-in-the-wool radical leftist, or did Franken not properly vet his new friend? Would he have cared even if he knew?

As the interview progressed—O'Reilly's patience waning—Glick became smug and obnoxious to the point that near the end of the interview O'Reilly couldn't stomach him anymore and cut off his microphone and threw him out.

How does Franken fit into all of this? Easy. O'Reilly hates Glick; so Franken loves Glick. Simple. On several radio programs since then, Franken has lied [by omission] about the Not in Our Name ad by dismissing it as nothing more than a "simple anti-war ad" that Glick signed. Furthermore, he has lied about what Glick said and implied during the interview with O'Reilly, even though Franken himself played excerpts from the interview on the air.

Here is a portion of the two-page Not in Our Name ad in the *New York Times*. It was titled "A Statement of Conscience."

> Let it not be said that the people of the United States did nothing when their government declared a war without limit and instituted stark new measures of repression.
>
> The signers of this statement call on the people of the U.S. to resist the policies and overall political direction that have emerged since September 11 and which pose grave dangers to the people of the world.
>
> We must first of all oppose the injustice that is done in our name. Thus we call on all Americans to RESIST the war and repression that has been loosed on the world by the Bush administration. It is unjust, immoral, and illegitimate. We choose to make common cause with the people of the world. . . .
>
> The mourning had barely begun, when the highest leaders of the land unleashed a spirit of revenge. They put out a simplistic of "good vs. evil" that was taken up by a pliant and intimidated media.
>
> In our name, the Bush administration, with near unanimity from Congress, not only attacked Afghanistan but arrogated to

> itself and its allies the right to rain down military force anywhere and anytime. The brutal repercussions . . . from the Philippines . . . to Palestine, where Israeli tanks . . .

The sixty-six thousand signers included such America haters as Noam Chomsky, Steve Earle (the America-bashing rocker from Air America), Ramsay Clark, Edward Said, Ed Asner, cop-killer Mumia Abu-Jamal, and Ben & Jerry's co-founder Ben Cohen.

Franken's first lie/smear against O'Reilly on his radio show was, "O'Reilly attacked him (Glick) for signing an anti-war petition."

Sorry, but this was no *anti-war* petition. This was an ugly bash-America ad, and O'Reilly didn't attack him for signing it, either. Contrary to how Franken reported the exchange, it became heated only toward the end of the interview as Glick kept insisting that President George H. W. Bush helped arm and train what would eventually become the Taliban and thus was somehow responsible for 9/11.

Franken never mentioned—not even once—Not in Our Name, knowing full well that once people read their stated objectives, it would diminish his argument that O'Reilly viciously went after a "poor boy whose only crime was that his father was killed on 9/11."

Excerpts from the interview, broadcast on February 4, 2003, are fascinating:

> **Bill O'Reilly:** In the "Personal Stories" segment tonight, we were surprised to find out than an American who lost his father in the World Trade Center attack had signed an anti-war advertisement that accused the USA itself of terrorism.
>
> The offending passage read, "We too watched with shock the horrific events of September 11 . . . we too mourned the thousands of innocent dead and shook our heads at the terrible scenes of carnage—even as we recalled similar scenes in Baghdad, Panama City, and a generation ago, Vietnam."
>
> With us now is Jeremy Glick, whose father, Barry, was a Port Authority worker at the Trade Center. Mr. Glick is a coauthor of the book *Another World Is Possible.*
>
> I'm surprised you signed this. You were the only one of all of the families who signed. . . .

Jeremy Glick: Well, actually, that's not true.
O'Reilly: Who signed the advertisement?
Glick: Peaceful Tomorrow, which represents 9/11 families, were also involved.
O'Reilly: Hold it, hold it, hold it, Jeremy. You're the only one who signed this advertisement.
Glick: As an individual.
O'Reilly: Yes, as—with your name. You were the only one. I was surprised, and the reason I was surprised is that this ad equates the United States with the terrorists. And I was offended by that.
Glick: Well, you say—I remember earlier you said it was a moral equivalency, and it's actually a material equivalency. And just to back up for a second about your surprise, I'm actually shocked that you're surprised. If you think about it, our current president, who I feel and many feel is in this position illegitimately by neglecting the voices of Afro-Americans in the Florida coup, which, actually, somebody got impeached for during the Reconstruction period. Our current president now inherited a legacy from his father and inherited a political legacy that's responsible for training militarily, economically, and situating geopolitically the parties involved in the alleged assassination and the murder of my father and countless of thousands of others. So I don't see why it's surprising." <Months later, Franken explained to his audience that Glick was nervous when he said "alleged assassination," though nowhere in the transcript do you see Glick stumble over any other words or seem nervous. In fact, Franken writes in his book how eloquently Glick composed himself during the interview.>

. . .

O'Reilly: You are mouthing a far left position that is a marginal position in this society, which you're entitled to. <Even with all the garbage coming out of Glick's mouth, O'Reilly is still keeping the interview moving along smoothly. Contrary to Franken's repeated distortion of the interview that O'Reilly was acting like a bully.>

. . .

O'Reilly: Here's why I care . . .
Glick: Let me finish. You evoke 9/11 to rationalize everything from domestic plunder to imperialistic aggression worldwide.

O'Reilly: OK. That's a bunch . . .
Glick: You evoke sympathy with the 9/11 families.
O'Reilly: That's a bunch of crap. I've done more for the 9/11 families by their own admission—I've done more for them than you will ever hope to do.

. . .

O'Reilly: All right. You didn't support the action against Afghanistan to remove the Taliban. You were against it, OK.
Glick: Why would I want to brutalize and further punish the people in Afghanistan?
O'Reilly: Who killed your father!
Glick: The people in Afghanistan . . .
O'Reilly: Who killed your father.
Glick: . . . didn't kill my father.
O'Reilly: Sure they did. The al Qaeda people were trained there.
Glick: The al Qaeda people? What about the Afghan people?
O'Reilly: See, I'm more angry about it than you are!
Glick: So what about George Bush?
O'Reilly: What about George Bush? He had nothing to do with it.
Glick: The director—senior as director of the CIA.
O'Reilly: He had nothing to do with it.
Glick: So the people that trained a hundred thousand Mujahadeen who were . . .
O'Reilly: Man, I hope your mom isn't watching this.

. . .

O'Reilly: As respect—as respect—in respect for your father, who was a Port Authority worker, a fine American, who got killed unnecessarily by barbarians . . .
Glick: By radical extremists who were trained by this government . . .
O'Reilly: Out of respect for him . . .
Glick: . . . not the people of America.
O'Reilly: . . . I'm not going to . . .
Glick: . . . the people of the ruling class, the small minority . . .
O'Reilly: Cut his mike. I'm not going to dress you down anymore, out of respect for your father.

Any fair and reasonable interpretation of Glick's position is that he espouses the extremely radical left-wing position that President

George H. W. Bush helped arm and train the Mujahadeen, who in turn bore Al Qaeda and the Taliban.

Later, on October 8, 2003, O'Reilly appeared on NPR to talk about his upcoming book, *Who's Looking Out for You?* and was asked about the Glick "takedown." O'Reilly said Glick accused the Bushes of "orchestrating" the attack on the United States. While Glick did not use the word *orchestrate,* he certainly did suggest or imply responsibility.

Here is how Franken portrayed the O'Reilly/Glick story on his radio program on July 21, 2004:

> **Franken:** This infuriates me. O'Reilly went after Jeremy Glick . . . Jeremy Glick's father died in 9/11—in the World Trade Center . . . Glick did not say that President Bush and his father were responsible for his father's death. He said President Bush's father had trained and had sent arms and money . . . to train the Mujahadeen . . . and the Mujahadeen is where Osama Bin Laden and Al Qaeda came out of . . . that's what he said.

Franken continues: "But he did not say Bush 1 and 2 'orchestrated' 9/11—An absolute lie! An absolute lie!"

See Franken's game? Because Glick did not actually use the term "orchestrate," O'Reilly's argument is somehow discredited.

One last point about how Franken deceives his audience. After portraying Glick as a sympathetic figure, he told his listeners to bear with him as he plays one more audio clip: "But it isn't that long, because O'Reilly tells him to shut up!" Franken then begins the interview (audio) from:

> **Glick:** So what about George Bush?
> **O'Reilly:** What about George Bush? He had nothing to do with it.

Franken ends the clip here. You can go back to the transcript and see for yourself what Franken didn't want his audience to hear, and how much of the pertinent portion he left out of the story. Again, this is called lying by omission.

In *Lies and the Lying Liars Who Tell Them*, Franken provides even less background about the incident. He begins on page 78, introducing Jeremy Glick and how he was attacked by O'Reilly. In the book Franken writes that Glick explained himself "modestly and eloquently. Until, that is, O'Reilly cut him off." Then Franken cites this part of the interview:

> **O'Reilly:** I don't want to debate world politics with you.
> **Glick:** Well, why not? This is about world politics.
> **O'Reilly:** Because, number one, I don't care what you think.

Franken then writes, "A little while later, O'Reilly told Glick to 'Shut up, shut up!'"

That's it. That's as much as Franken wants his readers to know about how "brutal" O'Reilly was on Glick.

In his book Franken says nothing about the anti-American Not in Our Name ad, nor does he mention how Glick compared the U.S. with terrorists. Nor does he discuss how Glick smeared the Bushes for allegedly paving the way for Bin Laden. All Franken cared about was how the mean old bully O'Reilly, who "attacked a young man whose only crime was that his father was killed on 9/11," by telling him to "shut up!"

Yet all the evidence, much of it omitted by Franken, shows that this kid is an arrogant America hater. It also shows how Franken, once again, engages his readers ("whom he respects") *honestly.*

Through the influence of his program, Bill O'Reilly was able to procure the millions of dollars raised by various charities for the families and survivors of 9/11. There is no record of Franken doing anything for any of these families other than use a willing pawn—Jeremy Glick—to attack O'Reilly.

20 Franken Wipes Pâté off His Face

On July 13, 2004, Franken played yet another of his "bash O'Reilly" audio clips. Weekly guest David Brock of Media Matters and he took turns laughing at an April 27, 2004, O'Reilly interview with Heather Mallick of the *Toronto Globe and Mail* about Americans deserting to Canada rather than serving in Iraq.

During the interview, O'Reilly informed Mallick that if Canada assisted American deserters, it ran the risk of an American boycott that would have the same dire economic consequences France suffered during the Iraq War. During the interview he referenced a French business publication called the *Paris Business Review,* which had reported on the impact of the American boycott on France's economy. Team Franken discovered that the *Paris Business Review* did not exist, proving again that "O'Reilly lies and makes things up."

David Brock chimed in by saying that in addition to the made-up name of a nonexistent French magazine, O'Reilly lied about the impact of the boycott. He claimed that French businesses did not suffer any backlash from angry Americans. On the same day, Brock's Media Matters group sent an e-mail alert: "O'Reilly Fabricated *Paris Business Review* as Source for Success of French Boycott."

Franken spent several days on this story, encouraging his listeners to call in to the show and make fun of O'Reilly. He suggested they come up with their own fictional French business publication. This was another delirious assault on O'Reilly that Franken thought he would get away with.

A quick Google search resulted in a number of hits dealing with the boycott against France. Then I found the French publication that O'Reilly had alluded to, the *Movement of French Enterprises*, similar in name to the *Paris Business Review* that Franken and his band of nitwits mocked.

Granted, O'Reilly got the name wrong, but he got the essence of the title correct. "Paris" is different from "French," and "Business" is different from "Enterprises." The important thing is that O'Reilly got the right publication. Mixing up the name of a journal just doesn't qualify as a lie. It may be an error, but it's not a lie.

As far as Franken's and Brock's claim that there were no economic repercussions for France, CNN.com reported that the U.S. boycotts had a significant impact on the French economy. O'Reilly got it right, and Franken and Brock got it wrong. From *CNN Money*, dated April 16, 2003:

> France's opposition to the Iraq war, which sparked an instant backlash against all things French in the United States last month, has begun to take a toll on one of its top exports to this side of the Atlantic—French wines.
>
> American importers of French wine are reporting sharp drops in sales in the past two months, and other French products also have been affected, according to a report in the *Washington Post* Wednesday. The *Post* said the nation's principal business federation took the unusual step of publicly acknowledging the problem and appealed to consumers and businesses to keep political differences from affecting commerce.
>
> Meanwhile, the *Movement of French Enterprises, MFEN,* said some French businesses are suffering because of France's opposition to the war.

The article also refers to the *MFEN* as the French Business Federation. Right about now, Franken and Brock should be wiping the pâté off their faces. The article goes on to say:

> Guillaume Touton, a Frenchman, who is president of wine distributor Monsieur Touton Selection Ltd. in New York, said anti-French feeling cost him $500,000 in sales last month.

Apparently people like Brock who receive funding from George Soros consider $500K just a drop in the bucket. Most Americans can appreciate Touton's sentiments that appear toward the closing of the article:

> He [Touton] said he thinks that business will pick up only when Chirac stops making anti-U.S. statements. "We want to send the message to the French side to please do something. Or, if you don't want to do anything, then please shut up."

I'm sure many Americans feel the same way. Touton had more courage to stand up to Chirac than Al Franken, David Brock, John Kerry, and most of the Democrats did. Or is Mr. Touton, like President Bush, also a squanderer of goodwill?

21 Bitch-Slapping a Bitch-Slapper: The MRC Responds to Franken's Attack on Bernie Goldberg

Maybe my title is a bit strident, but it's in response to chapter 6 of *Lies and the Lying Liars Who Tell Them:* "I Bitch-Slap Bernie Goldberg." Though the debate between Franken and Goldberg on *Donahue* in January 2003 was not as explosive as Franken *v.* O'Reilly at the Book Expo, it was raucous enough to justify rebutting it. Besides, refuting Franken on a story he seems so confident that he won is so much fun.

On page 28 of *Lies and the Lying Liars Who Tell Them,* Franken writes, "A couple of weeks after I did the [Donahue] show, I was stopped by a TV news producer [not from CBS] who said, 'Man, you really bitch-slapped Bernie Goldberg.'"

Well, Al and your TV producer friend, prepare to be bitch-slapped back.

• • •

Former CBS reporter Bernard Goldberg was attacked during an appearance on MSNBC's *Donahue* devoted to the question, "Is there a conservative bias in the media?" Franken begins with the thesis, "Here's the difference between the mainstream media and the 15 percent of the media that is Fox, that is the *Washington Times*, that is the *New York Post*, that's Hannity, that's Rush—they cheat. The mainstream media at least tries to be fair."

When he was asked for examples, Franken turned to chapter 12 of Goldberg's book *Bias,* which reprinted a slate of Media Research Center quotes. He took offense at the ridicule of John Chancellor's commentary from August 22, 1991:

> It's short of soap, so there's lice in hospitals. It's short of panty hose, so women's legs go bare. It's short of snowsuits, so babies stay home in winter. . . . It drives everybody crazy. The problem isn't communism. No one even talked about communism this week. The problem is shortages.

It's hard to take Chancellor's statement out of context unless you believe, as Franken does, that the Union of Soviet Socialist Republics had been liberated from communism in about 1985. So Franken demanded Goldberg answer his question, "Now what happened in the Soviet Union that day?"

When Goldberg conceded he didn't know, Franken asserted,

> That was the collapse of the coup, the hard-liner coup, at the Parliament. . . . You know that perestroika had been in effect for six years at that point? The point here is, Bernie, you regurgitate a quote that you got from some right-wing media watch group, and you didn't care to look at the context of it.

Franken then read Tom Brokaw's opening words from that night's newscast in which Brokaw described it as "the day when the power of the people in the Soviet Union proved to be greater than the power of the gray and cold-blooded men who thought they could return that country to the darkness of state oppression."

Franken asked sarcastically: "Boy, sounds like a pro-communist bias at NBC, doesn't it?" Actually, in the context of the day, with people risking their lives to defeat a communist coup, what else could Brokaw have said? In reality, the coup's end didn't immediately bring democracy, but the return of Mikhail Gorbachev.

Franken continued:

> But you know what, Bernie? You did not even bother to find out what the context of John Chancellor, who by the way, is dead and

> couldn't defend himself. You had no interest in finding out the context of what he was saying, and what he was saying was that after six years of perestroika, in which communism was gone—that the people, that the reason for these shortages was the transition away from communism. . . . And you have the nerve to say about John Chancellor, you call absurd his observation that the problem in the old Soviet Union wasn't communism, but shortages. The only thing absurd about this is your accusing John Chancellor of saying that.

Well, judge for yourself. MRC analyst Patrick Gregory transcribed Chancellor's commentary on the August 21, 1991, *NBC Nightly News:*

> The coup d'etat had no effect on the fall harvest which will be below normal, no effect on exports which are in a slump, no effect on the mountain of foreign debt. Billions of dollars in foreign loans must be paid this year, more food must be purchased abroad, and the country is desperately short of cash. It's short of soap, so there are lice in the hospitals. It's short of pantyhose, so women's legs go bare. It's short of snowsuits, so babies stay home in the winter. Sometimes it's short of cigarettes so millions of people stop smoking, involuntarily. It drives everybody crazy. The problem isn't communism. Nobody even talked about communism this week. The problem is shortages.

Later in the show Franken started pounding Goldberg again about Chancellor. Goldberg expressed disbelief at Franken's statement that "the fact that they don't have anything isn't the fault of communism, it's the result of shortages." I guess Franken doesn't understand that communism produces shortages.

"Al, you're a comedian," Goldberg replied. "You ought to use that in your routine."

Franken still protested that was not what Chancellor said: "The context was after six years of perestroika, after six years of dismantling centralized economy in the Soviet Union, that was when they had the worst shortages." He denied it when Goldberg asked him if capitalism was to blame, but added: "I'm saying that the mainstream media has standards, and you don't." To complete the mystery of

Franken's confused theories, he added, "Milton Friedman would agree with John Chancellor."

No doubt feeling victorious after his bitch-slapping, Franken continued his assault on Goldberg, going from the inaccurate to the inane. He accused Goldberg of "selective outrage" over liberal media bias. According to Franken, Goldberg had been in the business for so long, he had picked a quote from here, a little eavesdropping over there, and soon enough there was enough material to write a book about liberal media bias.

On page 33 of *Lies and the Lying Liars Who Tell Them,* Franken writes, "Why, Bernie asks, if CBS identifies the Heritage Foundation as a 'conservative' think tank, does it not identify the Brookings Institution as a 'liberal' think tank?" I would think that is a reasonable question, but I guess I'm just not as quick on my feet as Al Franken.

Franken's retort? "I don't know. Bias? Or could it be because the Heritage Foundation's website says their mission is to 'promote conservative public policies,' while the Brookings website says it is committed to 'independent, factual and nonpartisan research?'"

Wow, Al is *so* sharp. The answer is basic:

1. Most conservative Web sites and organizations identify themselves as conservative because they are proud of their ideas and don't run away from them. Liberal groups, on the other hand, dread being labeled as "liberal," so they call themselves anything but. The current label seems to be "progressive," but it is common knowledge that Brookings is a liberal think tank.
2. Just because a Web site doesn't label itself as liberal doesn't mean that its creators aren't. More often than not, a mainstream liberal anchor calls someone conservative simply to put them in their place. For instance, on October 18, 2004, at the National Press Club, host Marvin Kalb referred to guest G. Gordon Liddy as a "controversial conservative" but introduced Al Franken as a radio talk-show host and former comedian. I recently went to Liddy's Web site, and nowhere does he describe himself as a "controversial conservative."
3. The Center for American Progress also bills itself as nonpartisan and makes no mention of its liberal leanings, but it is

> one of the most viciously partisan progressive groups in existence. Would George Soros be pumping tens of millions of dollars into the organization if it was nonpartisan and not progressive or ultra-leftist?

Bernie Goldberg was right. There is a liberal bias in the media, but it seems like liberals are more defensive and obsessed about it than conservatives are. Sure the bias exists. But so what? Our side is winning in spite of being outnumbered in the media, because truth conquers all.

22 Franken Accuses Republicans of "Dirty" Politics

Listening to Franken's radio program and hearing him accuse Republicans of lying and playing dirty is nothing new. To listen to his program for fifteen minutes without hearing him say "Rush," "Hannity," "O'Reilly," or "Coulter"—now that would be new. Exposing his distortions and hypocrisy is not that difficult either, but every once in a while he comes up with something that forces me to go back into my political memory bank.

On his August 2, 2004, radio program, Franken denounced Republicans for "dirty tricks" in handing out new voter registration forms to newly sworn-in citizens with the box for "choice of party registration" checked off as Republican. This, according to Franken, is dirty politics.

Nothing illegal was done, and no one was being told how to vote on Election Day. It was simply smart politics. In politics this is known as outreach.

This is done every day in communities across the country by both parties. When a new family moves into a neighborhood, activists send out brochures and voter forms to enlist new members. There is nothing unethical, immoral, or dirty about it.

Speaking of dirty tricks and unethical voter registration tactics, though, I remembered a news story about how just prior to the 1996 elections Clinton Attorney General Janet Reno performed a massive swearing in for hundreds of thousands of new immigrants, many of whom had not yet been properly investigated or screened by the FBI to see if they had criminal records or other reasons that might disqualify them for citizenship. Unlike what the Republicans did, the Clinton administration short-circuited citizenship requirements for votes. *That* was dirty tricks.

On the *Newshour with Jim Lehrer* (March 4, 1997), the topic was "Good Citizens? Did Election Year Politics Play a Role in the Rules of Citizenship?" Here are some excerpts:

> **Kwame Holman:** The Immigration Service recently had to admit its speeded-up system of naturalizing immigrants sometimes resulted in their becoming citizens before the FBI completed required checks of their backgrounds. The Justice Department now puts the number of unscreened new citizens at 180,000.
>
> This afternoon, Republican Harold Rogers, Chairman of the House Appropriations Subcommittee that oversees the INS budget, grilled both Commissioner Meissner and Attorney General Janet Reno on a number of immigration issues. He called the incomplete FBI checks of immigrants in the Citizenship USA program the most serious of his concerns.
>
> **Janet Reno:** 71,000 rap sheets for the end—have been identified as having FBI records. 34,700 individuals have been arrested only for administrative violations, 25,500 individuals have been arrested for at least one misdemeanor but no felonies, and 10,800 have been arrested for at least one felony. The presumption was based on the FBI's processing estimates—the presumption was that if there was a record, it would be—it would be identified in 60 days and returned to us. If we did not hear anything, we assumed there was no record. That is the system that we had been operating—
>
> **Doris Meissner:** There are 10,000 cases that might have disqualifying arrests that we are reviewing.
>
> **Kwame Holman:** Chairman Rogers cited a report in today's *Washington Post* that suggests Vice President Gore's office had pressured the Immigration Service to increase the number of naturalizations before election day.

Do you see the hypocrisy once again? Republicans register newly sworn-in citizens who are here legally, and Franken cries foul. Yet when Democrats register new voters, many of whom are here illegally, that's acceptable.

Media Matters for America Defends Democrats' Dirty Tricks

In an October 2004 e-mail blast, Media Matters for America issued this alert: "Conservatives Distorted DNC Manual to Accuse Dems of Dirty Tricks."

> Following reports of a Democratic National Committee Election Day manual giving party workers advice on how to combat potential efforts to intimidate minority workers, conservative media figures repeatedly distorted the manual's content in order to claim that the Democratic Party's official policy is to make baseless allegations of voter intimidation against Republicans. In fact, the manual does no such thing; it simply advises party workers to use standard, uncontroversial communications tactics to raise public awareness about the potential for intimidation.

You can decide for yourself, based on the following instructions from the manual, if conservatives are making false accusations about the manual's contents.

> 2. If no signs of intimidation techniques have emerged yet, launch a "pre-emptive strike" (particularly well-suited to states in which their techniques have been tried in the past).
>   - Issue a press release:
>   i. Reviewing Republicans' tactics used in the past in your area or state.
>   ii. Quoting party/minority/civil rights leadership as denouncing tactics that discourage people from voting.
>   - Prime minority leadership to discuss the issue in the media, provide talking points.
>   - Place stories in which minority leadership expresses concern about the threat of intimidation tactics.
>   - Warn local newspapers not to accept advertising that is not properly disclaimed or that contains false warnings about

> voting requirements and/or about what will happen at the polls.

The actual manual cover can be viewed at http://www.drudgereport.com/dnc.jpg.

Once again, liberals like Franken and Brock charge Republicans with making baseless accusations and slurs against Democrats, and then arrogantly present the evidence that proves they are guilty of it themselves. Do they think people are too stupid to understand what the memo says? The manual clearly states, "If no signs of intimidation techniques have emerged yet, launch a 'pre-emptive strike.'" What is so hard to understand about those directions?

This must be what *Boston Globe* columnist and frequent Franken guest Thomas Oliphant was talking about when he said on the *Al Franken Show,* September 2, 2004, "My experience in public life is that people who are telling lies have defense mechanisms when they get caught in lies."

Yes, and that defense mechanism is to lie, then present the incriminating evidence against yourself in the hopes that your readers will be dumb enough to think that vindicates you.

23 Franken Uses U.S. Troops as Props

I tend to become cynical when I hear people brag about how good they are. It's one thing when young children do it; but when a grown man boasts about how good he is, it's a little off-putting. It's even more unappealing when Al Franken does it. At every opportunity, Franken toots his own horn.

This is just a small sampling:

- "Well this is my fourth USO tour, and I love doing the tours." —Interview with Paula Zahn, CNN, January 6, 2004
- "That's me with John Glenn on the second of three USO tours." —In reference to a picture in *Lies and the Lying Liars Who Tell Them,* page 21
- "I've gone overseas to entertain the troops on three separate occasions." —Back jacket of *Lies and the Lying Liars*
- "And I'm going on a—USO tour to Iraq at Christmas." —From *Topic A with Tina Brown,*" CNBC, September 10, 2003
- "I am doing my fourth USO tour this Christmas. . . . I love and honor our troops." —E-mail to me on September 24, 2003
- "I am doing my fifth USO tour." —January 26, 2005, the CBC's *The Fifth Estate*

Really, what is going on when a grown man says, "Look at me, look at me, look how good I am. I do USO tours, and you don't"?

I respect that he takes risks traveling to dangerous places to entertain our troops. And I'm certain that the troops appreciate his performances, regardless of his motivations. But it's really irritating when a grown man looks for recognition for a good deed.

If you think I'm exaggerating, consider this pity party Franken threw himself on his January 31, 2005, radio program. He was talking about his recent trip to Los Angeles where he met with investors and prepared for the launch of his program in the L.A. market. According to Franken, some media folks called Sean Hannity and his producer for comments about Franken's new launch and his recent USO tours. According to Franken, the only thing they would say was, "Franken is a moron." He then complained to his cohost, the adorable Katherine, that "they [Hannity and his producer] weren't even willing to acknowledge my USO tours."

"Wow!" I thought.

Or actually, "Are you kidding me? You have called Hannity every crude and vulgar name under the sun, and now you're upset that he didn't have any kind words for you? You say that you can't stand Hannity—that he's a bastard—and now you're fishing for compliments from a person you don't even like? I think someone needs a special moment with Stuart Smalley."

Franken's shameless self-promotion, however, caught up with him when he challenged Sean Hannity's patriotism during the Democratic convention on July 27, 2004. Franken managed to snag Sean for a brief and at times contentious interview. Toward the end of the interview the tone changed from uncomfortable laughter to outright indignation as Sean charged that the Left's rhetoric against President Bush was undermining our war on terror. Franken then angrily charged Sean with having done the same thing when he said that Bill Clinton "lacked the moral authority" when he began bombing Kosovo. Sean stood firm, denying that his comments were the same as what the Left was doing. Then Franken, about to pop a vein, barked at Sean, "How many USO tours have you done?" Realizing how foolish he looked, he spent the next few minutes saying, "I was just joking . . . it was a joke. . . ." Sean, having none of it, said, "It wasn't funny."

On July 10, 2005, while on Letterman's *Late Show*, however, Franken told a different story, telling Dave and his audience that conservatives don't have a sense of humor. "I was interviewing Sean . . . and I told him that my wife said, "You don't see Sean Hannity doing any USO tours." "Well, that's not fair, honey, Sean doesn't have any talent." Franken continued, "So it was clearly a joke and Sean said it wasn't funny, because he doesn't have a sense of humor."

But the real topper came when Franken was interviewed on a Canadian TV show called *The Fifth Estate* on January 26, 2005. While the Canadian reporter Bob McKeown slammed Fox News in general and Bill O'Reilly in particular, Franken was showcased as almost a saint (or at least the "good guy"). Franken even teared up on camera as he told McKeown of his upcoming USO tours and how much he loves this country. Later, when talking with Ann Coulter about Franken's watery eyes and USO tours, McKeown told her, "Nobody is that good an actor."

Listening to Al Franken tell it, you get the impression that he is the only person who does these tours. I guess no one loves our troops like Al does. More truthfully, no other celebrity is as insecure as Al, who seems to constantly seek approval from his peers.

Many celebrities do good things for the right reasons, but they don't go out of their way to bring attention to themselves the way Franken does.

I Blow $8.99 on a Franken CD

In getting to know Al Franken, I needed access to anything having to do with him, from his books, radio show, and guest appearances to the Al Franken alarm clocks and bobbleheads. So I went out and purchased a CD called *The O'Franken Factor Factor—The Very Best of The O'Franken Factor.*

I listened to the CD while driving to a friend's house. I thought I might have missed something important from his prior programs. You would think that out of twenty-seven tracks there would be *something* I could use, but it wasn't until track twenty-six that I found anything. It was a disgusting, humorless, shameless, below-the-belt, filthy parody mocking the troops and our military over the Abu Ghraib incident. Here are some excerpts from this ugly parody, a song titled, *Sorry:*

Sorry 'bout the prisoners
Sorry they got raped
Sorry they got tortured
Sorry it got taped. . . .

Believe me when I say their apology is sincere
I'm awfully sorry for that broomstick up their rear. . . .

The chorus of the parody is: "Oopsy, I made an oopsy."

In September of 2003, I was watching *The O'Reilly Factor,* and I saw a clip of Franken ripping into Fox News's Brit Hume: "And what an a—hole Brit Hume is. How f—ing shameless. . . . These people are so f—ing shameless," an obviously irate Franken ranted.

Wow! I thought. I mean I knew he didn't like Ann Coulter, or Rush, or O'Reilly, but Brit Hume? What on earth could Brit Hume have done to be on the receiving end of such a profanity-laced diatribe?

So, once again I e-mailed Franken, asking him what Hume had done to deserve that attack. Here was his response, dated September 23, 2003:

> Here's my beef with Brit Hume. On his August 26th *Special Report* he said, "277 U.S. soldiers have now died in Iraq, which means that statistically speaking U.S. soldiers have less of a chance of dying from all causes in Iraq than citizens have of being murdered in California, which is roughly about the same geographical size. The most recent statistics indicate that California has more than 2,300 homicides each year, which means 6.6 murders each day. Meanwhile, U.S. troops have been in Iraq for 160 days, which means they're incurring about 1.7 deaths, including illness and accidents each day."

Franken continued:

> There are, of course, 32 million people in California. There are 140 thousand troops in Iraq. . . . I love and honor our troops. What Hume said was absolutely false, and I don't apologize for getting angry about someone trivializing the danger that our troops in Iraq

> are in. What Hume said was obscene and insensitive to our soldiers in Iraq and to their families, especially those who have lost loved ones. . . . He was deliberately misleading his viewers."

This Franken response is a composite from three e-mails to me on the same subject. Franken claims that he actually carries this memo (Hume's comments) in his pocket every day.

The following statement was made on June 14, 2005, on the floor of the United States Senate following an FBI report on some interrogation conditions found at Guantanamo Bay:

> If I read this to you and did not tell you that it was an FBI agent describing what Americans had done to prisoners in their control, you would most certainly believe this must have been done by Nazis, Soviets in their Gulag, or some mad regime—Pol Pot or others—that had no concern for human beings. Sadly, that is not the case.

This was not another Brit Hume "careless analogy" or anybody else from Fox News. It was from the second highest ranking Democrat in the Senate, Dick Durbin.

Unlike Hume's comments, which obviously prompted Al to spend a lot of time researching the population of California versus that of Iraq, there was no ambiguity or vagueness about the meaning and intent of Durbin's comments. Durbin clearly stated that the treatment of Iraqi terror suspects—who get three square meals a day and time to pray five times day—is equivalent to the treatment of the millions of civilian prisoners in the Nazi death camps and gulags. Certainly, by any reasonable standard, his comments were at least as offensive as Hume's.

Was Franken driven to swear and curse at Durbin for the insensitivity directed at the troops and their families? Nope. Did Franken even bring up the vile smears against the troops he "loves and honors" on his radio show? Not until a week later, on June 21, when Franken briefly brought up Durbin's comments to *defend* him.

Franken appears to be of the mind that U.S. interrogators applying information-gathering techniques to terrorists arrested for engaging in or being in the vicinity of terror activity is comparable to the

Nazis' rounding up of millions of Jews from their homes, sending them to death camps, starving them to death, conducting laboratory experiments on them, and throwing them into the ovens of Auschwitz.

One of the most valuable sources I relied on for several chapters in this book was the Media Research Center. Here is their analysis of Hume's statements and Franken's rantings:

> Hume's statistical contrast may not match up to the risk of death for a U.S. soldier in Iraq vs. a citizen in California, but that was not his point. He was making an observation about media priorities. Whereas Franken says Hume was unfairly shilling for Bush with the comment, the reality is that he was quite fairly exposing the rest of the media's unfair shilling to liberal biases in their reporting and sensationalism over the deaths in Iraq. . . . Hume was trying to contrast raw numbers of murders occurring in the two places (hence the phrase "statistically speaking" opposed to "the value of human life speaking") in order to make a point about excessive media vulture focus on the casualty rate in Iraq as being inordinately high and newsworthy above all other developments. . . .

It appears that Franken's love for the troops is mostly because he can use them as yet another weapon to bash conservatives. After all, prominent Democrats and liberal elites have made comments about the war that did not raise Franken's shackles or draw his ire the way Hume's comments did. This is further evidence that Franken sees the troops as props for his schemes.

Here are just a few examples of obscene verbal assaults against our troops made by liberals. They didn't seem to offend Franken the way Hume's did:

- "I hope for a million Mogadishus." —Columbia University professor of anthropology Nicolas DeGenova at an April 2003 anti-war teach-in
- "The majority of Americans supported this war once it began. . . . Sadly, that majority must now sacrifice their children until enough blood has been let." —from Michael Moore Web site, "Mike's letter" April 14, 2004 (http://www.michaelmoore

.com/words/message/index.php?messagedate=2004-04-14)
- "We're making too big a deal about [9/11]. The odds of Americans dying from lightning are greater." —Ed Koch and Dick Morris paraphrasing what Franken pal Michael Moore had told them (from the DVD *Fahrenhype 9/11*)
- "The American people have questions about this war." —Senator Hillary Rodham Clinton (D-NY) to military leaders who were seeking encouragement and a morale boost in Iraq, Thanksgiving 2003
- "President Bush is probably holding Bin Laden until election day." —former Clinton Secretary of State Madeleine Albright to Fox News's Morton Kondracke (December 2003)

In order for the president to "secretly hold Bin Laden" until Election Day, hundreds of our troops would have to be in cahoots with this devious conspiracy. Is this how Democrats now honor, respect, and support our troops?

It's really hard to take anything Franken says about loving or honoring our troops seriously. Certainly he forfeits the moral high ground on sensitivity to our troops and their families.

Franken Just Doesn't Get It

In truth, I don't get Franken. For a guy who comes from a political party that has an image problem when it comes to our military and national defense, you'd think he would avoid putting himself in situations where he has to be on the defensive on such issues.

On June 10, 2005, in an ironic twist, Al Franken was awarded the Freedom of Speech award by *Talkers Magazine*. No, it was not a belated April Fools' joke. The one part of his acceptance speech that stood out was his saying, after talking about how much he loves our troops, that "we owe it to our troops to have an honest debate about the war."

I think this was Franken's defining moment: thinking that our young brave men and women are fighting in Iraq, losing friends to enemy fire and roadside bombs, so we can have an "honest debate."

"Honest debates" are *not* what we owe our troops. What we *do* owe them is our unconditional support, not attacking them for panty raids at Abu Ghraib, comparing them to Nazis, the Gulag, or Pol

Pot. Not making parodies of them and their stressful work or saying that "only poor kids from ghettos" enlist.

We owe them credit for liberating millions of Iraqis, for smoking out terrorist hideaways, for building schools and hospitals, for being extra careful to minimize civilian losses, for fighting in a dangerous place far away while miserable talk-show hosts and slimy politicians attack their work.

That's what we owe our troops!

It's Just About Sex

One of the biggest complaints from liberals about Abu Ghraib and Gitmo is how some of our troops humiliated "in a sexual way" the Iraqi prisoners. In truth, what some liberals regarded as criminal sexual conduct in Iraq is regarded as party night in New York City's Village.

Franken was, and continues to be, one of the most outspoken defenders of Bill Clinton, who committed perjury by lying under oath against charges of sexual harassment by saying, "He lied about sex. Big deal, he lied about sex." So let's get this right. It's morally all right for the president of the United States of America to lie under oath when it's "just about sex," but our troops, whom Franken loves and honors, are somehow criminals to be prosecuted for trying to get information from prisoners and terrorists by using sexual taunting and other kinky techniques to get information that may save the lives of thousands of our troops and innocent American and Iraqi civilians. Go figure!

Franken Should Rally His Listeners Behind Our Troops

With the influence Franken thinks he has, it would be nice to hear him ask his listeners to pray for the troops and their families, rather than using them as a tool to attack Republicans and conservatives. Then again, maybe Franken and his audience see prayer as a sign of weakness.

During the Democratic National Convention, O'Reilly had Michael Moore as a guest on his program. Moore asked O'Reilly if he [O'Reilly] were president, what he would say to the families who lost loved ones in a war that was fought on questionable intelligence.

I don't remember O'Reilly's response, but if *I* were the president, I would say, "The American people share in your grief. Your son (or daughter) served bravely and courageously, and the American people will be forever grateful for their sacrifice. They are heroes, and thanks to them, millions of Iraqis, who had lived under a brutal murderous tyrant, are now free."

How would Moore or Franken address these grieving parents? "President Bush lied to you. Your son (or daughter) died so that Bush and Cheney could give billion-dollar contracts to their war-profiteering buddies. So vote for John Kerry, who fought in Vietnam."

The Results Are In: 9.9999 Out of 10 Troops Prefer Rush to Franken

One of Franken's biggest problems is not knowing when to quit. In another delirious episode on March 1, 2005, Franken attacked Rush, who went to Afghanistan early in 2005 to meet our troops, for telling them that "some people in America are not behind you." According to Franken, Rush crossed the line by demoralizing our troops, "who we're all behind," of course.

Did Franken really think, before challenging Rush's visit with our troops, that there is any doubt whom our troops love and admire? Does Franken really want to go man-to-man with Rush as to which of them our troops would really prefer a visit from? Hasn't he figured out yet that if he can't beat Rush's #1 rating in New York City, where Democrats outnumber Republicans 5 to 1, he won't beat him with our troops?

In contrast, Captain Jeffrey Mull thanked Rush in an e-mail for the visit and his "demoralizing" message. Rush posted the letter on his Web site, a few comments of which appear below.

> Attached are some of the pictures of you and the 1st Texas crew (the "A" team) that flew you from Kabul-Herat to Kandahar. We just wanted to thank you for what you do every day back home and especially for what you do for the military. You are one of the big reasons why our morale stays so high. We know that everyday the real message and truth about what goes on over here is shared to millions of Americans tuning into your broadcast. . . . What you do for us is bigger than you'll ever know.

As I read this e-mail over and over, I didn't find anything about Rush demoralizing our troops. Funny, he didn't accuse Rush of being a chicken hawk, either.

24 Franken "Cheats" on His Research on Fox News

In *Lies and the Lying Liars Who Tell Them,* Franken seems to have lifted the research of a group called Fairness and Accuracy in Reporting (FAIR) in his chapter on Fox News and treated it as if it were the result of "painstaking" work by Team Franken. This is the kind of thing he accuses others of doing, which smacks of hypocrisy to me.

For instance, on March 17, 2005, Franken attacked Nevada congressman and war veteran Jim Gibbons, whose fiery speech delivered about a month earlier before a Republican audience had components very similar to a speech made in 2003 by Alabama state auditor Beth Chapman.

"Plagiarism!" Franken charged with great outrage. As he says, he takes "telling the truth" very seriously. Apparently he takes plagiarizing very seriously as well.

I don't know how big a deal this *actually* is. For all I know, cheating, stealing, or borrowing material from somebody else's report, speech, or book is commonplace, especially among political satirists.

Then I came upon a press release from David Brock's *Media Matters* excoriating author Edward Klein for "borrowing material without attributing it to the source." He accused Klein's *The Truth*

About Hillary of containing "several paragraphs that appear to have been borrowed from, or at least closely based on, Sidney Blumenthal's *The Clinton Wars.*"

Well, then. I guess it is a big deal.

The uncanny similarities between Franken's chapter and the FAIR report raised my eyebrows. First, FAIR claimed that viewing *Hannity & Colmes* is like watching a Harlem Globetrotters game—we know who's going to win. Franken made the same comparison in his book. Coincidence? I think not.

Franken appears to have plagiarized the FAIR report in several of his criticisms of Fox News. What follows are details of the striking similarities of thought and expression on several subjects:

1. On the Willie Horton ad that George H.W. Bush used against Michael Dukakis in 1988:

   FAIR: Ailes once jocularly told a *Time* reporter (8/22/88): "The only question is whether we depict Willie Horton with a knife in his hand or without it."

   Franken: It was Ailes . . . who directed the Willie Horton attack against Michael Dukakis (and it was Ailes who said "the only question is whether we depict Horton with a knife in his hand or without it"). (page 61)

2. On *Hannity & Colmes:*

   FAIR: Even Fox's "Left-Right" debate show, *Hannity & Colmes*—whose *Crossfire*-style format virtually imposes numerical equality between conservatives and "liberals"—can't shake the impression of resembling a Harlem Globetrotters game.

   Franken: If any program on the Fox lineup represents the network's credo "fair and balanced," it's got to be what has been called "the highest rated show in television. . . . It's a conservative-versus-liberal talking head show, kind of a combination between *Crossfire* and a Harlem Globetrotters game. (page 63)

3. On Sean Hannity:

   FAIR: On the Right, co-host Sean Hannity is an effective and telegenic ideologue, a protégé of Newt Gingrich and a rising star of conservative talk radio.

   Franken: Roger Ailes, who has a real eye for talent, personally chose the telegenic, soon-to-be superstar Hannity. (page 84)

4. On finding a partner for Sean Hannity:
   FAIR: Before the selection was made, the show's working title was *Hannity & Liberal to Be Determined.*
   Franken: The show's working title was *Hannity and Liberal to Be Determined.* (page 84)
5. On Alan Colmes:
   FAIR: "I'm quite a moderate," he told a reporter when asked to describe his politics. (*USA Today,* 2/1/95)
   Franken: "I'm quite moderate," he told a *USA Today* reporter. (page 84)
6. On Tony Snow:
   FAIR: A former speech-writer for the elder Bush, Snow often guest hosts the Rush Limbaugh show.
   Franken: Snow, a former speech writer for the first President Bush, was editorial page writer for the *Washington Times* and is a frequent host for the Rush Limbaugh radio show. (page 63)
7. On Brit Hume:
   FAIR: Fox's managing editor is Brit Hume, a veteran TV journalist and contributor to the conservative *American Spectator* and *Weekly Standard* magazines.
   Franken: Ailes went to work hiring his team. For managing editor, he chose veteran journalist Brit Hume, a contributor to the ultra-conservative *Weekly Standard* and the ultra-conservative *American Spectator.* (page 62)
8. On *Special Report with Brit Hume:*
   FAIR: Each episode of *Special Report with Brit Hume,* for example, features a three-person panel of pundits who chat about the day's political news at the end of the show. The most frequent panelist is Fred Barnes, the evangelical Christian supply-sider who edits the Murdoch-owned *Weekly Standard.*
   Franken: . . . which concludes with Brit moderating a three-person panel of pundits. The most frequent panelist is prominent conservative Fred Barnes, editor of the *Weekly Standard.* (page 63)
9. On Fox's coverage of the news in general:
   FAIR: "Stories favored by the journalistic establishment, Kim Hume says, are "all mushy, like AIDS, or all silly, like Head Start. They want to give publicity to people they think are doing good."
   —*New York* magazine (11/17/97), quoting Kim Hume, Fox News Channel Washington Bureau chief

Franken: For Washington Bureau chief, Ailes chose Brit's wife Kim, who was determined to change the tone of television journalism. Mainstream stories, she complained in 1997, are "all mushy, like AIDS, or all silly like Head Start." (pages 62–63)

10. On the right-wing echo chamber:
FAIR: This network of fiercely partisan outlets—such as the *Washington Times,* the *Wall Street Journal* editorial page, and conservative talk-radio shows like Rush Limbaugh's—forms a highly effective right-wing echo chamber.
Franken: The *Wall Street Journal* editorial page has a conservative bias and an agenda. And the *Washington Times* has a bias and an agenda, and talk radio has a bias and an agenda and in my book, I expose that and what that does to how it becomes part of the echo chamber. (Interview with Lester Holt, June 2, 2003)

In fairness to Franken, some of these quotes are probably used in everyday conversations and by other outlets. However, citing so many examples of "Fox News bias" by using the same or very similar wording as FAIR can't be dismissed as a mere coincidence.

Sometimes, though, what is omitted shows plagiarism as clearly as what is included. In its report on *Special Report with Brit Hume,* FAIR did not mention the daily "Grapevine Segment," a two-minute segment that covers headlines that are unlikely to appear in most media outlets (but that *can* frequently be read on the *Drudge Report).* David Brock of Media Matters clearly considers it important enough to monitor and report on.

FAIR apparently didn't think that the "Grapevine Segment" merited attention, which is fine. It's their report, so it's their call. But if Franken's chapter on Fox News was based on his own research, as he claims, isn't it a coincidence that he ended up ignoring the same story?

I Challenge a Dunderhead

I wanted to see how one of Franken's dunderheads would respond to this information, and so I sent one of them a copy of it to see what he would say. At first, he merely replied, "This is really funny. Did you do this yourself?" When he finally figured out that the press might take my charges that Franken plagiarized seriously, he replied that a number of the similarities I cited were "public domain" and available on other sites besides FAIR. He mentioned Tompaine.com. Thus, he said, my charges were ridiculous.

So, me being me, I went to the Tompaine.com Web site to see for myself if it had anything about Fox News. He was right! The site did have statements similar to the FAIR report. Was Franken off the hook?

Hardly.

You see, Tompaine.com *did* have the same analysis as the FAIR Web site. The difference is, TomPaine credited FAIR at the top of their page:

> **The True Facts About the Fox News Channel**
>
> Most of this text is from a web site called www.fair.org. I edited it and added some of my own words to it. I am in no way saying I wrote all of these words. I did spend hours finding and changing and adding pieces of it together and changed parts of it. For the actual unedited full story go to www.fair.org.

More Cheating ?

One of Franken's weekly guests is *Salon* and *New York Observer* columnist Joe Conason. Joe has written his own book, *Big Lies.* I started reading Conason's book just to get another perspective from another liberal author, but it turned out to be another dose of the same material I found in Franken's book.

Even more striking were the incredibly "coincidental" similarities between the Franken and Conason books. Conason's book, *Big Lies,* was published in May 2003. Franken's *Lies and the Lying Liars Who Tell Them* was published in August 2003.

On page 20 Conason writes about Ann Coulter saying, "Democrats actually hate working-class people." On page 8 of his book, Franken quotes her as saying, "Democrats actually hate working-class people"

On pages 30–32, Conason writes of Coulter complaining in *Slander* about "liberal media bias" even though she appeared on most of the networks. On page 5 Franken writes about her complaining in *Slander* about "liberal media bias" though she appeared on most networks.

On page 32 of his book, Conason writes that Ann wrote in *Slander* that the *New York Times* ignored for two days the death of NASCAR driver Dale Earnhardt. On page 6 of his, Franken writes that she wrote in *Slander* that the *New York Times* didn't report on Earnhardt's death for two days. Franken even provides the front page of the *Times* and circles the article on Earnhardt in his book (page 7).

On page 33, Conason writes of Bernard Goldberg complaining in his book, *Bias*, that conservatives are labeled as "conservatives" by the media, but liberals are rarely identified as "liberals." On page 33, Franken writes of Goldberg complaining in *Bias* how the Heritage Foundation is labeled conservative, but the Brookings Institution is not labeled liberal.

On pages 43–44, Conason writes about how the media compounded the Al Gore exaggerations of "inventing the Internet" and "discovering Love Canal." On pages 40–45, Franken accuses the media of jumping on Gore for his exaggerations on "inventing the Internet" and his "discovery of Love Canal." Franken denied that these were even exaggerations.

On page 45, Conason writes about the Pew study from 2000 showing that Gore received a much higher percentage of negative media than did George Bush. On pages 38–39, Franken writes about the Pew study and Al Gore receiving a much higher percentage of negative media coverage than Bush. In fairness to Franken, he did use really cute graphs to illustrate his point.

On page 60, Conason writes that the Newt Gingrich "playbook" instructed Republicans to attack Democrats by calling them sick, corrupt, anti-flag, and traitors. On page 139, Franken writes, "He (Gingrich) sent out a letter advising them to characterize their Democrat opponents with words like *corrupt, sick, pathetic, greedy,* and *traitor.*"

On page 112, Conason writes that Coulter says, "Liberals seek to destroy sexual differentiation in order to destroy morality." On page 9 of his book, Franken quotes Ann Coulter, "Liberals seek to destroy sexual differentiation in order to destroy morality."

One has to wonder. Did Al and Team Franken actually *research* Rush, Ann, O'Reilly, and other conservatives, or did they just *research* what others have written about them?

Hannity and Colmes and Franken

In what can only be described as another black eye for Team Franken's "get your facts straight" research, in chapters 14 and 26 of *Lies and the Lying Liars Who Tell Them,* Franken mocks Fox's "fair and balanced" credo because of the obvious domination of Sean Hannity over Alan Colmes on the hit show *Hannity & Colmes.*

In fact, the title of chapter 14 in his book is called "Hannity and Colmes." Get it? Hannity is more dominant, so Franken makes his name bigger—another example of Franken's inimitable humor.

Now I know that Franken knows what he's talking about when he says that Hannity and Colmes isn't "fair and balanced" because Franken monitors the show scrupulously.

For chapter 26, another chapter related to Fox News and *H&C,* Franken's title is, "I Attend the White House Correspondents' Dinner and Annoy Karl Rove, Richard Perle, Paul Wolfowitz, and the Entire Fox News Team." As I'm reading this, I'm trying to figure out what the point of this title is. Is he bragging that he got to attend a fancy shmancy dinner or is he trying to reaffirm what an immature pain in the ass he is? The answer is a little bit of both, particularly the part about annoying the Fox people.

Franken writes "I had been watching a lot of *Hannity & Colmes* during the war in Iraq and had something I thought Alan could use against Hannity" (page 208).

A little farther down, Franken writes that he grows frustrated with Colmes because he won't go after Hannity with his (Franken's) material.

Here is a part of that exchange:

Franken: "You're going to use it, right?"
Colmes: "Well, that's not the format of our show."
Franken: Not the format of your show?"
Colmes: We don't go after each other. We go after the guests."

This just had Franken riled.

First, everybody who watches the program understands the format. Certainly, I would expect someone like Franken, who not only "watches" the show but "monitors it" and has become enough of an *authority* to write about it, would understand that.

"Fair and Balanced" means that each side is given the opportunity to make their case and debate a highly qualified guest on the subject at hand. While Colmes may not match up "telegenically," as Franken and FAIR put it, the show provides plenty of balance to Sean's posture and ability. Here is just a sampling of the balance to Hannity, who appear regularly to challenge his conservative positions. Former Clinton counsel Lanny Davis, former DNC chairman Terry McAuliffe, attorney and former Dukakis strategist Susan Estrich, *Newsday* reporter and Regis Philbin soundalike Ellis Hennican, Democratic strategist Bob Beckel, racial agitator Al Sharpton, abortion rights advocate Patricia Ireland, Democratic advisor Howard Wolfson, Michael Moore pal Greg Palast, and the list goes on. There is never a segment (I'm sure one of Franken's researchers will now look for one) where the guest opposing Hannity's position isn't someone of stature or ability.

On his October 15, 2004, radio program, Franken had Alan Colmes as his guest and confessed that he hadn't understood the format of the show.

Now, I have to wonder: How does an individual put himself out front as someone who "holds himself to an impossibly high standard when it comes to telling the truth," reinforce that claim by stating he is using "fourteen Harvard students" (America's best and brightest) as researchers, go on the record as saying that he monitors the show, then get it *SOOOO* wrong on the format of the program?

But Alan Colmes is a nice and forgiving guy, and he gave Franken a pass. Of course, this isn't about Colmes; it is about Franken, time after time, attacking and smearing people who are better and smarter than he is, being allowed to get away with smear tactics. This *is* about Franken, who claims that he is "standing up to bullies."

Well pardon me, but is Alan Colmes a bully? Or maybe Franken thinks that for a liberal to have *any* credibility, he has to be as obnoxious, dishonest, and sloppy in his research as he is.

25 Paul Wellstone's Memorial Service: A Case Study in Blaming Conservatives for *Your* Mistakes

The chapter on Paul Wellstone's memorial service from Franken's book *Lies and the Lying Liars Who Tell Them* is probably his most passionate. His title for the chapter is "'This Was Not a Memorial to Paul Wellstone': A Case Study in Right-Wing Lies."

Anyone who saw the memorial broadcast on C-Span will know what I'm talking about. Anyone who didn't see it, well, nothing I write will do it justice. It was one of the biggest news stories prior to the 2002 elections.

According to media reports, many Americans who watched the memorial thought it was more of a political pep rally than a somber, respectful memorial for a decent politician who had recently died with his wife, daughter, and several members of his campaign staff in a tragic airplane crash. Following the memorial, the national media—print, radio, and television—were abuzz over the content and conduct of the service. Here are just a few of the headlines:

- *Time:* "Fallout from a Memorial: Did the Memorial Service for Paul Wellstone Cost Democrats the Election?"
- *CNN Inside Politics:* "Tone of Wellstone Memorial Generates Anger"
- *St. Paul Pioneer Press:* "Wellstone Memorial Service: Local Fame or National Infamy?"

- *New York Times:* "Wellstone Memorial Takes on Spirit of Rally"
- *Associated Press:* "Wellstone Memorial Was Political Theater Almost from the Start"
- *Bulletins Frontrunner:* "Poll Indicates Memorial Service Turned Independent Voters Towards Coleman"
- Associated Press State and Local Wire: "Moe Apologizes for Partisanship at Wellstone Memorial"
- *New York Times:* "Wellstone Tribute: Too Much Politics?"

In an interview with CNN on October 31, 2002, Dave Ryan, a Minneapolis radio talk-show host, said, "I guess the local radio stations here were swamped with phone calls from people who were angry because they had been sold a memorial that had turned into a political rally." Minnesota Democratic State Chairman Mike Erlandson complained, "The boos were unfortunate and inappropriate."

This is not how Franken saw it. There was little room, as far as he was concerned, for dissenting opinions. He writes on page 179:

> I was there. It was a beautiful memorial, sometimes incredibly sad, sometimes funny, sometimes rowdy, and sometimes political. Some people watching on television were offended. Some people were moved. But the Right saw an opening. They took moments out of context . . . and used it as a political club to attack the Democrats.

Throughout the chapter, he quotes and cites conservative talk-radio hosts, newspaper columnists, and writers from conservative magazines as part of a conspiracy to form public opinion that the memorial wasn't "what people saw." After all, *Al Franken was there and we weren't.*

He also claims that he watched the memorial on video together with Team Franken, and they agreed that the event was a respectful memorial. And—surprise!—they agreed that Rush and others were guilty of misrepresenting what really happened, leading other print media to go with what conservatives reported rather than what actually happened.

On page 200 he writes, "It was Rush, and the Republican Party, and *The Weekly Standard,* and the *Wall Street Journal*, and Fox—

and then it was CNN and MSNBC and all the newspapers that wrote hundreds of articles—that got it wrong. Some of them did it maliciously. Some of them just picked up the story. Some were evil, some just lazy."

He goes to great lengths to cite what every conservative said or wrote regarding the memorial, to paint them as "evil liars." Franken included Fox News as part of the propaganda machine, but he never cites their role, other than a brief comment by Mort Kondracke, who hardly represents conservative thinking on Fox News. Franken misleads (that is, lies), as he accuses his targets of doing, by lumping subjects or people into the same story and assuming that his readers won't challenge or research his accuracy. When a conservative does this sort of thing, Franken denounces it as a "lying lie."

More important than his lies about Fox News, Franken produces no evidence, other than wishful thinking, that the "right wing" poisoned the minds of millions of Americans. He writes of *one article* in the *Weekly Standard,* which hardly has the influence that the *New York Times*, *Los Angeles Times*, or *Washington Post* have to influence national public opinion. Exactly how many Minnesota Democrats read the *Weekly Standard*? His reference to the culpability of the *Wall Street Journal* is also limited to just one article by op-ed contributor Peggy Noonan. All of these combined hardly amount to a barrage by the right wing. His claims just don't stand up to the truth.

In an article published in the *New York Times* before Rush Limbaugh took to the airwaves the following day, Jodi Wilgoren called it "a touching memorial for beloved friends and a rousing political rally for Democrats desperate to retain control of the Senate." She wrote:

> The mourners wore green Wellstone buttons on their black suits. The closing hymn was a campaign song, "Stand Up, Keep Fighting"—only its refrain was edited, from "Vote for Paul Wellstone" to "Remember Paul Wellstone. . . ."
>
> [P]eople sprang to their feet as the face of Walter F. Mondale, the former vice president, who is likely to replace Mr. Wellstone on Tuesday's ballot, flashed on the Jumbotron. The spontaneous chant was a muddle of "Wellstone, Wellstone!" and "Mondale, Mondale!"

> Later, the Wellstones' youngest child, Mark, would lead the crowd in a roar of "We will win!" . . .
>
> The roar for Senator Edward Kennedy, Democrat of Massachusetts, was undercut by boos for Senator Trent Lott of Mississippi, the Republican leader. Gov. Jesse Ventura of Minnesota, an Independent, also was greeted with disdain.

Is Franken suggesting that the *New York Times* is now in the back pocket of the "right-wing machine"?

I later e-mailed Jodi Wilgoren to ask her if she wrote her article before or after Rush Limbaugh took to the airwaves the day after the memorial. Her response was clear and to the point:

> I was sitting in the hall writing and rewriting for editions as the event was going on. I thought it was political from the moment I stepped on the grounds, and that it built throughout the night, growing more political each hour. I heard nothing that Rush Limbaugh said about the event then or since.

I also exchanged e-mails with the author of "No Contest: Paul Wellstone's Memorial Service Turns into a Pep Rally," William Saletan, which was published by the online magazine *Slate* on October 29, 2002. Note that Franken has said, "We love William Saletan," on his radio show. Saletan wrote:

> But the solemnity of death and the grace of Midwestern humor are overshadowed by the angry piety of populism. Most of the event feels like a rally. The touching recollections are followed by sharp political speeches urging Wellstone's supporters to channel their grief into electoral victory. . . .
>
> But as the evening's speakers proceed, it becomes clear to them, honoring Wellstone's legacy is all about winning the election.
>
> Rick Kahn, a friend of Wellstone's, urges everyone to "set aside the partisan bickering," but in the next breath he challenges several Republican Senators in attendance to "honor your friend" by helping to "win this election for Paul Wellstone."

In an e-mail exchange with Saletan, I asked him why or how he came to a different conclusion than Franken about the Wellstone memorial. In his reply he said:

> I was sitting in the press room next to a *New York Times* reporter who, without speaking to me about it, reached the same conclusion I did. I doubt she was part of any right-wing conspiracy. . . .
>
> Ideological media do tend to be more "on message" and therefore amplify whatever they pick up. In this case they picked up the pep-rally aspect and amplified it. But they didn't create it. Kahn and his colleagues did. . . .
>
> I can't say Franken was wrong if his point was that the service was more than a pep rally. But if he thinks it wasn't a pep rally at all, he's certainly wrong about that.
>
> I don't have much patience for his (Franken's) sort of whining. That Senate race was the Democrats' to lose, and they lost it. All they had to do was conduct a normal, decent memorial service. Instead, they pushed it. Yeah, Limbaugh and company pounced at the opportunity the Dems gave them. But I'm a personal responsibility kind of guy. If you give the other side a tasteless gaffe like that, and they run with it, that's on you.

From his appearance on *Donahue* to his books and radio program, Franken has bellyached and smeared Rush Limbaugh and the right wing of this country. The fact is, conservatives like Rush Limbaugh *did* respect Senator Wellstone. It was the Left who tried to exploit his untimely death to achieve electoral victory at the ballot box.

On his radio program, Rush noted, "Wellstone was a down-the-middle liberal. He wasn't ashamed of it, and he didn't try to convince people otherwise. He didn't take polls to figure out where he stood on issues." That about says it all.

As William Saletan suggests, the Democrats blew it!

Franken Doesn't Just Smear Conservatives

Whatever charming qualities Franken may have, tolerance for the views of people who disagree with him isn't one of them. All that's needed to incur his wrath is to argue with him on something he insists can only be seen one way.

In a rather gratuitous cheap shot at Minnesota governor Jesse

Ventura, who was deeply offended by the tone of the memorial, Franken writes on page 185 of his book, "Now Jesse 'The Body' Ventura is not a man easily offended. In his 1999 autobiography, *I Ain't Got Time to Bleed*, Ventura proudly describes his visit to Nevada's Bunny Ranch, where he "fornicated with what my feminist friends refer to as a 'sex worker.'" Including that in his book, I believe, shows his true nature: a vicious attack dog and character assassin against anybody who disagrees with him.

Another Conservative Remembers Paul Wellstone

On October 25, 2002, Tony Snow filled in as host on *Special Report with Brit Hume*. In his book, Franken attempts to discredit and besmirch Tony Snow's integrity as a reporter by citing his conservative credentials. Some of Snow's comments on Wellstone were particularly touching.

> Normally in TV we script our thoughts, but tonight I'm going to go off-script for a couple of seconds to talk about Paul Wellstone. We have all mentioned here that Paul Wellstone was a happy warrior. He was a guy who wore his emotions and principles on his sleeves.
>
> But he was also somebody who was just a joy and a delight to know. One of the things that distinguished him from all the pack was he was a good human being. He was a good husband, he was a good father. And he was the kind of guy who could come off the senate floor after having a vehement debate or disagreement with somebody, shake hands, clap him around the back and say, Good job. This is the kind of spirit that has been missing way too long in Washington. . . .
>
> Paul Wellstone was a good guy. He was a role model. People may have disagreed with him, but all of us looked up to him.

I didn't know Paul Wellstone. But from what I have been able to learn about him, I believe he would have been deeply ashamed of how Al Franken used his memory to attack Republicans and conservatives.

26 Franken on the Cutting Edge of . . . Last Year's News

No, it's not quite a Peabody or a Polk Award, but winning the "rehashing last year's news" award is no slouch, either. And if anyone deserves this award, it's Al Franken.

On Monday, December 6, 2004, Franken began his program talking about Philadelphia Eagles quarterback Donovan McNabb's performance against the Green Bay Packers the previous day. In that game, which the Eagles won 47-17, McNabb threw for 464 yards on 32/43 passing with 5 touchdowns and no interceptions. Even though the Packers defense ranked among the league's worst in 2004, the stats were pretty impressive. They are even more impressive if you take into consideration that Donovan McNabb is a black man in twenty-first-century racist America.

On September 28, 2003, fourteen months earlier, new ESPN analyst Rush Limbaugh opined, "I don't think he's [McNabb] been that good from the get-go. I think what we've had here is a little social concern in the NFL. I think the media has been very desirous that a black quarterback do well."

In the firestorm that continued until Rush's resignation at the end of the week, the media, which Franken has accused of being afraid of their own shadow, was wall-to-wall "Rush made racially insensitive remarks. . . ." In his statement on the incident, Limbaugh explained, "My comments this past Sunday were directed at the media and were not racially motivated. I offered an opinion." Then he resigned, not wishing to be a distraction to ESPN and the NFL and not wanting to force his employers into having to respond to the accusations of the media about his comments that were intentionally misrepresented.

Rush's comments were clearly an indictment of the media, not McNabb, not black quarterbacks, not black people. The media and their friends on the Left knew that. But for the liberal elite media and the Franken types, Rush gave them an opening and they shamelessly grabbed it.

Was McNabb That Good in 2003?

Judging by any reasonable standard, McNabb didn't have a great year in 2003. He played sixteen games that season: In four of them he threw for less than 150 yards, in six for between 151 to 200 yards, in four between 151 and 200 yards, in one game between 251 and 300 yards, and in one game over 300 yards. These numbers were very similar to those of Detroit Lions quarterback Joey Harrington, whose team went 5-11 in 2003 vs. McNabb's Eagles, who were 12-4.

It wasn't until the fourth game of the 2003 season that McNabb threw his first touchdown of the season. At the time Rush made his comments, McNabb's completion percentage was less than 50 percent. He had thrown for no touchdowns, and had been intercepted three times.

Rush's analysis and opinions came just prior to game three in 2003, when McNabb's numbers didn't even justify being a starter, let alone being called a great quarterback. For the three weeks after Rush's resignation, his numbers were no better.

Yet one year and eight weeks later Franken makes sure to remind his audience that Rush said "McNabb was overrated as a quarterback because he's black." In making this statement, Franken lied about what Rush said and smeared him as a racist, which he is not.

Just to be fair to Franken, though, certainly more fair than he would ever be to his foes, I did a Google search on "Al Franken and football" on the Internet to see if he is a big football fan, and was not just exploiting a black person for his race—like so many in the Democratic Party—to attack Rush. As I expected, there were no hits other than those stories dealing with Rush's comments on McNabb and Franken's book on Rush.

On February 6, 2005, McNabb played brilliantly in the Super Bowl. Even though the New England Patriots defeated the Eagles, he threw for more than 300 yards. I certainly expected that on his program the next day I would hear Franken gloat some more about the great passing game. Not one word. Not a word about McNabb, not even a word about the game. Franken was not interested or even informed about football, just as he is uninformed about a whole host of issues. Franken's sole interest in an issue is in how he can use it to attack President Bush, Rush, or other conservatives. In this case, Franken's only interest in football was to smear Rush.

I look forward to hearing Franken's analysis of 2005 events sometime in mid-2006.

A couple of weeks earlier, on January 24, 2005, Franken tried to sandbag Mark Luther during his show's dittohead segment by playing Rush's 2003 clip criticizing McNabb's abilities, then asking Luther, "McNabb had a great game yesterday (in the January 23 NFC Championship game), didn't he?" Luther then fired back that Franken was being dishonest since Rush's comments were over a year old.

Franken, though, made no apologies. He neither acknowledged that what he was doing was dishonest nor said, "Omigod! How embarrassing!" like he felt O'Reilly should have responded to Franken's call about *Inside Edition* winning a Polk, not a Peabody, award. Instead, he became emboldened and asked Luther, "Would you like me to play more recent Rush racist comments?"

So Franken went on to play clips of Rush defending our troops against the charges made against them at Abu Ghraib, as if somehow the two are related, or that citing Rush's comments on Abu Ghraib justify lying about his comments on McNabb.

In conclusion:

1. Franken revives a story that is a year and a half old.
2. Franken distorts what Rush actually said about McNabb's performance.
3. Franken cites one game in the middle of the 2004 season to justify attacking Rush's comments from early in the 2003 season.
4. When caught by "resident dittohead" Mark Luther, Franken angrily replies, "Should I play other Rush racist comments?"

27 Did You Know Al Franken Lies?

Just when I thought I was the only guy in America set to launch a Web site exposing Franken's lies and deceptions, two others went up around the same time, the first week of January 2004.

One of them, Frankenlies.com, posts roughly twenty-nine separate instances where Franken's standards for telling the truth fall just a bit shy in practice. Below are references to just a few of them:

- On page 218 of the hardcover edition of *Lies and the Lying Liars Who Tell Them,* Franken writes that former Bush foreign policy adviser Richard Armitage "bolted" from a Senate hearing and "[knocked] over veteran reporter Helen Thomas, breaking her hip and jaw." Did Armitage really knock over and break this eighty-year-old woman's hip and jaw? I wrote her an e-mail in which I asked her if what Franken said was true. The next morning I received a reply, "Not true, thanks for your concern. Helen."
- On page 74 of *Lies and the Lying Liars Who Tell Them,* Franken tells his readers that Bill O'Reilly is not from Levittown, Long Island, New York. He claims O'Reilly is from the "affluent suburb" of Westbury, which, according to him, is "several miles apart" from Levittown. Yikes! On the April 12,

2004, episode of *The O'Reilly Factor*, Bill exhibited the actual deed from his boyhood home for all his audience to see. Only the street location was covered. [His mother still lives there.] The words "Levittown, New York" were clearly displayed in reference to the home's location.

- Franken and his fact-checkers really messed up when on page 163 of *Lies and the Lying Liars Who Tell Them* he writes, "[Former Georgia Senator] Max [Cleland] left three of his limbs in Vietnam. A VC grenade blew them off." He must not have read Cleland's book. Cleland is an inspiration to all disabled war veterans. He fought valiantly in Vietnam, but his tragic injury was the result of a horrible accident with a grenade from a fellow soldier. Senator Cleland wrote about this heart-wrenching incident in his eloquent memoir, *Strong at the Broken Places*.
- On page 110 of the hardback edition of *Lies and the Lying Liars Who Tell Them,* Franken writes that Barton Gellman of the *Washington Post* wrote that Clinton's was the "first administration to undertake a systematic anti-terrorist effort." In reality, Gellman's article attributes the statement to former National Security Adviser Sandy Berger. This may not seem like a big deal, except this is exactly the kind of thing that Franken attacks Ann Coulter for supposedly doing in her books. Hypocrisy, anyone?

Although Franken personally admitted this last error to me, the passage was not corrected for the paperback edition!

28 FactCheck.org

FactCheck.org is the Web site of the nonpartisan Annenberg Political Fact Check (APFC) organization. The APFC monitors the factual accuracy of what is said by major U.S. political players in TV ads, debates, speeches, interviews, and news releases with the goal of increasing public knowledge and understanding. A project of the Annenberg Public Policy Center of the University of Pennsylvania, it was established in 1994 by publisher and philanthropist Walter Annenberg to create a community of scholars within the University of Pennsylvania that would address public policy issues at the local, state, and federal levels.

This group's work is so respected that Vice President Cheney referred to them during his debate with John Edwards. Overnight, FactCheck saw visitors to their site grow tenfold, leading to a temporary shutdown of the server.

Franken referred to this site's findings and analysis regularly during the 2004 campaign as evidence that the Bush ads attacking John Kerry were lies. What he didn't think of is what happens when his listeners visit the site themselves and see how many Kerry ads are deceitful.

Political ads present their candidates in the most favorable light, while portraying their opponents in a less than flattering light. That's what political ads—as well as commercials for all kinds of products—do. If you don't get that, then I guess we can say that Pepsi lies because I didn't find myself surrounded by bikini clad beauties when I popped open a can of the carbonated beverage.

Franken, on the other hand, makes no such admission. "Bush's ads are lies, despicable lies," he thunders. John Kerry's ads, on the other hand, are all true. I know he believes this because he challenged a caller to his radio show to come up with *one* example of a lying Kerry ad.

Franken asks for "one example." How about if we provide more? I found the following from the FactCheck.org site:

AUGUST 11, 2004: DNC AD SAYS BUSH LOST MANUFACTURING JOBS

Fact Check: But even Clinton lost manufacturing jobs in his second term. Economists say changing the tax code won't do much to help. **Fact Check summary:** The DNC released an ad August 6 saying 2.7 million manufacturing jobs had been lost under Bush. That's true, but it ignores the fact that manufacturing jobs started their decline three years before Bush took office.

The ad also says "Bush protects tax breaks favoring corporations that move their headquarters overseas" and that Kerry would "end job-killing tax loopholes." But as we've said before, offshoring accounts for just a small fraction of jobs that are lost, and even Democratic economists say changing the tax code won't end the overseas job drain.

OCTOBER 18, 2004: KERRY FALSELY CLAIMS BUSH PLANS TO CUT SOCIAL SECURITY BENEFITS

Fact Check: It's not Bush's plan, and it wouldn't cut benefits. **Fact Check summary:** A Kerry ad claims, "Bush has a plan to cut social security benefits by 30 to 45 percent." That's false. Bush has proposed no such plan.

JULY 28, 2004: KERRY BLAMES CORPORATE TAX CODE FOR SHIPPING JOBS OVERSEAS

But economists say outsourcing jobs overseas is a minor problem that Kerry's plan wouldn't do much to fix.

DECEMBER 4, 2003: KERRY MAKES BOGUS COMPARISON TO GREAT DEPRESSION

He claims the United States suffers its greatest job loss since the 30s, which is not true.

Fact Check summary: In his September 2 speech in South Carolina, Kerry claimed the United States is suffering the "greatest job loss since the Great Depression." That's wrong.

JULY 9, 2004: ECONOMY PRODUCING MOSTLY BAD JOBS? NOT SO FAST

A new set of figures from the Bureau of Labor Statistics shows higher-paying jobs growing faster. A FactCheck.org exclusive.

Fact Check summary: A recent ad by some Kerry allies even shows a middle-aged man reporting for his new job wearing a paper hat at a seedy-looking burger joint. Well, hold on—here's strong new evidence to the contrary.

AUGUST 3, 2004: KERRY'S DUBIOUS ECONOMICS

He says new jobs are paying $9,000 less than the old ones. That's not a fact. . . . He [Kerry] bases that on disputed analysis from a liberal think tank.

Kerry also said "wages are falling" when in fact they are increasing.

OCTOBER 27, 2004: MEDIA FUND TWISTS THE TRUTH MORE THAN MICHAEL MOORE

Radio ad claims most air traffic was grounded when Bin Laden's family was allowed to leave. Not true. In fact, The FBI questioned twenty-two of them and found no links to terrorism.

Fact Check summary: The anti-Bush ad is among the worst distortions we've seen in what has become a very ugly campaign.

MAY 14, 2004: TWISTED FACTS AND FALSEHOODS IN MEDIA FUND AD

Democratic group's ad claims Bush turned White House into "corporate headquarters," but backs that up with false claims.

Fact Check analysis writes: It's hard to cram this much distortion into a mere 30 seconds, but Ickes' group is up to the task. <*Note:* Harold Ickes is a former Clinton aide and adviser.>

SEPTEMBER 14, 2004: A FALSE AD ABOUT ASSAULT WEAPONS

A new Moveon Pac ad implies machine guns are becoming legal, which isn't true. And it blames Bush, even though Bush said he would have extended the ban on assault weapons.

Fact Check summary: This latest ad from Moveon Pac is about as misleading as it can be.

It has been illegal to buy a machine gun without federal clearance since 1934, and it remains so.

JUNE 18, 2004: ANTI-BUSH AD OVERSTATES CASE AGAINST HALLIBURTON

Moveon Pac ad says administration gave contracts "on a silver platter," but government investigators say otherwise. <See chapter 29 for a discussion of the Clinton administration's relationship with Halliburton.>

When you accuse others of lying and maintain that you or your side never does, you better be sure that can be substantiated.

29 Democrats and Big Business

If you are a liberal, I suggest you close this book now or move on to the next chapter. Do not read any further.

Okay, you were warned.

For years you have been led to believe that Republicans are the party of "big business" while Democrats are the party that "cares" for the little guy.

Wake up! Use your head! Who do you think was paying for those $1,000-a-plate dinners and $100,000 coffee breaks with Bill Clinton? Some $40,000-a-year union electrician?

This chapter exposes how Democrats, the party of "the people vs. the powerful," and their left-wing allies love to denounce big business—until it comes time to pay their bills, when they then turn to "evil big business" for financial support. Furthermore, their hypocrisy is documented with countless examples of Democrats talking out of both sides of their mouths when it comes to dealings with Halliburton, the "outsourcing" of local jobs, and Ken Lay's Enron.

The Truth About Halliburton and How the Left Demonized Dick Cheney

Ask a Democrat why they hate President Bush or Dick Cheney, and they might respond, "Halliburton!" You would think they could use nouns, verbs, adverbs, and other parts of speech to express complete thoughts, but no. This is the kind of answer one might hear during Sean Hannity's "Man on the Street" segment when one of his interns or producers goes onto the streets outside WABC headquarters to mingle and ask questions of New York's brightest liberal minds. "Well, what about Halliburton?"

"Well, you know, uh, *Halliburton,* man."

They hear about Halliburton and know that it's, like, *really bad*, but most of them don't have a clue about what the company is or what it does.

During the presidential race, Team Kerry/Edwards kept shouting "Halliburton!" every time they wanted to paint Bush/Cheney as captives of corrupt, evil corporations that steal from hardworking taxpayers. But even John Edwards, the man who wanted to be the second most powerful officeholder in America, couldn't say exactly what Dick Cheney did wrong regarding Halliburton or that he used undue influence in getting them preferential treatment.

Here is an exchange with Chris Matthews of MSNBC in a broadcast aired shortly before the elections:

> **Matthews:** You raised the issue of Halliburton. Senator Kerry raised it again in the second debate I believe. What did Cheney do wrong, the vice president, actually do wrong in moving from being CEO of Halliburton and becoming vice president? If you could point to something nobody else should do again, what is it?
> **Edwards:** It's the vice president allowed, as part of his administration, Halliburton to get no-bid contracts when he had just left Halliburton to become the vice president of the United States.
> **Matthews:** How did he do that? You said he called someone to say—he called the defense department, the Pentagon and say give this contract to Halliburton? What did he actually do?
> **Edwards:** Well, the first thing they said was they had nothing to do with this and they had a memo or an e-mail that was released indicated that there was some. . . .
> **Matthews:** Corps of Engineers had run something by the VP.
> **Edwards:** Some coordination of some kind. The bottom line is this should not have been allowed to happen because at a minimum it creates the appearance of impropriety.

> **Matthews:** But isn't Halliburton—you know this better than I do. Isn't Halliburton the only corporation of that size that can handle these kinds of jobs in Iraq?
> <Edwards then gives a long, tortured response.>
> **Matthews:** Is he unethical?
> **Edwards:** Dick Cheney?
> **Matthews:** Yeah.
> **Edwards:** I do not think Halliburton should have been allowed to get this no-bid contract.
> **Matthews:** Well, was that his call?
> **Edwards:** I don't know what he had to do with it. He claims he has nothing to do with it.

Edwards would have looked smarter if he had just stuck to the script: "Halliburton, man."

What this exchange shows is that after all the accusations of wrongdoing—even according to the Democratic vice presidential candidate—the crime was, *It doesn't look right!*

I've noted that a great majority of Bush/Cheney haters throw out "Halliburton" to make themselves sound knowledgeable. Who wants to sound ignorant or uninformed about why they think the Bush/Cheney team is corrupt?

Certainly not Al Franken.

In chapter 18 of *Lies and the Lying Liars Who Tell Them,* "Humor in Uniform," Franken only *alluded* to Dick Cheney and Halliburton. He used the usual Democrat talking points without going into too much detail.

What would he write? And it's not like he doesn't hate Cheney enough to turn his fourteen Harvard researchers onto the Cheney-Halliburton corruption. You would think they could have come up with a lengthy chapter on the Cheney/Halliburton connection, instead of just a few paragraphs.

Maybe Franken, like Edwards, couldn't come up with anything more substantial than "homina, homina, homina" because there was nothing to find other than unsubstantiated claims and innuendo.

The only thing Franken offers his readers on where they can get more information about Halliburton comes from a letter sent by Rep. Henry Waxman (D-CA). He puts this information in his endnotes, the same thing he criticizes Ann Coulter for doing, since "her readers aren't going to bother looking for them."

National Review's Byron York wrote extensively about the Halliburton charges made by the Left, including the Waxman letter that Franken refers to in his book. In an article published on July 14, 2003, "Halliburton: The Bush/Iraq Scandal That Wasn't," he replies to the three accusations Waxman made about Halliburton: that their contract was given without competition, that the company overcharged the government, and that Halliburton's performance record was "troubling."

> Last year, as administration officials made plans for war in Iraq, they were greatly concerned that Saddam Hussein would set fire to his country's oil fields, just as retreating Iraqi troops had done in Kuwait at the end of the first gulf war. . . . Last November, the Corps assigned Kellogg Brown and Root (KBR), which has been a wholly owned subsidiary of Halliburton since the 1960s, to do a classified study of potential damage and repairs in the Iraqi oil fields. Contrary to Waxman's assertions, the work was done under a competitively awarded contract system known as the U.S. Army Logistics Civil Augmentation Program (LOGCAP). . . .
>
> LOGCAP is, in effect, a multi-year supercontract. In it, the Army makes a deal with a single contractor, in this case Halliburton, to perform a wide range of unspecified services during emergency situations in the future. The last competition for LOGCAP came in 2001, when Halliburton won the contract over several other bidders. Thus, when the oil-field study was needed, Corps officials say, Halliburton was the natural place to turn.

The big issue, it turned out, was how large the contract should be, and the army "assumed a worst-case scenario" when issuing an indefinite delivery/indefinite quantity (ID/IQ) contract to Halliburton. They decided that between $0 and $7 billion would be enough to handle any foreseeable problems. According to York, after the contract was explained to Waxman, "he immediately began calling the KBR deal a $7 billion contract," leaving out the fact that he had been told the contract "would not be worth anywhere near the cap amount."

Halliburton and the Clinton Administration

What? Bill Clinton had a relationship with Halliburton?

You didn't really think those corporate *evildoers* were paying $100,000 just for coffee, did you?

According to York and others who have looked into the issue, in 1992 four companies competed for the first LOGCAP, and Halliburton won. The contract was put up for bid in 1997, and when Halliburton lost, the Clinton administration overrode the process and issued a new contract to them anyway. Vice President Al Gore's National Performance Review lauded the company's performance, and in 2001 Halliburton was awarded the contract again after winning the bid.

Halliburton's contract with the Defense Department didn't seem to bother Waxman during the Clinton years. I wonder what caused his opinion to change.

Kerry/Edwards Halliburton Attacks Refuted

During the 2004 election, the Kerry/Edwards campaign smeared Dick Cheney in an ad that claimed Cheney got $2 million from Halliburton "as vice president," implying he was profiting from Halliburton's contracts in Iraq. According to FactCheck.org, that was not true. "The fact is," their report explains, "Cheney doesn't gain a penny from Halliburton's contracts, and almost certainly won't lose even if Halliburton goes bankrupt." All of the money he earned from Halliburton "was earned before he was a candidate, when he was the company's chief executive," they reported.

John Kerry's Plan to Stop "Outsourcing"

On October 20, 2004, Ted Koppel of ABC's *Nightline* interviewed John Edwards on the campaign trail through Ohio to discuss the issue of "outsourcing." It had become a sensitive subject in battleground states like Ohio. John Kerry had promised to end it while at the same time accusing the Bush administration of encouraging it.

Here are excerpts from Ted Koppel's interview with John Edwards (and again, wasn't Edwards supposed to have a great ability to communicate?):

Koppel: Let's talk in reducing things to simplicity. Outsourcing, bad.

Edwards: Yeah. It is bad.

Koppel: You know damn well that if you ever get to be vice president of the United States and John Kerry gets to be president of the United States, there will continue to be a huge amount of outsourcing. You can't live without it these days.

Edwards: But the choices you make matter. What we have right now is a president who has—his administration has actually said, in their economic report, that outsourcing is good for the economy. I don't believe that's right. They've also promoted policies that facilitate outsourcing. You know, they—support tax cuts that presently exist for companies that are taking jobs overseas. <Factcheck.org refuted this.> They have lobbied for more tax cuts for companies taking jobs overseas. We just think that's fundamentally wrong. . . .

Koppel: You can reduce it. You can't do away with it. And even . . .

Edwards: I don't disagree with that. That's true.

Enron and the Democrats

I have never understood how mega-millionaires like Ted Kennedy, John Kerry, and Jon Corzine and lesser millionaires like the Clintons and others could say with a straight face that they are for the working families and the Republicans are for the rich.

Early in the Bush administration, Ken Lay and Enron were caught in a major stock fraud costing thousands of people, including their own employees, tens and hundreds of thousands of dollars. For many investors, it was their life savings. Democrats immediately pounced and said, "Aha, a rich guy got caught in a major corruption scandal while his Republican friend is in the White House." Proof positive, once again, that Republicans are the friends of the wealthiest 1 percent. However, the Enron planning and stealing had gone on for years in the mid-1990s, unfettered by the Clinton administration.

On October 29, 2004, on the *Al Franken Show,* Franken, who blamed the recession on Bush policies that he said favored Enron, said, "Kenny, Kenny boy," referring to Ken Lay, and his alleged friendship with the Bush administration. (In chapter 25, which exposes Franken for using other people's material for his work, Joe Conason himself refers to Ken Lay as "Kenny Boy." Another coincidence?)

So let's look at the facts, something that Franken and his fourteen Harvard researchers just happened to have missed—again! In the 1990s, Christopher Dodd (D-CT) and Phil Gramm (R-TX) "pushed through two laws that, in effect, immunized Wall Street from lawsuits by investors whom it swindled," Dick Morris wrote in his book, *Off with Their Heads.* "These laws protected Enron [and their accounting firm], Arthur Andersen, so they could cook the books in peace. These senators also helped to stop the Securities and Exchange Commission (SEC) from curbing some of the worst abuses on Wall Street."

On January 13, 2002, the *New York Times* noted, "As Enron stock climbed and Wall Street was still promoting it, a group of twenty-nine Enron executives and directors began to sell their shares. These insiders received $1.1 billion by selling 17.3 million shares from 1999 through mid-2001."

Charles Lewis of the Center for Public Integrity commented, "Chris Dodd—here he is, chairman of the Democratic Party, but he's also the leading advocate in the U.S. Senate on behalf of the accounting industry."

In other words, the plotting, scheming, and ripping off of investors and employees began under the Clinton administration and was broken up in the first six months of the Bush administration. It was Senator Chris Dodd, reelected by Democrats in Connecticut, who pushed through laws in the Senate protecting corporate corruption, but by no means was he the only Democrat who was willing to *deal* with Enron.

- Enron donated $100,000 to Clinton's 1993 inauguration and an additional $25,000 to the Clinton 1993 celebrations.
- Enron senior vice president Terrance H. Thorn had coffee with Bill Clinton on March 5, 1996. <I wonder what they talked about over coffee.>
- In 1994, Enron's CEO Ken Lay surfaced on a list of attendees wishing to travel to Russia with Clinton secretary of commerce Ron Brown.

- Enron executives traveled on a profitable trade trip to India with Ron Brown, landing a major contract for a power plant.
- Enron executives also traveled in 1997 to Bosnia with Ron Brown in hopes of landing an energy deal. According to the *Chicago Tribune,* Enron made a $100,000 donation to the DNC just days prior to the trade mission to Bosnia.

The most damning evidence linking Bill Clinton to Enron is documentation that shows Enron received U.S. taxpayer monies in order to finance a corrupt deal with Indonesia. In a letter to the Indonesian minister for trade and industry, Ron Brown endorsed two Enron deals for gas-fired power plants with the corrupt Suharto regime.

In October 1995 Brown wrote another letter, this time to Hartarto Sastrosurarto, Indonesia's coordinating minister for trade and industry, pressing him to conclude the Enron power plant deals.

In November of 1996 Enron consummated its deal with Suharto.

30 Franken Debates Coulter and Defends the Integrity of *Fahrenheit 9/11*

I couldn't believe that Ann Coulter and the guy with a massive crush on her were on the same show at the same time. It was Thursday, December 9, 2004, on MSNBC's *Scarborough Country.* And there he was in all his glory: Al Franken.

The debate was over the Oscar nominations for *The Passion of the Christ* vs. *Fahrenheit 9/11*. I was astonished to hear, for the first time, Al "I hold myself to an impossibly high standard when it comes to telling the truth" Franken defend the integrity of Moore's movie. I knew they were friends, but I didn't remember ever hearing Franken say the movie was truthful.

Toward the end of the discussion, Ann commented how the Oscar nominators were willing to pick Moore's movie even though it was full of distortions. Franken challenged Ann to name "one untruth" from the film. Ann admitted that while she didn't see the movie, she did read different articles that pointed out the individual lies. Again, Franken said, "Name one." So she mentioned the part of the movie where Moore walks over to Congressman Mark Kennedy (R-MN) and asks him to sign a petition calling for members of Congress to send their family members over to Iraq. The congressman said that he had nephews there already.

Franken pointed out correctly that wasn't a lie, and he was right. Sure, it made Moore look like a jackass, but he didn't lie.

Or did he?

Here's what actually happened. After Kennedy told Moore about his nephews being in Iraq, Moore edited that statement out of his movie. I'm not sure if deleting people's words to satisfy your agenda is lying, but someone with impossibly high standards for telling the truth shouldn't tolerate it.

At this point President Bush had already been reelected and Moore had been exposed and refuted by a bevy of DVDs such as *Fahrenhype 9/11* and *Celsius 41.11,* not to mention the book *Michael Moore Is a Big Fat Stupid White Man.* You'd think Franken would be a little more cautious when claiming the movie is accurate.

Fahrenheit 9/11 basically has three villains: President Bush (obviously), the Saudi royal family (who, everyone agrees, aren't good guys), and the troops in Iraq (whom Al Franken, of course, "loves and honors").

To prove that the Bush family has close ties to the Saudi royal family, perhaps *too* close, Moore shows a number of photographs of George Bush or his father with different members of the royal family, shaking hands or laughing together.

Moore shows one picture of Saudi Ambassador Prince Bandar sitting comfortably on the arm of a sofa, dressed very casually in a pair of jeans, while the president is also dressed casually with his cowboy boots. The obvious intent is to show a couple of "rich oil buddies" having a friendly talk.

However, this is not what was going on when the photograph was taken. They were at the president's ranch in Crawford, Texas, where the environment was anything but friendly. In reference to that meeting, the Associated Press reported on August 27, 2002, "President Bush is opening his ranch to Saudi Prince Bandar . . . [to] help thaw relations chilled by the September 11 attacks and questions about the Kingdom's commitment to defeating terrorists." Why would there have to be a thaw in relations almost one year after the terror attacks on the World Trade Center, if the "Bushies" were buddy-buddy with the Saudis? The article also reported a recommendation that "the Arab ally be given an ultimatum to stop supporting terrorism or face retaliation."

Another Associated Press story, dated August 23, 2002, reported, "Saudi Arabia has made clear to Washington—publicly and privately—that the U.S. military will not be allowed to use the Kingdom's soil in any way for an attack on Iraq." That's not exactly the kind of tone one would expect from a couple of buddies.

In an appearance on the Letterman show in 2000, then candidate George W. Bush was asked, "Why do you want to drill [for oil] in ANWR [the Arctic National Wildlife Refuge]?" Bush's response was, "We need to look for other sources, because the Arabs have us over a barrel."

These statements do not demonstrate a closeness or fondness for the Saudi government.

Another villain in the movie, or in this case villains, are the troops. Moore shows interviews in which U.S. troops tell the interviewer what kind of heavy-metal rock music they listen to for the adrenaline rush they need before going out to kill Iraqis. This brief clip makes our troops look like heavy-metal, rock 'n' roll, reckless, immature, heartless savages.

In the same clip Moore shows the troops mistreating Iraqi prisoners. In a voice-over Moore says, "These are basically good kids . . . immoral behavior [the war] begets immoral behavior [troop conduct]." So now Moore is not just critical of what a few troops did in Abu Ghraib, now he's denouncing all of our troops for participating in an "immoral war."

For all the Frankens and Democrats out there who "love and support" our troops, where is the outrage at Moore's demeaning remarks about them?

I must also ask, who perpetrated a greater disservice to our troops and their families? Brit Hume's innocent mistake (in his analysis of the safety of our troops in Iraq), which was viewed by no more than 1.5 million people (an average number of viewers per night), or Moore's grotesque portrayal of our troops, viewed worldwide by 25 to 30 million people?

Where's the outrage, Al?

The strongest message you can send to the Michael Moores and Al Frankens of the world is to show your support for the troops by donating to those charities that are helping them and their families.

Tony Snow of Fox News Radio supports a charity called

Wounded Warrior Project. The organization assists the men and women of our armed forces who have been severely injured during the conflicts in Iraq, Afghanistan, and other hot spots around the world.

Sean Hannity has helped raise nearly $6 million over the last two years through the Freedom Alliance Scholarship Fund.

Bill O'Reilly supports and promotes the Families of Military Casualties. Bill also supports many charities including the Candles Museum, which is dedicated to the children of the Holocaust and those subjected to the experiments of Dr. Mengele.

Or you can send your jokes to Al Franken for his next USO tour.

31 A Letter for Michael Moore and Air America

Yes, I am one of those conservatives who saw *Fahrenheit 9/11*. I saw it for free on DVD.

I did not see the "genius" of Michael Moore as so many people had claimed. I didn't laugh when he played the Go-Gos' hit song "Vacation" in a clip of the president vacationing.

I didn't get any sick feeling when he showed our troops—the ones Franken loves and honors—telling him what kind of heavy metal they like to listen to before turning into killing machines.

I didn't become uncomfortable when he showed pictures of the Bushes and Saudi royalty. In other words, I wasn't conned by this awful movie the way so many other Americans appeared to have been when they called it "eye-opening," rather than a con job.

Many articles and numerous organizations have already thoroughly exposed the movie for what it was: a deceitful anti-America piece of propaganda. The organizations include the Ethics and Public Policy Center (EPPC), which presents in great detail a point-by-point rebuttal to Moore's movie under the title *War Lies, and Videotape: A Viewers Guide to* Fahrenheit 9/11. It can be viewed at http://www.eppc.org/publications/pubid.2189/pub_detail.asp.

But what I did find powerful and "eye-opening" was an article by Michael Niewodowski regarding Moore's movie. Michael is a chef at the Windows on the World restaurant. He was to have reported to work at the restaurant atop the World Trade Center at 9:00 a.m. on September 11, 2001. The first plane hit at approximately 8:46 a.m.

July 26, 2004
Michael Niewodowski on Michael Moore

From Here to Eternity
Tora! Tora! Tora!
In Harm's Way

These are three films made about Pearl Harbor. There have been more than 20 films made about Pearl Harbor, and over 200 films made about World War II. These films inspire patriotism, courage, and nationalism. They tell us about the honor and bravery of the soldiers and the nation that supported them.

Two and a half years after the attack on Pearl Harbor, the world watched American forces fight on D-Day. Two and a half years after the September 11 terrorist attacks, the world is watching Michael Moore's *Fahrenheit 9/11*.

Moore's film is the first major motion picture about September 11, 2001. This bears repeating. When future generations look back on the Sept. 11 massacre, their first impression, through the medium of film, will be a work in which the president and the government are blamed for the attacks, and the soldiers who are protecting this country are defamed. Instead of a film version of Lisa Beamer's book, *Let's Roll,* or Richard Picciotto's *Last Man Down,* we are presented with this fallacy.

How could this happen?

It would be a colossal insult to insinuate that Franklin D. Roosevelt or the U.S. government were in any way responsible for the attacks on Pearl Harbor.

Can you imagine the indignation of the men and women who lived during that period?

Fahrenheit 9/11 is indicative of a nation that has become too apathetic, ignorant, or deceived to face the enemy at the gate.

America. Where is your fury?

On September 11, 2001, I stood across the Hudson River watching the Twin Towers burn, knowing that if the plane had struck at 9:46 a.m. instead of 8:46 a.m., I would be dead. As a survivor and witness to the attack on the World Trade Center, I am more than insulted by this film. I am outraged.

This film is based on conjecture, hearsay, and propaganda. At a time when this country desperately needs to rally in support of our brave soldiers and our strong leaders, Moore is content to spread discord and divisiveness. The base of his argument is that the Bush administration had strong ties with the bin Laden family. However, sound facts are conspicuously absent from this "documentary."

The 9/11 Commission did not indict President Bush. According to the report, the president's actions before, during, and after the attacks are fully justified, including the military action in Iraq. The commission did not find a direct link between Saddam Hussein's Iraq and the September 11 terrorist attacks. A similar commission in the 1940s would not have found a direct link between Hitler's Germany and the attack on Pearl Harbor. In both instances, the threat was imminent; the president and the military acted decisively.

Could we have been more prepared for a terrorist attack on September 10, 2001?

Certainly.

Could we have been more prepared for an attack on December 6, 1941?

Most definitely.

In the weeks and months following Pearl Harbor, there were reports and criticisms that the government and military should have been more prepared. The difference is that the people of the nation did not waste a lot of time pointing fingers at each other. Rather, they unified and engaged the enemy head-on. I guess that is why we call them "The Greatest Generation."

How will future generations refer to us?

So how do we explain Moore's film to future generations? I wonder.

More than that, I wonder how I would explain this film to Nancy D., Jerome N. or Heather H. I am sure you don't know their

> names, but their faces haunt me day and night. How would I explain to them that a film was made accusing the president and vilifying the soldiers——the same president and soldiers who are attempting to avenge their murders and protect other citizens.
>
> Moore has not only insulted the nation, he has insulted the victims of the terrorist attacks.
>
> During his acceptance speech at the Oscars, Moore said, "Shame on you, Mr. Bush."
>
> Well, I say, "Shame on you, Michael Moore."
>
> Shame on everyone who supports this travesty of a film. Shame on a society that allows this sham of a film. You have weakened the nation.
>
> (source:http://www.webcommentary.com/asp/ShowArticle.asp?id=tseugmn&date=040726))

And shame on you, Mr. Franken, for defending the integrity of Moore and his film.

32 David Brock: A Sick Boy's Cry for Help . . . and Media Matters Splattered

"You're an inspiration. You are living proof that someone can see the errors of their ways and make a huge change for mankind."

—Al Franken to David Brock of Media Matters for America (MMFA) on November 10, 2004

That is rather high praise from a man who makes a living by lying and smearing his opponents to another guy who makes a living by lying and smearing people Franken doesn't like. You have already been introduced to David Brock and Media Matters in earlier chapters. If you now think he's a Franken sycophant, then I've done my job.

David Brock rose to prominence in the early 1990s for writing a book about Anita Hill, who herself rose to prominence by trying to derail the confirmation of U.S. Supreme Court Justice nominee Clarence Thomas. Her main charge was that he "talked dirty" to her approximately ten years earlier when they worked together at the Equal Employment Opportunity Commission. Brock worked for the *American Spectator,* where his most famous accomplishment was reporting how Arkansas state troopers said they saw Bill Clinton having sex with Paula Jones and other Arkansas beauties. Brock changed teams and became a left-winger's left-winger in the late 1990s.

This chapter is primarily a compilation of Media Matters' e-mail alerts, which are supposed to serve as a warning against conservative misinformation. As a recipient of his alerts, I have come to a different conclusion: many of them are meaningless or incoherent, and the rest are distortions of the facts or simply irrelevant.

As Franken's radio show was supposed to counter conservative talk radio and the Center for American Progress was supposed to counter the Heritage Foundation, Brock has convinced himself that his group is the counter to the Media Research Center.

I'm not alone in my criticism of Brock. On March 27, 2002, Timothy Noah of *Slate,* a liberal online magazine, wrote an article titled "David Brock, Liar: A lifelong habit proves hard to break." Here are some excerpts from his column, "Chatterbox," in which Noah reviewed Brock's book, *Blinded by the Right:*

> Whiny, histrionic, and so factually unreliable that *Chatterbox* practically gave himself a migraine trying to figure out which parts of Brock's lurid story were true, and which parts were false. . . .
>
> *Blinded by the Right* offers plenty of evidence that for Brock, lying has been a lifelong habit. . . .
>
> How can we trust a writer who won't even summarize his own book truthfully?
>
> He now runs a snarky little "club" called Media Matters for America, or MMFA. MMFA began as a media watchdog, monitoring conservative talk radio, cable news, and other outlets exclusively. But it recently changed its focus and now monitors and cites any media that report positively on Republicans and/or negatively on Democrats. . . .
>
> Brock also appears as a weekly guest on Franken's show to share his news "alerts" with Franken's audience. It sometimes gets embarrassing to listen to these two gush over each other.

While Franken is pretty much a one-trick pony whose daily lying and smearing of his opponents are growing rather monotonous, Brock wears different hats at different times. Sometimes he's a little "Cindy Brady" tattletale, other times he advocates censorship, and yet other times he flat-out lies and ignores evidence that would refute his claims. Worse, however, is when he tries to take credit for something he had nothing to do with.

On September 30, 2004, MMFA sent the following e-mail alerts to their subscribers:

> Salon.com, *Roll Call:* Republican pollster canned at MSNBC
>
> Upon hearing that MSNBC planned for Republican pollster Frank Luntz to conduct on-air focus groups as part of the cable network's debate coverage tonight, David Brock of the media watchdog group Media Matters sent MSNBC executive Rick Kaplan a letter of complaint. It looks like Kaplan listened.
>
> [Brock stated,] Looks like the letter had an impact. It is encouraging that MSNBC responded to criticism in a constructive way. Clearly they realized that employing a partisan pollster does not reflect well on them as a responsible media outlet.

As someone who knows Frank Luntz and is familiar with his reputation in the polling industry, I was furious that MSNBC would allow themselves to be cowed by a pipsqueak like Brock. Immediately, I decided to send an e-mail myself to MSNBC to see if they jump at every e-mail complaint they get.

> I am deeply disappointed, and extremely concerned by a number of recent e-mail blasts I have received from David Brock's Media Matters, and his "influence" over your network.
>
> Over the last ten days, Brock has targeted Luntz because of his ties to the Republican Party.
>
> My question is, so what?
>
> Luntz has been on MSNBC for years, and there never seemed to be any controversy over his "methods" until Brock began his "Jihad" against conservatives. If you think I'm exaggerating, just visit Brock's website.
>
> David Brock is attempting to silence the conservative viewpoint, and I cannot believe that MSNBC would be in cahoots with him, especially since Luntz only performs focus groups (for MSNBC) and does not espouse any kind of ideological perspective as part of his service.

I was pleasantly surprised that once again I had caught a Franken wannabe in a lie. That morning, I received a reply from MSNBC:

> You should know that the decision not to use Frank had nothing to do with David Brock. We made a decision not to use focus groups in our debate coverage PERIOD. Unfortunately, Brock is taking credit for our decision.

In a recent letter to his subscribers, Brock listed his accomplishments of the previous year, including getting Luntz canned from MSNBC.

As I said earlier, Brock wears "different hats" depending on the mood of the day. Here are some examples of when David is in his "Cindy Brady" tattletale mood:

- "O'Reilly and guest Ralph Peters took potshots at Dean." (August 12, 2004)
- "*US News'* Roger Simon likened Kerry to 'French candidate.'" (August 18, 2004)
- "WABC's Levin compared UN to KKK." (September 27, 2004)
- "Limbaugh got a big hug from the president at the White House." (December 20, 2004)
- "Falwell's Thanksgiving message: 'I thank G-d for Hannity, Limbaugh, Newsmax, WorldNet Daily, and the Drudge Report.'" (November 24, 2004)
- Hyman called ACLU the "Anti-American Criminal Liberties Union" (September 14, 2005)

Isn't the Left lucky to have someone like Brock to alert them to these right-wing attacks? On other days when Brock isn't feeling like a tattletale, he turns into "free speech censorship man."

- "MMFA Asks Secretary Rumsfeld to Remove Limbaugh's Radio Show from Taxpayer-Funded American Forces Radio." (July 9, 2004)
- "MMFA asks NBC not to feature Limbaugh on election night." (October 26, 2004)

- "MMFA sends letter to Wal-Mart, Amazon.com, and Barnes & Noble asking these top booksellers to review policies on selling *Unfit for Command.*" (August 20, 2004)
- "William Safire: Fit to Print?" (November 15, 2004)
- "Hannity promoting 'disgusting' book that even O'Reilly has criticized." (June 21, 2005)

I suppose these "alerts" are less lethal than having a pie thrown at you. But isn't it eye-opening the lengths that the "tolerant free speech" advocates of the Left will go to suppress the rights of others to be heard?

Have you ever heard of Rush, Sean, O'Reilly, or David Horowitz attempting to block the publication of left-wing hit books?

On September 27, 2004, "Cindy Brady" alerted us, "Fox's Wallace echoed GOP talking point that Kerry is inconsistent on Iraq."

The *only* thing Kerry was consistent on during his 2004 campaign for the presidency was his inconsistency. It's not exactly a GOP talking point if the whole world knows about it.

In a December 3, 2003, interview, Sean Hannity asked John Kerry about Joe Lieberman's comment that if Howard Dean had his way, Saddam Hussein would be in power, the world would be a much more dangerous place, and the American people would have a lot more to fear.

After a long pause, Kerry replied that he was glad Saddam Hussein was gone.

A few months later, Diane Sawyer asked him on *Good Morning America* (September 28, 2004) if the war in Iraq was worth it. He replied that, knowing the information we know today, we should not have gone to war.

Kerry and Sawyer went back and forth as she sought to get a clear and straight answer from Kerry.

> **Sawyer:** So it was not worth it?
> **Kerry:** We should not—depends the outcome ultimately. . . .

Kerry should have said what he really meant. If the war helps President Bush's poll numbers, it wasn't worth it, but if it hurts him, it was worth it.

Another MMFA alert dated May 21, 2004, reported: "Ann Coulter slander on Fox, MSNBC: She smeared Bill Clinton, Nancy Pelosi, Ted Kennedy, and Michael Moore."

She had been a guest on MSNBC's *Scarborough Country.* Here's how she "smeared" Michael Moore:

> **Scarborough** (reading a letter from Michael Moore to his Web site visitors): "I oppose the U.N. or anybody else risking the lives of their citizens to extract us from our debacle in Iraq. The majority of Americans supported this war once it began and sadly that majority must now sacrifice their children until enough blood has been let that maybe, just maybe, G-d and the Iraqi people will forgive us in the end."
>
> Ann Coulter, is that [what Moore wrote] treasonous? . . . Because I personally, I don't know how that is not treasonous when you say more young Americans need to die over in Iraq.
>
> **Coulter:** Yes, I think it's hard to get around that. No, they root against their own country. I think that is an unavoidable conclusion.

Did Ann smear Moore, or did Moore smear our troops and their families?

Brock Clears Things Up for His Subscribers

On November 16, 2004, MMFA sent this alert: "Falwell distorted 1969 Bill Clinton letter, suggested that Clintons 'abhor the military.'" According to Brock, Rev. Jerry Falwell had lied about what Clinton said about the military when he appeared on C-Span two days earlier. Falwell had said, "Hillary is committed, clearly, she has a distaste for, she and her husband, at one point said, he did, we, I abhor the military. . . ."

Coming to the defense of Clinton, but more importantly, to the defense of *truth against conservative misinformation*, Brock wrote, "Clinton never said, 'I abhor the military.'"

So what did Clinton write in his 1969 letter? "I am writing, too, in the hope that my telling this one story will help you to understand more clearly how so many fine people have come to find themselves still loving their country but loathing the military. . . ."

So you see, Clinton didn't *abhor* the military, he *loathed* it. We salute David Brock and MMFA for making this correction, and for not letting Reverend Falwell get away with his distortion.

But wait! Brock wears yet another "hat" when he either doesn't get it or seems to be in denial.

Within hours after Dan Rather's broadcast about the forged documents that allegedly showed George Bush ducking out of his National Guard service, which Rather used in an attempt to derail the Bush presidency, credible evidence from Internet bloggers, such as littlegreenfootballs.com and others, exposed the documents as a fraud. It wasn't too long before CBS and Dan Rather themselves had to admit that these documents were not what they had claimed.

Even Franken had enough sense to stay away from this story just in case the refutations were true. But that didn't stop Brock and his "alerts" from attacking conservatives and other media outlets for being just a little suspicious of these dubious documents.

Brock even tried to distract his subscribers with a release on September 16, 2004: "Media's memo obsession has enabled conservatives to distract from Bush's lies about service." He attempted to make George Bush the real villain by citing Michael Moore's, and DNC Chairman Terry McAuliffe's claims that President Bush was AWOL during his National Guard service. On February 11 and 12, 2004, the nonpartisan group Fact Check.org posted two alerts proving that President Bush did fulfill his requirements.

Franken and Brock Smear Vets Against Kerry

I salute John Kerry for his service in Vietnam, but that does not mean I would vote for him as president. It does not matter to me if he went voluntarily or was denied a deferment and had to go. I do not care if he served four months or four years. I do not care if he won five medals, fifteen medals, or zero medals. The fact is, he served four months longer than I did, and I owe him respect for it.

In 2004 an organization known as Swift Boat Veterans for Truth was formed by many of the men who served in Vietnam at the same time as John Kerry. In the spring they published a book critical of his service and of his comments about war crimes he claimed to have seen them and other soldiers commit. The book, *Unfit for Command,* enjoyed sales success as they also released a series of television ads that challenged the very basis of his campaign for president, namely that he was a highly decorated war hero.

Within a day or two after the first ads were played, Franken went nuts on his radio show. He called them "liars, disgusting liars . . . working with the Bush campaign." It's fair to say that Franken has never interviewed any of the Swift Boat Vets. Based on my monitoring of Franken on his show and television appearances, I believe he has never read the best-selling book *Unfit for Command,* yet he has no problem calling them liars.

Here is a man who says over and over again how much he honors our troops. Yet he attacks John O'Neill and the more than sixty Swift Boat vets who, like John Kerry, served in Vietnam. According to Franken, Kerry's four-month tour qualifies him to be commander in chief, but vets like John O'Neill and the rest of the vets who contributed to the book, all of whom served longer than Kerry and many of whom won medals, deserve to be smeared and savaged.

Basically, this makes Franken a hypocrite. If he has a political litmus test to determine which vets he supports, he is no friend of the military. How do you say you are "for the military," but then try to silence veterans with whom you disagree? Can any fair-minded, decent American really stand there and say the Swift Boat Veterans were not entitled to be heard?

Davie Brock was even worse than Franken (at least Franken does USO tours). He waged an Internet smear campaign against people whose shoes he is not fit to shine. Brock, who attempted to smear John O'Neill, actually posted O'Neill's e-mail address and phone number on his Web site and e-mail alerts so his subscribers could harass him.

Here are some examples from MMFA demonstrating the extent to which Brock and his fellow creeps went to denounce and silence the Swift Boat heroes:

- "On Fox, Sabato called Swift Boat Vets' lies "true." (August 31, 2004)
- "Kondracke echoed discredited Swift Boat Vets charge." (August 24, 2004)
- "Only one of 15 newspaper editorial boards found merit in Swift Boat Veterans' Charges: An MMFA survey." (August 25,

2004) <*Note:* Brock's headline was intentionally misleading in that he wanted his subscribers to believe that fourteen out of fifteen editorials trashed the Swift Boat Veterans' charges. However, if you read carefully* it is clear that only nine of the fifteen cited editorials attacked the Swift Boat Vets, and all of them were from liberal publications like the *Los Angeles Times, St. Petersburg Times,* and *Boston Globe.*>

- "MMFA sends letter to Wal-Mart, Amazon.com, and Barnes & Noble asking these top booksellers to review policies on selling *Unfit for Command.*" (August 20, 2004)
- "Conservatives echoed false accusations that Kerry lied about Cambodia." (August 25, 2004)
- "The lies of John O'Neill: An MMFA analysis. . . . Swift Boat Vets' founder has told repeated untruths about himself, Swift Boat Vets, *Unfit for Command.*" (August 24, 2004)
- "Take Action: Contact Sinclair Broadcasting Group" (Urging them not to broadcast *Stolen Honor*, October 10, 2004)

In response to charges from the Swift Boat vets and others that Kerry was withholding some of his military records, MMFA sent out the following e-mail: "Coulter and Limbaugh accused Kerry of refusing to release military records; they're posted on his Web site" (August 17, 2004).

Truth

During the campaign, Kerry biographer Douglas Brinkley stated that Kerry should release all his military documents. Kerry never signed Form 180, which meant that many of his official records were never released, contrary to Brock's repeated e-mail "alerts" that Kerry had posted *all* his records. And to this day there are still questions as to whether Kerry's Form 180 has finally been signed, and if signed, whether it has actually been sent in to the navy.

Neither Brock nor Franken, nor their like-minded compatriots, had the moral right to attack and demonize John O'Neill and his group the way they did. Do not kid yourselves. If the Swift Boat Veterans could be demonized now as they were, years from now the

*Source: http://mediamatters.org/items/200408250006

same left-wing groups could demonize our brave troops now serving in Iraq.

One of the biggest smears made against the Swift Boat Veterans for Truth (from Kerry supporters in general and Brock and Franken in particular) followed their charge that "John Kerry did not deserve all his medals." The Kerry campaign and their supporters charged the Swift Boat Vets with lying.

On August 24, 2004, the Swift Boat Veterans for Truth backed up their claims in a press release that announced the Kerry campaign had changed its story on his first Purple Heart award.

> In a reversal of their staunch defense of John Kerry's military service record, Kerry campaign officials were quoted by Fox News saying that it was indeed possible that John Kerry's first Purple Heart commendation was the result of an unintentional, self-inflicted wound. (*Special Report with Brit Hume,* August 23, 2004)
>
> This is not the only incident in which Kerry campaign officials have changed their story concerning Kerry's prestigious war medals.

Furthermore, with regard to the medal Kerry earned for pulling Jim Rassmann out of the water:

> Kerry officials were forced to acknowledge that Kerry's boat actually left the scene when another swift boat—operating on the other side of the river—was damaged by an underwater mine. Kerry officials now admit that Kerry's boat returned after several minutes to pull Rassmann from the water while three other swift boats remained on site to render assistance to the injured crew of the one damaged boat. Campaign officials once claimed that Kerry returned to the scene under withering hostile fire to rescue Rassmann after all the other swift boats left.

A month later, on September 20, *US News & World Report* reported that "Kerry was hurt because at least some of the SBVT charges proved true. On August 11, his spokesman admitted that he was not on an illegal mission in Cambodia at Christmas time 1968—the memory of which, he said on the Senate floor in 1986, was 'seared—seared—in me.' . . . He has not authorized release of his military records."

In a September 15, 2005, report titled "New Kerry Medal Flap," the *New York Post* reported yet another inaccuracy in Kerry's biography:

> A newly surfaced document from John Kerry's Navy record says he shot a lone, wounded enemy who was running away in the incident that led to his Silver Star, his highest military decoration . . . this report was obtained from the navy archives by syndicated TV commentator Mark Hyman of *The Point*. A Navy official confirmed its authenticity.

The next day, September 16, in an article in Cybercast News Service, "Navy Contradicts Kerry on Release of Military Records," it was reported that even more details of Kerry's military record were incorrect:

> The U.S. Navy released documents Wednesday contradicting claims by Democratic Presidential candidate John Kerry that all of his available military records have been released.
>
> The Navy, responding to a Freedom of Information Act request from the legal watchdog group Judicial Watch, also referred interested parties to Kerry's campaign web site for government military documents. . . .
>
> In additional correspondence with Judicial Watch dated Sept. 15, the Navy stated that it did not have a copy of Kerry's Discharge Certificate (DD Form 256N), adding that the Navy did not keep files of the certificate in its records.

Clearly, these news reports and press releases both vindicate the Swift Boat Vets and expose the despicable vilification of Vietnam vets by smear merchants like Franken and Brock. How ironic it is when you consider how Al Franken defended Jeremy Glick, "whose only crime was that his father was killed in the WTC," against Bill O'Reilly. Franken himself bullied people like John O'Neill, whose only crime was fighting for this country.

Brock Should Quit While He Is Still Behind

Any time Brock attacks Bill O'Reilly, he demonstrates just how out of his league he is. Brock has sent out numerous "e-mail alerts" defending George Soros against his questionable activism and "philanthropy." O'Reilly has condemned Soros for his questionable financial contributions and activism on more than one occasion.

A Brock alert dated September 17, 2004, attacked O'Reilly for telling his viewers of a Soros/ Brock connection. According to Brock, there was no such connection.

> Fox News Channel host Bill O'Reilly denied having told lies about progressive financier and philanthropist, George Soros. But Media Matters for America has documented several instances of O'Reilly both lying about and smearing Soros. Introducing a segment about Soros on the September 15 edition of Fox News Channel's *The O'Reilly Factor,* O'Reilly claimed Soros "is funding some pretty nasty websites." <O'Reilly was referring to MMFA.>

Then Marc Morano of the Cybercast News Service reported on March 3, 2005, that MMFA was backpedaling on the Soros funding issue:

> After initially claiming on Dec. 1, 2004, that "neither Media Matters nor its president and CEO David Brock has received any money from Soros or from any organization with which he is affiliated," the group is no longer disavowing any connection with groups "affiliated" with Soros. . . .
>
> A Cybercast News Service examination of Brock's financial records and public documents showed that the heavily funded Soros liberal think tank, The Center for American Progress, (CAP) was instrumental in getting Brock's media group off the ground.
>
> Former Clinton administration chief of staff John Podesta, the current president of (CAP), also confirmed to the New York *Sun* that his group provided office space and logistical assistance to Brock in 2004.
>
> Soros has reportedly given $3 million to CAP and its senior

vice president, Morton H. Halperin, who also is the director of Soros's Open Society Institute.

Judge Not, Lest Ye Be Judged

For weeks in the spring of 2005, both Franken and Brock reported over and over how back in 1968 the Republicans filibustered President Lyndon Johnson's nomination of Abe Fortas to be chief justice of the Supreme Court. Hence, the Democrats could point to Fortas as proof that once again Republicans and their shills in talk radio are lying when they say, "It's (filibustering of judicial nominees) never happened in the history of the United States Senate."

So were the Democrats right? Do Republicans have egg on their faces? Are they just as guilty of playing politics with judicial nominees as Democrats are?

No!

Once again, the record has been distorted and manipulated. Let's look at some of the deceptions of Franken and David Brock.

DISTORTION # 1

Unlike President Bush's judicial nominees, Abe Fortas was already a Supreme Court justice. "What's that?" you ask? Unlike President Bush's nominees, who were being held up and denied a hearing or vote by Senate Democrats for cheap partisan political gain, Abe Fortas was already a Supreme Court justice.

DISTORTION # 2

Franken and Brock would have their listeners/subscribers believe that it was the Republicans who blocked (filibustered) the nomination of Fortas. The truth is that nineteen Democrats joined twenty-four Republicans in blocking the Fortas nomination. Eventually Fortas stepped down from the Supreme Court over ethical concerns of his having accepted Wolfson foundation money that was tainted. (Official vote: page S11688, vote 254, 90th Congress 2nd session, vote taken October 1, 1968)

DISTORTION # 3

This is really more Brock than Franken, and it is very clever if I do say so myself. Franken would call it a lie if a Republican did it. Brock distorted the truth by running sentences and phrases together to make them look as if they were part of the same story. In this case, Brock is trying to sanitize lies by distorting the facts.

Brock writes at some points that Republicans filibustered a judicial nominee (just as Democrats are doing now), and at other times writes that Fortas was a Supreme Court justice seeking an elevation to chief justice. But he blurs the truth to make it look like the current "unprecedented" filibuster situation, which Republicans are "unjustly" accusing Democrats of.

From an MMFA alert dated May 18, 2005:

> But Republicans initiated a filibuster against a judicial nominee in 1968, forcing Democratic president Lyndon Johnson to withdraw the nomination of Associate Supreme Court Justice Abe Fortas to be chief justice. . . .
>
> And these are merely instances when Republicans filibustered Democratic presidents' judicial nominees.

From an earlier MMFA alert dated March 16, 2005:

> Finally, Republicans did sustain a filibuster against the promotion of a Democratic president's judicial appointee in 1968. The *Washington Post* reported on December 13, 2004: "In 1968, Republicans filibustered President Lyndon B. Johnson's choice of Supreme Court Justice Abe Fortas to be chief justice, but Johnson withdrew the nomination in the face of Fortas's likely rejection by the Senate."

From an MMFA alert dated April 28, 2005:

> Republicans first used the filibuster against a judicial nominee in 1968.

How many of Franken's listeners or Brock's subscribers were able to distinguish between Fortas the "judicial nominee" and Fortas the "Supreme Court justice" seeking a higher position, especially when this is repeatedly stated in the context of "Republicans did it first"? This is the kind of "blurring" that Franken has frequently attacked Ann Coulter for.

I might be giving Brock more attention in this book than he deserves, but exposing him proves that "birds of a feather flock together." Franken and Brock are smear merchants who conspire with the Left to demonize conservatives and opposing viewpoints. Since the Left can't win the war of ideas against the Right, it has to fight back with smears and distortions.

And just as it will be a cold day in the desert before Franken can truly be a "liberal Rush Limbaugh," it will be a cold day in the desert and pork will become Kosher before MMFA is regarded as the liberal Media Research Center.

33 Were Americans Really United After 9/11?

Al Franken seems to think so, or at least he wants his listeners to be misled into thinking so, and that it was President Bush who "disunited" us.

Ah, yes, I still remember Al Franken, Michael Moore, Ted Kennedy, (and Saddam Hussein) telling America that now is the time to get behind President Bush. A *USA Today* article published in November 2003 quoted a speech that Franken gave to the Commonwealth Club of San Francisco the month before. "I felt like after 9/11 this president had a chance. We were united in a way that I had never seen."

See what I mean? We were all united.

But those good feelings didn't seem to last very long. Al had a book to write, people to attack, and money to make. In a satirical section of *Lies and the Lying Liars Who Tell Them*, Franken wrote, "G-d said that after 9/11, George W. Bush squandered a unique moment of national unity."

That's right, rather than react forcefully as leader of the free world, President Bush should have bent over and said, "Thank you, Muhammed. May I have another?" John Kerry tried that approach, and the American people rejected his candidacy.

Addressing delegates at the Democratic National Convention, as reported by the *Milwaukee Journal Sentinel,* "Franken echoed Bill Clinton's claims that President Bush squandered an opportunity to unite the country and world after 9/11."

While I, too, believe that most Americans were united after 9/11, there were *some* folks who seemed upset that President Bush had been handed an opportunity to unite the country behind him. Some in the media were even cynical enough to ask, "How would Bill Clinton have handled this?"

What kind of question is that? Thousands of people were killed in a devastating terrorist attack, and they want to know how *Clinton* would have handled it? Go back and reread chapter 16 if you really want to know how Bill Clinton would have handled it. I'll tell you how Bill Clinton dealt with terrorists like Yasser Arafat: He invited them to the White House. Maybe *that's* why Bin Laden was so angry at America. "Yasser gets more than forty White House invites and I get none?"

No, President Bush did not squander the opportunity to keep Americans united. Instead, cynical Democrats were determined not to stay silent while the president rallied the country for a common cause.

I did some Google and Nexis searches and found some very ugly and frankly moronic statements by some prominent Democrats following the 9/11 attacks. It seems to me that the only purpose of these comments was to sow doubt and discord in the minds of Americans about who might have been responsible for 9/11.

At Georgetown University on November 7, 2001—less than two months after the attacks—in comments about 9/11, Bill Clinton told the audience:

> Here in the United States, we were founded as a nation that practiced slavery, and slaves quite frequently were killed even though they were innocent. This country once looked the other way when a significant number of native Americans were dispossessed and killed to get their land or their mineral rights or because they were thought of as less than fully human. And we are still paying a price today.
>
> In the First Crusade, when the Christian soldiers took Jerusalem, they first burned a synagogue with 300 Jews in it and proceeded to kill every woman and child who was a Muslim on the

> Temple Mount. I can tell you that story is still being told today in the Middle East and we are still paying for it.

In a story reported by World Net Daily on December 20, 2002, Senator Patty Murray (D-WA) asked students to consider why Bin Laden is more popular than the United States. She asked the students:

> We've got to ask, why is this man so popular around the world? Why are people so supportive of him in many countries that are riddled with poverty?
>
> Out in these countries for decades, building schools, building roads, building infrastructure, building day care facilities . . . and the people are extremely grateful. We haven't done that.
>
> Your generation ought to be thinking about whether we should be better neighbors out in other countries so that they have a different vision of us.

Where did she get such foolish, un-American ideas? Even more shocking, when you come to think of it, is how in this country left-wing activists in the media have completely blacked out news about the good things we are doing in Iraq: building schools, infrastructure, and hospitals, to name just a few, the very things Senator Murray claims are the reasons for Bin Laden's "popularity."

The leftist group FAIR took offense that for a brief moment Americans were willing to put aside partisan politics for the good of the nation. Instead, they focused on the "folly" of the Right for taking the position that "we're better than they are."

In an October 2001 update (one month after 9/11), the extremist liberals at FAIR put out a very biased piece titled "Why They Hate Us." The article cites people like Sean Hannity, George Will, and retired air force general Charles Boyd who essentially "tow the party line" that "they hate us because of our values, our freedom. . . ." FAIR took exception to this "self-congratulatory rhetoric." They seemed to prefer, at least in tone, the "blame America" attitudes of other sources, such as *Newsday* on September 12, 2001, just *one day* after the attacks (and probably written much less than twenty-four hours after the attack):

> But none of these explanations address the United States' deep involvement in Mideast politics, including military actions over the past two decades involving such countries as Libya, Lebanon, Iraq, Iran. Bringing up this history would have complicated one of the themes of media discussion, that of America's "lost innocence"—as in "we must grieve for our nation, which has lost its innocence."

Jim Wooten on *ABC World News Tonight,* on September 12, 2001 (one day after the attacks), reported that "Arabs see the U.S. as an accomplice of Israel: . . . The most provocative issues include economic sanctions against Iraq, which have been seen to deprive children there of medicine and food." In 2003 the press reported that Saddam Hussein had looted the money the UN had sent to pay for food shipments.

In the *Washington Post* on September 16, 2001, Caryle Murphy wrote: "If we want to avoid creating more terrorists, we must end the Israeli-Palestinian conflict quickly. . . ." Did you catch that? If "we" want to avoid creating more terrorists? We?

According to FAIR, the analyses of Murphy and Wooten are much more honest and illuminating about how the United States has given rise to Middle East extremism, whereas self-flattering American pundits like Brit Hume are delusional. They scoffed at Hume's September 23, 2001, analysis:

> Some of these views that you're hearing now that blame America, that say that this country was responsible for what happened in one way or another, that all of this grows out of American support of the state of Israel, this sort of thing: . . . We can now see these views for what they ultimately are. They are a critique of this country . . . the views of people to whom anti-Americanism is a political philosophy in itself.

The Left doesn't understand or refuses to accept that America has enemies who hate us and hate our democracy. It's much easier for them to blame us for terror attacks perpetrated against us than the actual perpetrators. It's ironic that the party of victimhood wants to make the terrorists the victims and the *actual* victims, the aggressors.

It's nice to know that FAIR, Senator Murray, and the careless words of an ex-president still seeking the limelight were united with other Americans before President Bush came along and blew it!

For the Left, it's much more enlightening and intellectual to romanticize the thoughts and ideals of the terrorists than to actually read what these terrorists say themselves. It may come as a shock to a few people, but it appears that the Islamo-killers agree with Hannity and the Right.

An article put out by the Foundation for the Defense of Democracies on January 3, 2005, makes the point that it *is* our values that they despise so much, contrary to the wishful thinking of the Left that we are "too self-congratulatory."

> WHY TERRORISTS OPPOSE DEMOCRACY: The Army of Ansar al-Sunnah, an Iraq-based terrorist group linked to al-Qaeda, issued a statement last week saying: "Democracy is a Greek word meaning the rule of the people, which means that the people do what they see fit." This concept is considered apostasy and defies the belief in one God—Muslims' doctrine.
>
> Earlier, the group had posted a manifesto on its Web site saying democracy amounted to idol worship—because to believe that humans, rather than Allah, has the power to make laws is to "idolize" human beings.

Liberal Democrats don't seem to get this. It makes them feel better to say that it is *our* fault that they hate us, bomb us, and behead us. Shortly after 9/11 Rep. Cynthia McKinney (D-GA) wrote a letter to Saudi Prince Alwaleed bin Talal, whose $10 million check was thrown back in his face by New York City Mayor Rudy Giuliani after the prince suggested to the mayor that 9/11 may not have happened if America had a different foreign policy in the Middle East. Here are some excerpts from her letter:

> Your Royal Highness, many of us here in the United States have long been concerned about reports . . . that reveal a pattern of excessive and often indiscriminate use of lethal force by Israeli security forces in situations where Palestinian demonstrators were unarmed and posed no threat of death or serious injury to the security forces. . . . Indeed your Highness, all people of good conscience

> understand that this kind of mistreatment breeds a hotbed of anger and despair that destabilizes peace in the Middle East and elsewhere. Until we confront the realities of events in the Middle East our nation and the nations of the Middle East will be at risk.

So tell us again, Al, how it was President Bush, and not the "blame America first" crowd, who sought to divide us? Who questioned our greatness as a nation, and who was determined to blame us as the president tried to unite us to fight our real enemies?

If the Left were truly interested in uniting behind the president, even if only on this one issue, there is more than enough ample evidence depicting the true horrors of Saddam Hussein. That includes the movie *Buried in the Sand*, which documents Saddam's secret police ripping out people's tongues, beating the soles of their feet, and other forms of gruesome torture. After they throw up the way I did, let them come back and talk about Israeli repression and destabilizing effects in the Middle East as the reason we should look inward as to why they hate us.

It is intellectual laziness to suggest that peace in the region and around the world could be produced by a simple agreement between Israel and the Palestinians. There are twenty-one Arab and Islamic countries in the region and one Jewish state. If the Arab leaders cannot bring themselves to come to an agreement with Israel, there is nothing America can or should do.

America did not cause the Arab-Israeli conflict; the Arab dictators did. This is not our battle, and shame on those Americans who have allowed themselves to believe that it is our problem to solve. Israel is an ally, a democratic ally with values and principles similar to America's. That is why we support them.

Our enemies hate us because we are better than they are. They merely use Israel, as Jew-haters have throughout history, as a scapegoat.

What Did We Do?

We heard more outrage and condemnations from the Left against what happened in Abu Ghraib and Guantánamo Bay than we heard when our own people were slaughtered and beheaded. At least the prisoners still have heads to put panties onto.

Lest I be too vague and evasive, let me identify a handful of these outspoken folks on the Left. Leading Democrats like Pat Leahy, Teddy Kennedy, and Joe Biden; Amnesty International; the American Civil Liberties Union; and the cheering section at Air America. I don't believe we've ever heard any of these people complain that Muslims are having an image problem in America.

How is it that these people, who supposedly fall under the category of "Americans who love America like grown-ups," can suggest that what a handful of (brave) U.S. troops did to some rotten, despicable monsters rises to the same level of jihadists? Why would Senator Biden seem more concerned that America work to improve *its* image problem while not demanding that Muslims worldwide need to improve *their* image, not only to America but among the civilized peoples around the world?

My question is, When was our image in the Muslim world ever positive? If we bowed down to them and kissed their feet, would it matter? Did Jimmy Carter's or Bill Clinton's repeated overtures to the Palestinians ever "enhance" our image in the Arab world?

Why aren't liberals and leftists calling for the closing down of mosques that serve as gathering places for terrorists and storage facilities for guns and explosives?

Why aren't Muslims yelling at one another to improve their own image in America?

Why is it considered free speech and "artistic" to depict the Virgin Mary in elephant poop, but a catastrophe of epic proportions when urine comes into contact with a Koran?

Why was Rudy Giuliani depicted as a Nazi for wanting to end funding for Christian-bashing museums, but Senator Biden was hailed as a hero for wanting to shut down military prisons that allegedly don't respect Islamic sensibilities?

And yet, many on the Left wonder why some on the Right question their loyalty to this country.

It's My Pa-arty and I'll Cry If I Wa-ant To

On June 15, 2005, *The Al Franken Show* began with an attack on *New York Times* columnist Thomas Friedman. "Thomas Friedman?" I thought to myself. What on earth did he do to get into Franken's crosshairs and bring him to the cusp of crying?

I couldn't figure out if Franken was accusing him of lying or if this was a cynical ploy to draw attention to himself. As it turns out, it was a bit of both. But it wasn't Friedman who was lying; it was Franken. Big surprise.

In his June 15, 2005, column, titled "Let's Talk About Iraq," Friedman wrote about the absolute need to fight this war to the end and what he believes is necessary to win the war. Nothing controversial there.

That's not how Franken saw it. In fact, he said, he put in a call to Friedman, who was away from his desk. Here's the part of the column that upset Franken. As will become clear below, this was a complete deception ("a lie" in Frankenspeak). The column said:

> Liberals don't want to talk about Iraq because, with a few exceptions, they thought the war was wrong and deep down don't want the Bush team to succeed.

When I first heard Friedman's quote on Franken's radio program, my initial thought was that he was pointing out that liberals are afraid to acknowledge the positive aspects of the campaign in Iraq because it would take away a campaign issue. As I wrote earlier, there were many liberals who were upset at the prospect of having to give President Bush credit for doing anything positive, particularly when it came to anything they are against.

How did Franken read the column? Literally: that liberals don't want to talk about it. Franken responded, "We talk about Iraq every day!" As Franken was holding back those tears of pain, he declared, "These are our guys!" as his eyes started to swell up.

Well, bravo, Al! But I think the point Friedman was making was that liberals don't want to talk about the positive things that have come out of the Iraq war, not that they *literally* just don't want to talk about Iraq.

Duh.

To back his claim that "we talk about it every day," Franken cited a list of his recent guest authors who had trashed the war in Iraq. Is Al just plain stupid, or did he just simply miss the point because he is so desperate not to acknowledge it?

There's an even more important aspect to this story. The bigger story is that Franken lied and completely distorted the context of the story. Friedman's column was *not* a "bash the liberals" article as Franken would have had us believe when he said, "It's one thing to hear Rush say this kind of stuff, but to hear it from Thomas Friedman . . ." The reality is, Friedman's column was a "bash everybody" article for all the mistakes that were made leading up to the war and the yet-unconcluded effort in stabilizing Iraq.

Here's what Friedman wrote prior to the passage Franken cited about liberals:

> Conservatives don't want to talk about it because, with few exceptions, they think their job is just to applaud whatever the Bush team does.

Throughout the article, Friedman lays the blame squarely at the feet of Donald Rumsfeld. He accuses him of fighting this war on the cheap, of not sending in enough troops, of not doing enough to maintain a strong and independent Iraqi force to stabilize the region.

In other words, Franken completely misrepresented the context of the story in order to throw himself a pity party and to elevate himself, while once again having a segue into talking about "our guys" (the troops he visits on his USO tours), and to give himself a reason to cry for the television audience for his program on the Sundance channel.

34 What Goodwill? What Allies?

First Franken complained that the president "blew it" when it came to uniting the American people, but it seems that the president can never catch a break with this Franken guy. Not only did Bush "blow it" with Americans who hate America, but he blew it with our friends and allies who hate America. If I had a nickel for each time I heard Al Franken talk about how President Bush "squandered the goodwill of our allies"—at the very least, I would have a lot of nickels.

Here are four nickels' worth of examples:

- "And after 9/11 . . . the world was behind us. . . ." —From an interview on CBS's *Early Show,* August 6, 2004. Of course they were behind us. They couldn't stab us in the back when they were in front of us.
- "And that Bush squandered another surplus. The surplus of goodwill from the rest of the world that he had inherited from Bill Clinton." —From *Lies and the Lying Liars Who Tell Them.* Ah, yes, the "surplus of goodwill." It sounds so poetic.
- "Almost the whole world was behind us" —Franken interview in the *New York Times,* March 23, 2004. First the "whole world" was behind us; now it's "almost" the whole world? Just out of curiosity, Al, could you name some of these "almost

whole world" supporters?

- "He gets in there and alienates the rest of the world." —*Al Franken Show,* October 29, 2004

Let me begin by acknowledging that I do have a prejudice against France [aka the "whole world"]. Both of my parents were born in Paris, and both barely escaped being sent to Auschwitz. Members of my family died in the camps. So you will have to excuse me if I am repulsed when I hear people like Al Franken and John Kerry talk about "our friends, the French."

I know I shouldn't hate the whole country because of what happened sixty or so years ago. So is it okay to despise them for turning a blind eye to the savage and vicious anti-Semitism that is growing in their country today? Is it okay to loathe them for siding with Yasser Arafat and treating him like a statesman all these many years while he was murdering Jewish civilians? Is it okay to be repulsed by those *baguette*-eating, *beret*-wearing, P*epe le Peu*–stinking French for their undermining the country that saved their rear ends during World War II?

John Gibson, host of Fox News's *The Big Story,* wrote a terrific and timely book called *Hating America.* In it he documents the attitudes about and toward America from "our friends," whom President Bush has "walked away from" and Franken and Kerry are eager to embrace again.

Gibson quotes former French President François Mitterrand telling his longtime confidant Georges-Marc Benamou, "France does not know it, but we are at war with America. Yes, a permanent war, a vital war, a war without casualties, at least on the surface." Now was this before or after President Bush became an alienator?

Gibson quotes dozens of other sources citing similarly snide comments from French officials and journalists toward this country before and shortly following the 9/11 attacks. They occurred during the period when, according to Franken, the "whole world was behind us."

Gibson cites *Business Week* contributor John Rossant, who wrote in an article that appeared just two weeks after 9/11, "Members of France's center-left coalition also are starting to chime up. . . . Green Party member Noel Mamere: 'The reality is that

American policy could only result in the kind of terrorism we've just seen.'" The Left in France thinks just like the Left in America. It's our fault we were attacked.

In a post–9/11 report, *Business Week* noted a surge of incensed calls to the popular Radio France Internationale. "What is so special about the American dead?" one caller asked about the September 11 victims. Looks like Michael Moore and Ward Churchill have fans in France.

The French journal of world politics, *Le Monde Diplomatique,* described the French attitude post–9/11 as, "It's too bad for the Americans, but they had it coming."

Please bear with me for one final quote from Gibson's book. This one comes from the time when "our greatest president," Bill Clinton, was in office. Remember, he was the president who left President Bush a "surplus of goodwill," which Bush in turn "just squandered."

John Vinocur wrote in the *International Herald Tribune* that "while Clinton was still in the White House, French political figure Bernard Kouchner 'described anti-Americanism as the motor of French foreign policy.'"

The Hatred Began a Long Time Ago

In an op-ed piece in the *New York Times* on January 3, 2005, John J. Miller, national political reporter for *National Review* and co-author of *Our Oldest Enemy: A History of America's Disastrous Relationship with France,* wrote:

> In 1965, when President Lyndon Johnson sent marines to the Dominican Republic to protect American citizens during a violent civil war, President Charles de Gaulle of France condemned the intervention. In a secret message to Washington, however, he asked for help defending the French Embassy. Johnson did so, but never heard a word of thanks, in public or private. Instead, de Gaulle went on to demand that the United States withdraw from Vietnam and, eventually, to pull his own forces out of NATO.

Miller identified Gaullism as the root of the problem. More than just a form of nationalism, "Gaullism insists that France must exert an outsized influence on the course of human events." Miller then, quite correctly, observes that in world politics the French are much more aggressive:

> Before the invasion of Iraq, Paris didn't just express reservations—it tried to sabotage American goals in every feasible venue, from the chambers of the Security Council to the committee rooms of NATO. Since then, it has issued a raft of demands, including the hasty transfer of sovereignty to an ad hoc Iraqi government, as well as a date certain by which the United States will remove its troops, no matter the circumstances.

. . . And They *Still* Hate Us

In the online magazine *Slate,* Chris Suellentrop wrote on January 29, 2003, "The French never really liked the Clinton administration, either. In June 2000, during Clinton's last year in office, France was the only one, out of 107, to refuse to sign a U.S. initiative aimed at encouraging democracy around the world." The article continues with a complaint from State Department spokesman, James (Rubin) Amanpour: "The French oppose the United States, quite simply, for what it is—the most powerful country on earth."

Now, if Suellentrop is correct and France was the only country not to sign this declaration, doesn't that mean they acted "unilaterally"? And yet I couldn't find anything on Google or Nexis that the French citizenry or media attacked their government for acting "unilaterally," or "walking away from their allies." Maybe the French Left doesn't hate *their* government the way the American Left hates theirs.

Claudia Rosett of the Foundation for the Defense of Democracies wrote an article that appeared in the *Wall Street Journal* on July 28, 2004, in which she looks at many countries to see how the "goodwill" we had under Bill Clinton was "squandered" by George W. Bush. In biting prose she brings us face-to-face with reality:

> Mr. Clinton was finished in January 2001, by which time Al Qaeda's training camps, on Mr. Clinton's watch, had already churned out thousands of terrorists we've been trying to catch ever

> since. By that time, the September 11 plot was just eight months from completion; Iran had already been working for at least half a decade toward its nuclear bomb; North Korea had already been cheating for years on President Clinton's "agreed framework" nuclear freeze; Arafat's intifada had crowned the Clinton photo-op forays into the Middle East; and Saddam Hussein, having kicked out the UN weapons inspectors in 1998, was busy cashing in big time on the Clinton-launched United Nations oil-for-food program, buying influence and blackmail opportunities among our allies, some of them the very same allies President Bush has alienated.

With regard to China, she wrote: "China was one of the countries where people cheered and threw parties to celebrate the attacks of September 11. Also, President Clinton angered China with his ambiguity on the one-China plan, with a non-committal response on Taiwan."

On South Korea she concluded that "Anti-American sentiment started around 1994 after Clinton, and 'free-lance ambassador' Jimmy Carter hammered out a strategy of appeasing North Korea by promising food, fuel, and nuclear reactors to a dictator . . . who was cheating, lying, and starving his own people."

On Russia, she pointed out, "It was during the Clinton administration that Russia was providing nuclear knowhow to our enemies, like Iran."

On Africa: "It was during the Clinton administration that over a half million Rwandans were massacred by their fellow countrymen in a battle of tribes."

It is absolutely sickening that the Frankenoids on the Left are mostly concerned about getting back into the good graces of other countries who do not share our values or concerns, all while attacking and demonizing their fellow Americans who disagree with them philosophically. Or as Al likes to call it, "scorn and ridicule."

When I saw the movie *Hotel Rwanda,* I was left trembling and unable to sleep. It was based on events that took place in Rwanda in 1993 and 1994, when Bill Clinton was president of the United States, Kofi Annan was in charge of peacekeeping in Rwanda, and America had "surpluses of goodwill" from around the world.

So what happened? Oh, not much, just the slaughter of nearly one million Africans (Tutsis) at the hands of other Africans (Hutus). Who in government cared? These were just black people being butchered.

Bill Clinton, America's "first black president," didn't lift a finger. Kofi Annan, who now sits as secretary general of the United Nations—supported by Al Franken against attacks from Rush Limbaugh and Senator Norm Coleman—ignored warnings of an impending slaughter and did nothing. Our great humanitarian European allies did nothing. Other left-wing groups like the NAACP and the Congressional Black Caucus, who decry George Bush's military adventurism, stood by while their brethren were being massacred.

If ever there was evidence that America must not wait to see what our allies and the United Nations say and do, Rwanda was it.

And that is why, if for no other reason, America is fully within its right to decide when and where we act, when and where we intervene.

Our Allies

Franken and the Left constantly bellyache about how President Bush "abandoned our allies." Just for once I'd love to hear from one of those We-support-our-troops-but-are-against-the-war activists say, "Man, I can't believe our allies abandoned us."

Maybe they don't know what the word *ally* means. So I pulled out my Franken "Liberal to American" dictionary and voilà! I found it:

> *Ally:* A country or countries that has used America to protect its sorry ass for the last hundred years but now resents us for being smarter, stronger, richer, and more G-d fearing, and won't help America in its time of need. Furthermore, gives aid and comfort to those on the political fringe in America who seek to destabilize us.

One of my favorite gems that reveals liberal foolishness appeared in the February 23, 2005, issue of Britain's *Daily Telegraph*. One word of caution, especially for you liberals: duck real fast before the egg hits you in the face.

> BRUSSELS—Senior European Union officials, for all their disdain toward the United States in recent years, have been squabbling this week over who gets more "face time" with President Bush.

Ooohh. That had to hurt!

Fox News Supports Terrorism

I wouldn't have believed it if I hadn't heard it from Al "Bush-abandoned-our-allies" Franken myself. Franken claimed that some people at Fox News were happy about the attacks in England on July 7, 2005. And all this time I thought it was the Left that took some sickening and depraved pleasure whenever the United States or its allies were struck by terror!

On July 8, 2005, he singled out *Fox and Friends* hunk Brian Kilmeade for "being happy about the attack."

Why would Kilmeade be happy about a terror attack against England, one of our friends whose goodwill President Bush did *not* squander? I mean, it's not like these Islamo-killers blew up the Eiffel Tower or bombed Rue de Fromage.

So before Franken played Kilmeade's "happy" message, I asked myself what a "happy" Kilmeade would sound like. I played a few different scenarios in my head. They went like this: "YES!!! Those damn British finally got what they had coming to them."

Now that sounds sort of happy. Or how about "I woke up to the great news that the queen mum got a bomb up her royal bum!"

Mmm, nah, this doesn't sound like such a happy Kilmeade, either. So just what does Al Franken consider a happy Kilmeade?

> **Kilmeade:** First to the people of London, and now at the G8 summit, where their topic Number 1—believe it or not—was global warming, the second was African aid. And that was the first time since 9-11 when they should know, and they do know now, that terrorism should be Number 1. But it's important for them all to be together. I think that works to our advantage, in the Western world's advantage, for people to experience something like this together, just 500 miles from where the attacks have happened.
>
> **Stuart Varney** [of Fox News]: It puts the Number 1 issue right back on the front burner right at the point where all these world leaders

are meeting. It takes global warming off the front burner. It takes African aid off the front burner. It sticks terrorism and the fight on the war on terror, right up front all over again.
Kilmeade: Yeah.

According to Franken, Fox News and Brian Kilmeade were "happy" that more than fifty innocent civilians were murdered and hundreds wounded in the subway and bus bombings in England. Why? So that terrorism would be back as the most pressing issue that unites civilized nations, while putting global warming and aid to Africa on the back burner.

Bad, Kilmeade. How dare you think that combating international Islamo-Fascism is more important than combating the impact that SUVs have on our environment!

Franken then went on to say that global warming and death and disease in Africa are just as important as confronting radical Islam, which threatens international terrorism until Islam dominates the world.

Really?

Is that what Franken tells our troops when he does his infamous USO tours? That their fighting and dying in Iraq are no more important than confronting global warming?

Is this what Tom Daschle meant when he said, "We [Democrats] had the right message, we just didn't get it out"?

Well, Tom, the message is out, and it doesn't sound too good.

35 Liberals Play the Nazi and Race Cards

Al Franken has written and often speaks of the superiority of liberals over conservatives when it comes to intellect, debating, civil discourse, and "loving America." Limbaugh and Hannity, he claims, "are like WWF wrestlers." That's right. And Al Franken and his cronies are like female mud wrestlers.

Franken, who is lucky that conservatives haven't yet mastered the art of pie throwing, portrays Rush and Sean as "sleazy, vicious, underhanded." Yet it is the Democrats who frequently play the intellectually inferior Nazi card in their attacks against Republicans.

The comedian Dennis Miller says this is one of the reasons he changed his political affiliation and became a Republican. He could not remain with a party that compared America's mayor, Rudy Giuliani, and Attorney General John Ashcroft to Nazis. It's sad that there aren't more Americans like Dennis Miller.

What great intellect it must take for these liberals and leftists to accuse others of Nazism and Fascism! If you ever visit a left-wing Web site or blog, in addition to the Nazi and Fascist name-calling and the vain imagination of intellectual superiority you might read, try counting how many times you read the F-word.

The only knowledge many of these people have of Nazism seems to come from the '60s sitcom *Hogan's Heroes,* which portrayed Nazis as bumbling idiots. Nazis were anything but.

The Nazis deeply and personally affected my parents, relatives, and parents of friends. Killing six million Jews and millions of others is easy to gloss over today. After all, it happened more than sixty years ago.

Try to picture men knocking on your door at midnight and arresting your father or husband, whom you will never see again. Imagine watching your children tortured right before your eyes in order to get information out of you. Imagine. And yet leftist leaders throw the word *Nazi* around as if it's no worse than calling someone an idiot or a jerk.

Here are some examples of "we're-more-cultured-than-you-are" leftists calling their political foes Nazis:

- At a 2004 Democrat fund-raiser, comedian Margaret Cho said, "Regarding this whole Nazi thing. . . . He (Bush) could be one if he only f—ing applied himself."
- Air America talk-show hostess and Franken colleague Randi Rhodes: "The difference between Hitler and Bush is that Hitler was elected."
- Singer Linda Ronstadt (quoted in *USA Today,* November 17, 2004): "People don't realize that by voting Republican, they voted against themselves. . . . I worry that some people are entertained by the idea of this war. They don't know anything about the Iraqis, but they're angry and frustrated in their own lives. It's like Germany before Hitler took over. The economy was bad and people felt kicked around. They looked for a scapegoat. Now we've got a new bunch of Hitlers." (This quote was reported by the Media Research Center and awarded the Barbra Streisand Political IQ Award for Celebrity Vapidity for 2004. This is just one more example of what Franken refers to as "grown-up" love of America.)
- Rep. Major Owens (D-NY) warned a group of feminists that the "Bush administration is taking America into a pit of Fascism. . . . They [the Bush administration] spit on democracy and are leading this country down a path reminiscent of Nazi Germany." (September 1, 2004)

- MoveOn.org financier George Soros said that President Bush's comments that "you are either with us or against us" was "reminiscent of Nazi propaganda during World War II." (Reported by the *Washington Post,* November 12, 2003)
- When asked about President Bush a few weeks after the 2004 election, Columnist Helen Thomas told a reporter, "My G-d, the man is a fascist—a fascist, I tell you."
- Former Sen. John Glenn (D-OH): "You've just got to separate out fact from fiction. . . . Too often, too often, in this country, if you hear something repeated, it's the old Hitler business." (Mike Allen and Lois Romano, "Closing Laps in Race to November," *Washington Post,* September 4, 2004)
- From the New York State Democratic Convention, May 16, "As an Honor Guard of Albany police officers entered the convention hall . . . they were spat upon and called Nazis." (Bob Just, "Fascism, Corruption, and My 'Democratic' Party," World Net Daily, July 25, 2000)
- "As I watched Tuesday night's network coverage of the unrelenting political propaganda hour known as the Republican National Convention, the first thought that came to mind was of old newsreels of those self-congratulatory Nazi rallies held in Germany during the reign of Adolf Hitler." (Hugh Pearson, *Newsday* columnist, September 2, 2004)

One of my favorite columnists is good guy Jeff Jacoby of the *Boston Globe.* On December 30, 1999, he penned a column titled "A Year of Ugly Slurs." In it he compiled a list of some of the most vitriolic smarm to come out of the mouths of Democrat and liberal leaders and pundits against Republicans:

- Atlanta Mayor Bill Campbell said the Center for Individual Rights and the Southeastern Legal Foundation—which oppose racial preferences and quotas—"are . . . a homogenized version of the Klan. They have traded in their sheets for suits . . . but it's the same old racism."
- *Newsweek's* Eleanor Clift, reacting to the House managers who led the impeachment against Bill Clinton, "Frankly, all they were missing was white sheets. They're like night riders."

- The left-leaning *Arkansas Times* wrote that Kenneth Starr is "cunning, ruthless and about as well-mannered as Heinrich Himmler."
- "Whenever I hear Trent Lott speak, I immediately think of nooses decorating trees, big trees, with black bodies swinging." (Karen Grigsby Bates, *Los Angeles Times,* January 15, 1999)
- New York congressman Major Owens said: "Republicans opposing a minimum-wage hike are like foreign leaders who support 'ethnic cleansing.'"
- Florida state Senator Skip Campbell fretted over whether to approve license plates bearing the logo "Choose Life," claiming that next state senators would be asked to approve a plate reading "Be a Nazi."

On January 25, 2005, the Drudge Report posted former CNN founder Ted Turner's address at the National Association for Television Programming Executives. In it he compared Fox News's popularity to that of Hitler as he rose to power in Nazi Germany.

If he were a news reporter, would Senator Robert Byrd (D-WV) write, "Hitler may have killed 6 million Jews, but he also tried to end the filibuster"? After all, he did slander and smear President Bush and the Republican Senate as they threatened to end the judicial filibusters, saying this would be no different from the tactics employed by Adolf Hitler. In a speech delivered on the Senate floor on March 1, 2005, he complained:

> Many times in our history we have taken up arms to protect a minority against the tyrannical majority in other lands. We, unlike Nazi Germany or Mussolini's Italy, have never stopped being a nation of laws, not of men. But witness how men with motives and a majority can manipulate law to cruel and unjust ends. Historian Alan Bullock writes that Hitler's dictatorship rested on the constitutional foundation of a single law, the Enabling Law.

He continued:

> Hitler needed a two-thirds vote to pass that law, and he cajoled his opposition in the Reichstag to support it. Bullock writes that

> "Hitler was prepared to promise anything to get his bill through. . . . Hitler never abandoned the cloak of legality; he recognized the enormous psychological value of having the law on his side. Instead, he turned the law inside out and made illegality legal."

At that point Byrd drew a direct parallel between Republican plans and Hitler's tactics: "And that is what the nuclear option seeks to do to Rule XXII of the Standing Rules of the Senate." He used the imagery of the Holocaust by alleging that the GOP's leadership in the Senate would "callously incinerate" the rights of the Democratic minority.

What response did Byrd's colleagues have to his offensive, highly inappropriate comments? One, Teddy Kennedy (D-MA), declared, "Once again, the Senator from West Virginia has spoken eloquently and passionately about this institution and about this Constitution."* I guess we should be thankful he didn't accuse the Republicans of wanting to drown their opponents.

At Least Hitler Was Consistent

Byrd had a different take on changing the filibuster rules in 1975. Democrats wanted the rules to change to give them an advantage in the Senate, but there was no talk of Hitler- or Nazi-like tactics then. He sponsored a proposal to reduce the super-majority in the Senate from two-thirds to three-fifths. He claimed that changing the rules governing their procedures only required a simple majority of senators.

> Senate Majority Leader Mike Mansfield (D-MT) said, "We cannot allow a minority" of the senators "to grab the Senate by the throat and hold it there." Senators Leahy, Kennedy, Byrd, and Biden all agreed. So thirty years ago Senator Byrd was a leading proponent of changing the rules of the Senate to lower the threshold of votes the Democrats would need to impose their will on the minority.**

Double Standards on Race

Nobody plays the race card better than the Democrats. If Republicans or conservatives say something that can be twisted

---

*Source: Congressional Record, March 1, 2005.

**From the CATO Institute Web site, *The Filibuster,* Ronald Rotunda, July 16, 2003. http://www.cato.org/dailys/07-16-03.html

to appear insensitive to minorities, the Democrats and the media will hype it up for a week or more; but when Democrats and liberals make overtly racially insensitive remarks, the media gloss over it.

What is also despicable is the way that Democrats play to the fears of minorities by scaring them into thinking that Republican issues or legislation are "code words" to harm the black community. Talk-show host and columnist Larry Elder gave examples of these tactics in a December 19, 2002, column:

- Congresswoman Diane Watson (D-CA) demands Lott's resignation. Watson, then a California state senator, opposed California's Proposition 209, the ballot initiative to rid the state of race- and gender-based preferences. About Ward Connerly, the black businessman who spearheaded the effort, Watson said, "He's married to a white woman. He wants to be white. He wants a colorless society. He has no ethnic pride. He doesn't want to be black." At least Lott apologized, whereas Watson later defiantly said, "That's right. I said it."
- Congresswoman Maxine Waters (D-CA) denounces Lott, but she once called former Los Angeles Mayor Richard Riordan "a plantation owner" and during a police-incident-turned-racial by Waters said that she never sees the cops abuse "little white boys."
- Donna Brazile, Al Gore's campaign manager, called the Republican Party "the party of the white boys." "A white boy attitude," explained Brazile, "is, 'I must exclude, denigrate and leave behind.' They don't see it or think about it. It's a culture." She later said of black Republicans Rep. J. C. Watts of Oklahoma and now-Secretary of State Colin Powell that "they'd rather take pictures with black children than feed them." Both Powell and Watts called her comments "racist."
- Al Gore, in a campaign stop at a black church, called the 2000 presidential election a matter of "good vs. evil." He also said that when George W. Bush used the term "strict constructionist," this hearkens back to a time when blacks were "three-fifths of a human being."
- Rep. Charles Rangel (D-NY) said of the 1994 Republican

Congress, "It's not 'spic' or 'nigger' anymore. They say, 'Let's cut taxes.'"

- Jesse Jackson called Jews "Hymie" and New York "Hymie-Town." Al Sharpton called Jews "diamond merchants" and denounced "white interlopers." They both apologized, and the matter quickly died. Never mind that Sharpton jump-started his career by falsely accusing a white district attorney of rape in the fraudulent Tawana Brawley case. Sharpton never apologized.
- California's lieutenant governor Cruz Bustamante, a Democrat, received comparative kid glove treatment when, incredibly, in a speech before a group of black trade unionists, he referred to blacks as "niggers." After Bustamante's profuse apologies, the story died.
- Colleagues call Senator Robert Byrd (D-WV) the "conscience of the Senate." Yet, after a Lexis-Nexis search of thirty-two years of media reports, NewsMax.com reported that the former Klan member never used the "A-word" or the "S-word" ("apology" or "sorry") in renouncing his membership. Last year, Byrd apologized for using the term "white nigger," and the storm quickly subsided.
- In Chicago, white Alderman Thomas Murphy, a Democrat representing a predominantly black district, attempted to join the city council's black caucus. "The only reason I was given [for the denial]," said Murphy, "was that I'm not an African-American elected official. I believe that the purpose of the caucus was to represent the interests of the black residents of this city. Apparently, they think otherwise." No story.

Elder concluded by writing, "This in no way excuses the boneheaded, offensive remarks made by Lott. But let's apply the same standard to non-Republicans. Lott's implosion proves the opposite of what those with race-colored glasses claim: that racism remains a potent force in American life. As Denny's, Texaco, and John Rocker learned, white racism long ago withered as a growth industry. . . . So here we are. An alleged segregationist goes on a channel called Black Entertainment Television to apologize for suggesting support for racial separation. Only in America."

As vile and ugly as racism is, we will never be able to address it properly until those who make a living under the guise of fighting it are exposed and ostracized.

Left-Wing Anti-Gay Bigotry

Sure liberals love black people—as long as they are liberal, vote Democrat, and remember their place. Sure they are the party of women's rights—as long as those rights mean the right to kill an unborn child. Sure they are the party of gay rights—even as they put their finger in the wind to see if the gay marriage issue is a nail in their political coffin—as long as you are a liberal gay person.

In February 2005 it was discovered that one Jeff Gannon had slipped through the White House press credential security check and had managed to snag a position in the press conference area. Even worse, he was one of the selected few who got to ask President Bush some questions. It was reported that Gannon wasn't a real journalist; he was a partisan activist affiliated with a Republican organization. His apparent objective was to ask the president "softball" questions.

We can debate all day long who or what a real journalist is. According to liberals, it's anybody who attacks Republicans. And we can ask how Gannon managed to get press credentials and how he, of all the reporters present, was selected to ask some questions of the president during briefings.

Those are all fair questions, I suppose. But if you read the liberal online reviews or Democratic Web sites about how Gannon was exposed as a "journalistic fraud," you will see that his crime wasn't passing himself off as a legitimate journalist. Heck no! His crime was that he was gay, a Republican, a male hooker, and an escort!

A February 14, 2005, story in AmericaBlog, "A Man Called Jeff," displayed pictures of Gannon in sexually explicit poses. This was done for no reason other than to hurt and embarrass him.

An article that appeared in *The Advocate* on March 29, 2005, reported, "When not asking the president conservatively slanted softball questions, with invented facts occasionally thrown in, Guckert [Gannon's legal name] apparently had another job: as a $200-an-hour (or $1,200-a-weekend) escort advertised on the sites HotMilitaryStud.com, MaleCorps.com, and others."

Even the flame-haired Bush basher Maureen Dowd couldn't hold back her acerbic tongue when writing in her March 17, 2005, op-ed for the *New York Times*, "I may have gotten a presidential wink, but I still don't have my regular White House pass back. (Maybe I'd get it back if I became a male escort?)"

There were hundreds, if not thousands, of attacks against Jeff Gannon for being a gay man whose ideological sympathies lay with the Right.

Never mind that Media Matters' David Brock's social life has never become a target or story, and conservatives have never attempted to make it one. Why? Because it's not important.

I will leave it to others to sort out how America is racist or conservatives are homophobic, but history has shown—over and over—that when it comes to demonizing people of color or of homosexual tendencies who forget which team they are *supposed* to be on, no one can compete with the Left.

Consider the slam against veteran New York political consultant Arthur Finkelstein from none other than former president Bill Clinton on April 12, 2005. Finkelstein married his male partner in a civil ceremony in Massachusetts in December 2004. A few of his conservative clients were at the nuptial.

"He went to Massachusetts and married his longtime male partner, and then he comes back here and announces this," Clinton said at a Harlem news conference. "I thought, one of two things. Either this guy believes his party is not serious and is totally Machiavellian in his position, or there's some sort of self-loathing there. I was more sad for him."

Clinton's decision to bring up Finkelstein's sexuality hearkened back to a similar remark made by John Kerry in the October 13, 2004, presidential debate. In responding to a question of whether homosexuality was a matter of choice, Kerry said, "I think if you were to talk to Dick Cheney's daughter, who is a lesbian, she would tell you that she's being who she was, she's being who she was born as."

It may or may not be true that gay people are born gay; there is scientific evidence to support both opinions, and I am not qualified to interpret the information. But nobody is born to be nasty, vitriolic, or a character assassin. That's a choice. Unfortunately, some people are very comfortable with the choices they have made.

36 How Al Franken and the Left Dehumanized Terri Schiavo

On March 23, 2005, Franken opened his last segment of the day by saying how tragic the Terri Schiavo case was. For once in his life he was right: it was tragic. He also said that he wasn't going to cast aspersions as to the motives of Republicans who supported keeping Terri alive.

Franken's second caller of the day told Al that it was okay for him to not cast aspersions, because he would do it for him. Did Al say, "Now, now, this is not the time for that?" No. Franken thanked him for launching the ugly personal attacks.

Way to take the high road, Al!

But this moron caller didn't just agree to play the role of smear merchant, he attacked Republicans as hypocrites for meddling in the affairs between a husband and wife, although the husband was living with another woman with whom he had two children. "I thought these guys believed in the sanctity of marriage?" yelled Franken's irate caller.

The Democratic Underground Web site used the same technique to chide John McCain (who suggested that Michael Schiavo could simply divorce Terri and end this controversy) by proclaiming, "Republicans are constantly harping on about the sacred bond of marriage between a man and a woman."

The *New York Times'* Maureen Dowd praised Rep. Debbie Wasserman Schultz (D-FL), who excoriated Republicans over the weekend for trying to save Terri. "It is particularly hypocritical when you have people who say they advocate on behalf of the defense of marriage who now insert themselves between a husband and his wife," Schultz railed.

It's incredible that the party that defended Bill Clinton's zipper problem for eight years is now the party advocating for the sanctity of marriage.

So the debate has gone from defending a woman's right to live to what the Left sees as yet another way to indict President Bush and Tom DeLay. In the war on terror, when the Left says, "Of course we support our troops, and that's why we want them to come home," it actually means, "Let's give the savage killers of Iraqi civilians free rein." When it comes to Terri Schiavo, the mantra is, "Of course it's tragic, but President Bush and Tom DeLay are hypocrites."

On March 23, 2005, Joe Scarborough had the always affable and informed Al Franken on as his guest to discuss "this tragedy." Since Franken is not a doctor, a lawyer, or a philosopher, all he could offer is what his callers might be saying about this issue, and this is exactly what Scarborough asked him at the beginning of the segment. Once Franken replied, "We don't have many callers," that should have been the end of the exchange. But of course it wasn't.

Franken quickly attacked Scarborough's integrity for promoting a Dr. Hammesfahr, who was a guest earlier in the week, as an expert on the Schiavo case. Apparently, Dr. Hammesfahr, a neurologist who has been in practice for twenty-three years and was nominated for a Nobel Prize for his work in medicine, had some credibility problems when it was made public that, according to reports, his nomination was suspect. Four times during the show Scarborough mentioned that the doctor was nominated for a Nobel Prize in medicine. (On May 24, 2005, Franken testified before the Conyers Committee on media bias that Scarborough mentioned it ten times.)

But Franken's shameless and disgraceful attacks didn't end with conservative talk-show hosts. Apparently he had decided he was qualified to determine who is a doctor and who isn't. Together with David Brock, he portrayed Dr. Hammesfahr as a quack who got his medical degree from a box of Cracker Jacks. Franken followed

Brock's lead on the vicious attacks. On March 22, 2005, MMFA posted the following headline on their site: "Dubious doctor touted as Nobel Prize nominee by Hannity, Scarborough." Both Franken and Brock not only dehumanized Terri, they attempted to discredit and smear anybody who chose to recognize her as a viable human being.

What did Dr. Hammesfahr do to deserve being slimed as a dubious doctor? He presented himself as someone who had been nominated for a Nobel Prize for his work in medicine. The nominator, however, was a congressman rather than a member of the Nominating Assembly, or select committee, and congressmen are not qualified to make such nominations.

Brock and Franken took this new revelation to attack the work of Dr. Hammesfahr, a man who had been in practice for twenty-three years and who was a leader in discovering new treatments and therapy, healing stroke victims, and who had treated a host of other victims of head and neck injuries.

In point of fact, though, the "unqualified" nomination was actually a letter of recommendation from Congressman Mike Gilirakis (R-FL), who cited numerous cases of patients who had made miraculous recoveries thanks to Dr. Hammesfahr's breakthrough treatments. In the letter, the congressman went on to cite other groups such as the Traumatic Brain Injury Association in the state of Florida, Viet Nam Veterans of America, The International Police Chiefs Federation, and the American Burn Survival Foundation, all of whom also wanted the Nobel Prize Committee to recognize this doctor's great work. But maybe Franken and Brock regard these groups as dubious, too. The congressman's letter of recommendation can be viewed at: http://www.hnionline.com/nobel_prize_nomination.htm.

So excuse us all, Al Franken and David Brock, if the doctor's nomination didn't exactly follow the proper nominating protocol. While Dr. Hammesfahr has been out saving lives and giving hope to people who might otherwise have none, what have you done to improve anyone's life? Oh, yeah, you call people liars.

It is utter folly to suggest that Hannity and Scarborough repeatedly misled their audiences with disinformation. If they thought his nomination was valid—they had no reason to suspect otherwise—

repeating it was appropriate. It would have been different if they had repeated it after the truth was disclosed. This clearly did not happen, but truth-teller Al Franken wanted his listeners to believe it did. He was looking to demonize both of them. As a sidebar, would it have made Franken and Brock happy had the doctor been promoted as someone who received a letter of recommendation for his great work with stroke and other paralyzed victims?

During his Scarborough appearance, Franken made an absurd charge. "George Bush is a hypocrite, because as governor of Texas he signed a law that allows hospitals to disconnect life support even against the mother's wishes." Franken later threw in how, according to this bill, the hospitals had the right to disconnect a respirator if the patient couldn't afford to pay.

Indeed, on March 15, 2005, life support was disconnected for a baby from Texas named Sun Hudson, who was born with a rare genetic disease called thanatophoric dysplasia. With a tiny chest and lungs too small to support life, young Sun had been on a ventilator since birth.

According to an NBC5 *HealthWatch* story dated March 15, 2005, the critically ill five-month-old boy "was taken off life support and died Tuesday, a day after a judge cleared the way for doctors to halt care they believed to be futile. The infant's mother had fought to keep him alive."

Nothing in the story suggested that doctors had cut off life support because the mother "couldn't afford the hospital bills." Wanting to demonize President Bush, Franken made up the money angle so he could portray him as being captive to the wealthy and big insurance.

• • •

Let's examine this a bit more closely, though, and try to get some insight into Franken's diabolical mind.

1. The baby was born with a rare condition, and a team of doctors—the hospital's ethics committee—ethicists, nurses, and clergy ruled that further care was futile and that the baby was going to die very shortly. In Terri's case, she had lived for fifteen years in her "brain-damaged" state and only needed water

and food to be kept alive. Unlike the baby, she was not going to die.

2. Though the baby's mother, like the Schindlers (Terri's parents), wanted the hospital to keep her baby on life support, Terri's parents were willing to take care of her themselves.
3. The bill signed into law by Governor George Bush that applied to this baby mandated that the hospital allow ten days for the mother to find another hospital or facility to take the baby once all medical attention was deemed "futile." In Terri's case, the judges prohibited everybody, including Terri's parents, from doing anything that would sustain Terri's life, including bringing her ice chips. Some children who were demonstrating in support of Terri were arrested for attempting to bring her cups of water.

Comparing the two cases, which are totally different from each other in every imaginable way, is obscene. But then again, we are talking about Al Franken.

Here is the actual transcript of Franken's appearance on *Scarborough Country:*

Scarborough: What were your callers telling you today?
Franken: We don't take that many calls. . . . [E]veryone believes this is a terribly sad thing. And the tragedy happened. A lot of people say the tragedy happened fifteen years ago. There has been an exploitation of this, that—this is what I believe and a lot of our listeners believe—by members of Congress and a lot of hypocrisy. And I'll give you one example. Where were you, Joe, last week when the—a tube was pulled from a six-month-old baby in Texas, against the wishes of his parents, because of a law signed by George W. Bush which allows hospitals, if they've decided that the care is futile, to remove life support, or to remove in this case, it was a breathing tube, even if the parents . . .
Scarborough: When you say if the care—if the health care is futile, what do you mean, if the baby can't be saved?
Franken: Yes. In other words, the same situation essentially . . . <No, Al, it was two completely different cases, with no similarities. The baby was going to die, and Terri wasn't.>

Scarborough: But, in this case, her life can be saved. If they feed her, she lives.
Franken: No, it . . .
Scarborough: If you take the feeding tube out, she dies.
Franken: Yes, but you're talking about—first of all, this was against the parents' wishes. And part of it was—and let me continue . . . <Franken is now saying that a feeding tube is the same as a respirator.>
. . .
Scarborough: And how are we taking care of this lady? Let's not make this a Republican or a Democratic issue.
Franken: I'll tell you how we're taking care of this lady. Most people in the polling that's been done would not want to live like she's living. <So let's kill her because the polls say so.> She's brain-dead. Now, here's where a lot of misinformation has been passed, including by you, Joe. The other night, you said this and you said it four times. This is how you teased this. "And a Nobel Prize-nominated neurologist who has treated Terri Schiavo; he says Terri should live and that her husband is perpetrating a hoax that is just aimed at killing his wife."

This Dr. Hammesfahr is not a "Nobel Prize nominee." You said that four times. He did not treat her. You said that four times. You have to do your research, Joe. There is no such thing as a "Nobel Prize nominee." Now, he claims to be a Nobel Prize nominee because a letter was written to the Nobel Committee by Representative Mike Bilirakis. Is that how you pronounce his . . . <So now we're off of Bush and this becomes about Joe, and how it's Joe's fault for not finding out how the Nobel nomination process works, for had he done that, he would have known that it wasn't a proper nomination. By Franken's own standards, he should have walked off the show after being asked about "his callers" since thorough research would have shown Scarborough that Franken doesn't have callers.>
Scarborough: I know you want to get down in the weeds. And if you want to come back on some other night . . .
Franken: This is not getting down in the weeds. <No, it's getting down in the gutter.>
Scarborough: . . . and you want to debate me on Dr. Hammesfahr,

who—it's amazing. He had a great reputation until he went after Schiavo's husband.

. . .

Scarborough: You're trying to change the subject. I'm asking you, why are we allowing this lady to starve to death?

Franken: Because the court has decided that she is brain-dead and that this would be her wish. And most Americans who are in this position would want to die. <Franken has now become an arbiter as to when and if Americans would want to die.>

Scarborough: You say that. But you know what? And this is the problem. I'm trying to have a conversation with you. You're turning it into a political fight.

Franken: No. I'm not.

This exchange went on for several minutes with no other guests for Franken to contend with. Yet when Franken testified before the Conyers Committee in Washington, D.C., on May 24, he declared that Scarborough cut his mike off much earlier in the interview following the point where Franken initially brought up the Hammesfahr and the Nobel Prize nomination issue.

FRANKEN FRAUD EXPOSED

Let's go over what Franken did on this show point by point:

1. Franken was invited to give the perspective of his left-wing callers on the Schiavo case. But since Franken takes few, if any calls, on any given day, he came prepared to make a case against George Bush and Joe Scarborough.
2. Bringing up the baby from Texas was absolutely obscene. It served no purpose other than to allow him to make a personal attack against Scarborough and President Bush. Asking "where were you when this baby's tube was being disconnected" was a gratuitous cheap shot. Whereas the Schiavo case garnered international headlines, few people outside of Texas even knew about the baby. And where was Franken's concern for the baby when this was happening? The answer is, nowhere. Because at the time, this poor baby's death served no purpose for Franken and his attack machine.

3. Franken had said several times on his radio program, as well as his appearance on Scarborough, that the bill Bush signed as governor allowed doctors to disconnect life support if the patient was unable to pay for medical expenses. That is a lie of the most imaginable scope. The bill made no such statement. In fact, the bill requires the hospital to allow the patient's family ten days to find another facility if the hospital deems further care to be futile. If Terri had been afforded that same consideration, we wouldn't have been talking about this case. Terri's brother, sister, and parents were begging for the right to take Terri home and watch over her.
4. On his show Franken repeatedly stated that Dr. Hammesfahr "never treated Terri Schiavo," contradicting reports that said he did. I am not sure what constitutes "treating" a patient versus "examining" a patient, but Dr. Hammesfahr did spend ten hours with her, and I can't imagine what he did in that time that wasn't directly related to her condition.

Democrats Become More Desperate or Ridiculous

Democratic strategist Victor Kamber said on CNN's *American Morning* (March 21, 2005), "Republicans who sanctify marriage, uh, and talk about marriage to intervene on a family situation, a personal situation like this. Uh, I mean, it just—it is—for—for Congress to come back on a weekend, for the president to fly back, um, uh, from his vacation when he wouldn't even come out for two days after the tsunami, wouldn't deal with the [sic] 9/11, hasn't been to a single funeral for one of our Iraqi [sic], uh, soldiers, I mean there are so many outrages here."

The only outrage here was how the political party of partial-birth abortion and "if it feels good, do it" all of a sudden took the side of sanctity of marriage and quality of life. *Boston Globe* columnist Jeff Jacoby wrote a brilliant article on March 24, 2005, on the Terri Schiavo case. In that article he talked about what he and his wife have been asked to consider as part of their living will, should they ever find themselves in a similar situation as Terri:

> My wife and I have been working on healthcare proxies that specify how we wish to be cared for should the worst ever come to pass.

> The scenarios we have been asked to consider are wrenching. For example: If you were in a coma or vegetative state and you had no hope of regaining awareness, would you wish to receive nutrients and fluids artificially? How about electric shock to keep your heart beating? A breathing tube? Kidney dialysis? Major surgery? Pain medications? Should you be given blood? Antibiotics? Invasive diagnostic tests? What if there was a small chance you would recover fully? What if, instead of being in a coma, you had irreversible brain damage? What if you also had a terminal illness such as incurable cancer? Which medical procedures would you definitely want? Which would you not want? Which would you want only as long as there was improvement in your condition?
>
> Even as hypothetical questions, these are tough issues to wrestle with. Do you want your loved ones to keep you alive once your personality and intellect are gone? Would you ever want them to withhold medical care even if you weren't in pain and your condition weren't terminal? Is the sanctity of life your highest priority? Should financial cost be an issue? Some answers are clear. Others are anything but.

The only thing Michael Schiavo brought to the table was, "Terri told me that she wouldn't want to live like this."

I am not a doctor, a lawyer, or a member of the Schiavo family, but I take an interest in the news. I saw a poor woman who could not speak for herself. And while she didn't seem to be living "a quality life," she was not dying. She was able to breathe on her own, and she did not appear to be suffering. What I could see was a husband with questionable motives seeking to end her life even though her brother, sister, and parents wanted to take care of her.

Much has been said about Dr. Hammesfahr, including the criticisms leveled against him by Franken and others. What do we know about the doctor chosen by Michael Schiavo?

The neurologist chosen by Michael Schiavo, Dr. Ronald Cranford, is a member of the board of directors of the Choice in Dying Society, which promotes doctor-assisted suicide and euthanasia. He was also a featured speaker at the 1992 national conference of the Hemlock Society (a right-to-die organization), a group that recently changed its name to End of Life Choices.

In 1997 Dr. Cranford wrote an opinion piece in the *Minneapolis Star-Tribune* titled "When a Feeding Tube Borders on Barbaric":

> Just a few decades ago cases of brain death, vegetative state, and locked-in syndrome were rare. These days, medicine's "therapeutic triumphs" have made these neurologic conditions rather frequent. For all its power to restore life and health, we now realize, modern medicine also has great potential for prolonging a *dehumanizing* existence for the patient. (Emphasis mine.)

If you want to get a better understanding of dehumanizing someone, you need look no further than how Air America described Terri on the headline they posted: "Appeals Court Rejects Request to Force-Feed Brain-Dead Woman."

First, they lie about force-feeding. The only thing "forced" was the removal of her feeding tube. Second, look at how they deprive her of humanity and dignity by referring to her as the "brain dead woman." All of America watched Terri's suffering; yet Air America couldn't bring themselves to refer to her by her name.

Oh, that liberal compassion!

But Air America's despicable conduct didn't end there. After I clicked on the "brain-dead woman" headline, I was brought to the actual story, which came from CNN.com: "Appeals Court Denies Parents' Request to Rehear Schiavo Case."

How did Air America report it? "Appeals Court Rejects Request to Force-Feed Brain-Dead Woman." Air America dehumanized Terri with its ugly headline. They might just as well have come out and said, "Polls: Most Americans Favor Killing the Retard." On his radio program, Franken discussed how "offended" he was by the media repeatedly playing the clip of Terri in her hospital bed, appearing to be attentive and responsive. Though I didn't hear any complaints from liberals when the media played the tapes, repeatedly, of Rodney King being beaten by the LAPD.

David Brock's Media Matters also chimed in on the controversy on March 22, taking exception with Fox News, which had more pro-Terri guests than those who wished to see Terri starve to death. The headline read: "Fox News Alert: *Hannity & Colmes* Schiavo Case Guest List Not 'Fair and Balanced.'"

> On the March 21 edition of the program *[Hannity & Colmes]*, co-host Sean Hannity promised his audience, "We'll also meet a congressman who voted against the resolution [calling for a review of the Schiavo case in a federal court] last night, to get the other side." But that congressman, Rep. Michael Capuano (D-MA), was the only guest who opposed the involvement of Congress in the Florida state courts' decision ordering removal of Terri Schiavo's feeding tube. Overall, the March 18 and March 21 editions of *Hannity & Colmes* featured thirteen guests who argued for replacing Schiavo's feeding tube and prolonging her life.

Reading Brock's e-mail alert leaves one with the clear impression that he wanted to hear more from those who supported leading Terri to a slow, debilitating death. This seems to contradict another Brock e-mail, from March 23, that implies any suggestion Democrats don't support keeping Terri alive is unfair: "Only on Fox: John Gibson suggested that 'Republicans stand for parents' right and life, and Democrats have sided for questionable husband and dying.'"

According to Brock, forty-seven Democrats supported the bill in support of Terri, which means that approximately 75 percent of Democrats were opposed to sustaining her life.

Relying on Polls

There's nothing that demonstrates how much of a real politician a person is like seeing them wait until the polls tell them what to do. Franken argued that Terri should be denied food and water because "the majority of Americans agree with me." More accurately, the polls show that Franken waited to hear what others had to say before staking his position. When Franken was on *Scarborough Country,* he argued for following the lead of the polls before Joe swatted his polls as bogus. "Bogus?" Franken demanded. Actually, he didn't respond to Scarborough until the next day on his radio show.

Yes, the polls were bogus. They were leading—actually *mis*leading—they didn't give the full picture, and they asked people to give a quick answer during a phone call without discussing the issue with their families. Here are the poll questions about the Schiavo case. Note how they were worded:

1. Schiavo suffered brain damage and has been on life support for fifteen years. Doctors say she has no consciousness and her condition is irreversible. Her husband and her parents disagree about whether she would have wanted to be kept alive. Florida courts have sided with the husband, and her feeding tube was removed on Friday. What's your opinion on this case? Do you support or oppose the decision to remove Schiavo's feeding tube?
2. If you were in this condition, would you want to be kept alive, or not?

Here is how these questions were grossly misleading:

- Terri was not on life support for fifteen years, she was on a feeding tube. The difference is very significant. Once you disconnect life support—a respirator—the patient dies within minutes. In the case of a feeding tube, a patient can continue living for more than ten days. In fact, Terri lived for thirteen days after her feeding tube was removed.
- Because of the first misleading question, the second question was going to be based on misinformation as well.
- The question refers to her "husband" but makes no mention that this man has since moved on with his life and has two children with another woman. Knowledge of this would clearly raise questions about why he was so eager to remove her feeding tubes.
- The poll question makes no mention of the fact that Terri's parents, brother, and sister had begged for the opportunity to assume all responsibility for Terri's medical care. The poll question says, "Her husband and parents disagree." The truth is, *They don't disagree; they hate each other.* How many people would side with the husband if they knew how the husband was estranged from her parents?
- The question makes no mention of the fact that her husband didn't claim that Terri wished "not to live like this," until seven years after she assumed a "vegetative" state (and after he had been awarded millions of dollars in a legal malpractice suit).
- The question made no mention that there were disagreements

among some neurologists as to whether all appropriate tests had been performed on Terri prior to her husband's decision to remove her feeding tube.

On March 29, 2005, Franken opened his show with, "Now that we know that House Majority leader Tom DeLay supported pulling the plug on his own father when his dad was in a Schiavo-like situation, people think he should resign . . . but we want him to stay so he can bring down other Republicans with him."

If Al Frankenstein were an actual doctor like he's a "highly talented talk-show host," he'd be guilty of malpractice.

Tom DeLay's father, Charles DeLay, was not in a "Schiavo-like" situation. His father had been in an accident and had major organ damage. He was in a coma and was breathing through machines. Terri, on the other hand, was breathing on her own and needed only a feeding tube.

In the case of Charles DeLay, the entire family decided together on what they thought was the appropriate decision. In Terri's case, there was no consensus. Michael, who was living with another woman and had children with her, was an adulterer who had an obvious conflict of interest.

Then Franken had the gall to attack DeLay for politicizing Terri's situation. However, Franken himself clearly said he hoped to use DeLay's "hypocrisy" to bring down the Republican Party. Go figure.

Franken Attacks Peggy Noonan

On March 28, 2005, Franken opened his program with a blistering attack on Peggy Noonan, who had written an op-ed on the Schiavo case for the *Wall Street Journal* on March 24, 2005. Here is the opening of the article:

> God made the world or he didn't.
>
> God made you or he didn't.
>
> If he did, your little human life is, and has been, touched by the divine. If this is true, it would be true of all humans, not only some. And so—again, if it is true—each human life is precious, of infinite value, worthy of great respect.
>
> Most—not all, but probably most—of those who support Terri

> Schiavo's right to live believe the above. This explains their passion and emotionalism. They believe they are fighting for an invaluable and irreplaceable human life. . . .
>
> They do not want an innocent human life ended for what appear to be primarily practical and worldly reasons—e.g., Mrs. Schiavo's quality of life is low, her life is pointless. They say: Who is to say it is pointless? And what does pointless even mean? Maybe life itself is the point.
>
> I do not understand the emotionalism of the pull-the-tube people. What is driving their engagement? Is it because they are compassionate, and their hearts bleed at the thought that Mrs. Schiavo suffers? But throughout this case no one has testified that she is in persistent pain, as those with terminal cancer are.

Franken complained that her column was "one of the ugliest pieces she has ever written." He attacked her on several levels.

He complained, "We're not committed to her death. We're committed to the rights of families to make private decisions." But that was exactly *not* what was at stake, and Franken seemed to gloss over it intentionally: *it was not a family decision.* The husband, whom it would be more accurate to call an ex-husband, had an ulterior motive for wanting her out of the way. The rest of her family—her brother, sister, and parents—wanted to take care of her. There was no "private family decision."

He also asked the rhetorical question, "Where was Peggy two weeks ago when a Texas hospital pulled the plug on a five-and-a-half-month-old baby against his mother's wishes because of a law signed by Governor Bush?" Here we go again. This charge has already been refuted above, and it's very difficult to make any comparison or find its relevance to Terri's case.

Furthermore, he sarcastically asked whether Noonan wasn't being hypocritical for referring to those calling for the tube removal as "pro-death" when she supports the death penalty. This is not a case of Noonan's hypocrisy so much as it is a case of Franken's stupidity. Is he saying that Terri Schiavo should be treated like Charles Manson, Ted Bundy, or Scott Peterson—all of whom earned their death penalties?

He also claimed that "regardless of the outcome, her dying or being kept alive in her present state, it's no good." Wrong! Doctor Frankenstein has no right to decide whose life is worth living and whose isn't. The *situation* is a tragedy; her life is not.

Terri Schiavo RIP

So Terri died and went to heaven on March 31, 2005, at 9:03 in the morning. May her soul find peace.

My heart ached after watching the poor, defenseless woman murdered by the state of Florida. She suffered an agonizing death after thirteen days of starvation and dehydration.

If Michael Schiavo had a shred of decency, he would have walked away. Even under the influence of his death-obsessed lawyer, he could so easily have said, "I know that Terri didn't want to be kept alive like this, because she told me. But it's obvious that nobody believes me and that I am causing great and needless pain to her parents who love her. I have moved on. I met a new woman whom I love, and we have two beautiful children. If the Schindlers want to take responsibility for Terri, I am willing to let them."

Nobody in America would have looked down on him. No one would accuse him of breaking his promise to Terri. To the contrary, he would have been looked upon as a hero, a man of great decency.

37 *Outfoxed* Defanged

Nothing says "I'm a little whiner" more than liberals complaining and bellyaching about "how unfair Fox News is." Liberals had CNN, ABC, NBC, and CBS, not to mention left-wing newspapers and magazines for so many years. How dare some network come along and give conservatives a fair shake?

In the summer of 2004, while the country was watching Michael Moore's propaganda film accusing President Bush of being in collusion with our enemies and our troops of being nothing more than heavy-metal crazed killing machines, Robert Greenwald produced a little flick called *Outfoxed: Rupert Murdoch's War on Journalism.* It was nothing more than a distortion of the operations at Fox News.

According to the Left, *Outfoxed* showed the true face and modus operandi of Fox News and their "shilling ways" for the Bush administration. After looking at it, I'd have to say that Michael Moore probably could have cooked up something like it when he was in first grade.

So what did this film accomplish? If you already hate Fox News, you'll probably say, "I told you so." And if you like Fox, you probably didn't waste your time watching it.

But since 2004 was the year of "liberal bitching and moaning," it was just another example of how liberals manipulate and distort the news to show how unfairly *they've* been portrayed.

Outfoxed begins with audio clips of President Bush talking about the clear danger Saddam Hussein and his weapons programs pose to America and the world. Then we hear a voice-over saying, "Were we wrong?"

Immediately, we see a smiling Saddam Hussein standing on his palace balcony, waving to his throngs of supporters, an obvious attempt by the filmmakers to portray Hussein as a likable character unfairly targeted by the lying Bush administration, rather than showing him towering over the carcasses of his hundreds of thousands of victims.

Next we are told about the "neoconservatives"—the Left's term for pushy, warmongering Jews who are less than regular conservatives—who pushed President Bush into war. The words are accompanied by pictures of "these smarmy Jews" Paul Wolfowitz and Elliott Abrams.

One of the guests who appeared throughout the film was Larry Johnson, a former counterterrorism expert and Fox News consultant. What did he bring to the table to prove Fox News's bias? It was that the network insisted the "suicide" bombers blowing Israeli civilians to bits be referred to as "homicide" bombers, because that was the term, according to Johnson, the administration was now adopting. Johnson complained that "homicide" bomber wasn't necessary since anybody who kills others is committing a "homicide"; therefore "suicide" bomber was more appropriate.

But Johnson was wrong, and his bias against Fox News and Israeli victims was wrong. Using the preferred liberal term, "suicide," makes the killers look more sympathetic.

Early on during these "homicide" campaigns, the Palestinians would say, "Look, the Israelis are driving us to commit suicide." As if these attacks on buses and pizza parlors were acts of desperation, instead of cold calculated acts of wanton, brutal murder. For some reason, the networks are expected to either sympathize with Palestinian and Arab terrorists or, at the very least, not pass judgment and treat both sides as if they are equally to blame for the cycle of violence.

Another opinion maker in *Outfoxed* was Jeff Cohen. Whenever he appeared on screen, he was identified as formerly of MSNBC and Fox News, but a more accurate description would have been founder of Fairness and Accuracy in Media (FAIR)—the ultra-left-wing media watchdog group that appears earlier in this book.

The film was full of distortions from beginning to end, but just a few of them are reported below.

Fallacy # 1: Fox News Repeated the White House Term "Flip-Flop"

In one of the later segments of the film, the producers tried to show how Fox News coordinates their "language" with the White House. They showed a collage of different Fox News reporters and anchors saying "Kerry flip-flops," as if they created this Kerry caricature that had never existed before.

However, it was supporters of Howard Dean—not Fox News, the White House, or lying conservatives—who, during the primaries, launched "flip-flops footwear" as Christmas gifts to their supporters in a direct attack against John Kerry. In fact, one of the deceptive clips shown in *Outfoxed* shows Chris Wallace talking about "flip-flop footwear." What the film doesn't say is that the Wallace piece was a report of what the *Deaniac*s were doing, not part of a coordinated effort by Fox News.

But since we're talking about "coordinated campaigns" and "staying on language," how many times did we hear different networks and anchors reference the term *gravitas* when discussing the Bush for president candidacy in 2000?

Fallacy # 2: O'Reilly Saying, "Shut Up"

Taking a page from the Franken book of distortion, they jumped on O'Reilly and his "bullying" tactics. First, they showed a clip of O'Reilly (on *The O'Reilly Factor*) responding to a letter from a viewer accusing him of being "rude" to his guests for always telling them to "shut up." O'Reilly responded by saying that he only told a guest to "shut up" once. Then, they played a series of segments where O'Reilly said "shut up" repeatedly to other guests, proving once again that O'Reilly is a bully and a liar.

Here is the intellectual dishonesty. The one time O'Reilly told a guest to "shut up" he was speaking to punk boy Jeremy Glick, who clearly deserved it (and a flogging to boot). The film then shows that O'Reilly lied because he used the words "shut up" in other places. The problem is, telling someone to shut up because you have nothing more to say to them, as in the Glick interview, is different from suggesting that someone "shut up" as a matter of strategy, which clearly is what O'Reilly was doing in these other clips.

Suggesting to an atheist who got himself into trouble for "outing" himself while in the Boy Scouts that he should have "shut up" and not advertised his views was advice from O'Reilly to protect himself, not a *rude* command. Telling Americans that once the war against terrorism started, we should "shut up" and get behind our troops is completely appropriate (unless you love America like a "grown-up"). O'Reilly was also correct when he advised a gay student—in order to protect himself from other students—that he would have been better off by just "shutting up."

The dishonesty illustrates the slimy influence of people like Al Franken.

Fallacy # 3: More Smears Against O'Reilly

If you go to the *Outfoxed* Web site, you can watch trailers and ads that you won't see in the film. One of them is about how Bill O'Reilly lied on Tim Russert's show when he squared off against Franken puppet Paul Krugman (August 7, 2004). Here is a point-by-point rebuttal with scenes from *Outfoxed*. (*Note:* Neither Paul Krugman nor Tim Russert appear in *Outfoxed*.)

This trailer features O'Reilly, with Krugman to his right, making a statement, then an *Outfoxed* participant rebutting it. But these are not rebuttals, they are complete distortions.

- **Clip 1:** O'Reilly says, "We put more liberals on the air than conservatives." *Outfoxed* then shows a clip from a FAIR study: "*Special Report with Brit Hume*—ratio of Republican to Democrat guests Republicans 5 to 1 over Democrats." This is a lie: O'Reilly was talking about *his* show having more liberals as guests than conservatives; the FAIR study was for a different Fox show, *Special Report with Brit Hume*. Also, it studied a segment that appears on Hume's show every evening featuring guests who are experts on the topic being discussed. It is *not* a debate segment as *Outfoxed* (mis)leads its viewers to believe.
- **Clip 2:** O'Reilly says, "We have a tally every day of what we put on," then the viewer hears a voice-over say that Fox News

has 83 percent to 17 percent Republican over Democrat "partisan guests." Again they mislead the viewer because the FAIR study is for Brit Hume's show, not O'Reilly's.

- **Clip 3:** The next clip shows O'Reilly saying he has more liberal guests than conservatives. Then Clara Frenk, described as a former Fox News producer, appears, saying Fox brought on liberal guests who were very weak. If you regard guests like Al Sharpton, Rev. Barry Lynn, Patricia Ireland, Susan Estrich, Ellis Hennican, and countless other well-heeled attorneys, doctors, police detectives, and civil rights activists who are invited to debate with O'Reilly as weak, then there's just not much to discuss here.
- **Clip 4:** Here Paul Krugman charges, "Fox News takes its marching orders from the Republican Party." Then O'Reilly denies that they take marching orders from anyone. *Outfoxed* comes to his rescue and provides memos of "marching orders" together with former Fox employees backing up that claim. The distortion that makes the segment a lie is that the so-called marching orders and memos do not come from the White House or the Republican Party, as *Outfoxed* implies, but from Fox News vice president John Moody. His job, like that of any news executive, is to determine the stories the network wants covered that day.
- **Clip 5:** This one has O'Reilly accusing *Outfoxed* of putting together a collage of him repeatedly telling his guests to shut up. On screen, O'Reilly referred to advice he gave to a gay student that he should "shut up about sex." Where *Outfoxed* thinks they "got" O'Reilly occurs where he told Russert that the film cut him off at "shut up," when in actuality it shows him saying "shut up about sex."

Nothing in this changes the tone or the substance of what O'Reilly said.

Fallacy # 4: Rupert Murdoch and World Domination

This segment portrays Rupert Murdoch as a media-hungry animal whose objective is to dominate the world and control what news features and stories people will be forced to watch and digest night after night. The movie shows all the entities in media and other outlets owned by Murdoch, and reveals that his empire reaches 280 million homes. However, Fox News is only viewed by 2 to 3 million viewers per evening.

Fallacy # 5: Fox News's "Internal Memos"

The movie shows a series of internal memos from Fox vice president John Moody to the anchors what they should focus on for the day. I cannot imagine that any other news network doesn't function the same way. One of these memos even dared to suggest that the network "refer to [American] snipers in Iraq as sharpshooters" as it is less negative than snipers.

What an exposé! And then the Left wonders why many people on the Right criticize them for attacking and bringing down the morale of our troops! The folks at *Outfoxed* want to make an issue over Fox News preferring to use a term that doesn't conjure up negative images of our troops. How terribly terrible!

Fallacy # 6: Fox News Anchors Say "Some People Say . . ."

Peter Hart, of Fairness and Accuracy in the Media (FAIR), complained about a Fox News tactic in which the anchors use the phrase, "some people say," as a "clever way of inserting political opinion when you know it probably shouldn't be there."

In fact, "some people say" is an expression used regularly by all news networks. When *Outfoxed* began running continuous clips of Fox anchors saying, "Some people say," the majority came from a couple of individuals being shown again and again in rapid sequence—twenty-three times to be exact. Furthermore, these anchors are the lesser known anchors. Brit Hume and Jim Angle (the more recognizable faces) said,"Some people say" once each. There were no clips of any other of the Fox stars saying it.

So much for *Outfoxed* making its case. Again.

Fallacy # 7: Hannity Becomes "Incensed" with His Guest

In another segment, Larry Johnson complained that Hannity became "incensed at my temerity to argue with him . . . over our military's capability to fight two wars—Afghanistan and Iraq—at the same time." But the clip shows no anger or yelling, and no one looked "incensed." It seems Mr. Johnson forgot that people argue and debate on *Hannity & Colmes,* and sometimes they raise their voices. But his description of Hannity's anger just doesn't come through on the clip they selected.

Fallacy # 8: Fox News Piles on Richard Clarke

Jeff Cohen points out Fox News's "attack tactics" in the way they piled on and tried to discredit former security adviser Richard Clarke. Clarke himself clearly made completely contradictory statements regarding the different approaches taken by Clinton, then Bush, in planning and strategizing an effective front against Al Qaeda. The simple fact is, Fox News and spokespersons in the Bush administration were 100 percent correct in their criticism of Clarke. The question ought to be, What was going on at the networks that gave Clarke, who was hocking a Bush-bashing book at the time, a free pass?

A *Newsmax* report dated March 26, 2004, reported that, according to a Fox News transcript, Clarke said, "There was no plan on Al Qaeda that was passed from the Clinton administration to the Bush administration." In the transcript, Clarke goes on to say that in the first eight months of the Bush administration, they adopted a "new strategy that called for the rapid elimination of Al Qaeda." Yet in the *Outfoxed* clip they conveniently showed only Clarke blaming the negligence on the Bush administration and apologizing for his role.

Fallacy # 9: Fox Viewers Are Less Informed Than PBS/NPR Listeners

To prove that Fox News watchers are "Kool-Aid drinking zombies," this segment reported on a study—the PIPA/Knowledge Networks Poll: Misperceptions, the Media and the Iraq War, October 2, 2003—that "proves" Fox News watchers were much more likely to believe erroneous information and news than those who watch and listen to PBS and NPR. Franken frequently cites this study on his radio program, and even referred to it while testifying before a Democratic committee on media bias on May 24, 2005. One of these polls showed that an overwhelming number of Fox watchers believed that Saddam Hussein was linked to Al Qaeda, while only a small percentage of PBS/NPR viewers/listeners believed it.

After the study was released, many on the left, including FAIR and Al Franken, continued to cite the report as proof that Fox News was biased and spread false information. PIPA apparently became annoyed at being used as a source of disinformation and issued the following clarification of its study: "Clarifications on the PIPA study re: Misperceptions, the Media and the Iraq War."

> First, the purpose of the study was to analyze the role of misperceptions in policy attitudes about the Iraq war. **The findings were not meant to and cannot be used as a basis for making broad judgments about the general accuracy of the reporting of various networks or the general accuracy of the beliefs of those who get their news from those networks.** Only a substantially more comprehensive study could undertake such broad research questions. . . .
>
> The fact that we reported that respondents who say they primarily get their news from Fox News had the highest frequency of misperceptions has generated a good deal of attention. **Some have suggested that we have effectively claimed that we have demonstrated that Fox News, prompted by ideological bias, is misleading its viewers. We want to clarify emphatically that we are not making this assertion.** (Emphasis mine.)

I have no doubt that Fox viewers may have been predisposed to believe Middle East terrorists are all linked together (which they are) and have similar evil intentions. The far-Left PBS/NPR viewer/listener is predisposed to the opposite view. The way *Outfoxed* used the poll was meaningless, intellectually dishonest, and purposely misleading.

On another topic in the PIPA study, once again, Fox viewers overwhelmingly believed that Iraq possessed WMDs, while PBS/NPR viewers/listeners did not. Are they smarter than we are? Are they more informed than we are? Or are they ignorant and prefer to be blinded to the threats that emanate from the Arab world?

Fallacy # 10: Fox News Called the Election for President Bush

In this clip *Outfoxed* wants viewers to believe that on election night 2000, Fox News conspired to call Florida for George Bush, thus handing him the keys to the White House. They show Fox News calling for Bush at 2:16 a.m. with the other networks sheepishly falling in line and calling it for Bush as well. But wait! According to the film, the person at Fox who called for Bush wasn't Brit Hume or Sean Hannity, but Bush cousin John Ellis. Conspiracy, anyone?

Here's what *really* happened. At approximately 7:48 p.m. eastern time (6:48 p.m. in Florida's panhandle), the polls were still open in Florida when NBC called Florida for Gore. Either ignoring the fact that the polls were still open or simply being inexcusably ignorant of it, all of the networks fell into line behind NBC.

I don't know if Gore had a cousin working at NBC, but clearly the "unbiased" NBC, ABC, and CBS networks rushed to call Florida for Al Gore prematurely, leading thousands of Floridians living in the heavily Republican panhandle to believe that their votes for President Bush wouldn't count. In many polling places, large numbers of voters who had been standing in line left and went home. Others who had plans to vote before the polls closed stayed home instead.

It wasn't until 2:00 a.m. that Fox News, Bush cousin or not, got the story straight. Only then did the other networks acknowledge their earlier mistake and follow the Fox lead. (*Note:* In *Fahrenheit 9/11,* Michael Moore's depiction of these events was even more deceitful.)

Outfoxed Concludes

The film concludes with a conspiracy theory that even Oliver Stone couldn't concoct. John Nichols, author of *Dick: The Man Who Is President,* says:

> When you have one network that is so powerful and so intent upon warping the dialogue, it limits that discourse. It actually influences it to be a narrower discourse and that's what I think citizens should be up in arms about. We can't accept this anymore. If we do accept it, we're handing onto our children and our grandchildren a less Democracy than we inherited. And that's the one thing we don't have a right to do.

So Fox News (Bill O'Reilly) saying "shut up" and its two million viewers is a greater threat to Democracy than:

- ABC (Mark Halperin), "This is Kerry's race to lose."
- NBC (Tom Brokaw), "The GOP convention is a 'con game.'"
- CBS (Rather-gate)
- PBS (Bill Moyers)
- CNN (Ted Turner), "Christianity is a religion for losers."
- *New York Times* (Daniel Okrent), "Sure, we're liberal."
- *Los Angeles Times* (Give all terror suspect detainees a lawyer, and maybe they'll like us.)
- and their over forty million viewers and readership?

Using David Brock in the film—he not only appears repeatedly throughout, but he was responsible for providing content and information—shows you why liberals can't win or gain any traction with the mainstream. Here is a guy who has admitted writing "hit piece" books for the Right, then coming over to the Left and doing the same thing. If I were doing a serious exposé, like Greenwald purported to be doing, I would demand certain psychological profiles from my contributors. Brock certainly would not make the cut, and my earlier chapter on him certainly makes that case.

38 You Know You Are a Liberal Hypocrite When . . .

For all the resentment the Left claims to have toward conservatives and their claims that "we think we are better than they are," it certainly hasn't stopped them from pontificating to us what values they think we should have.

It's easy for the liberal elite to tell us we should keep our kids in public schools while they send their kids to the most elite and prestigious private schools.

It's easy for John Kerry to talk about the "rich paying their fair share" while he and his wife use tax shelters.

It's easy for Rosie O'Donnell to talk about taking guns off the streets when she has armed body guards.

You Know You Are a Liberal Hypocrite on Taxes and Jobs When . . .

- You are against tax cuts, but you look for every loophole to avoid paying taxes.
- You claim tax cuts are for the rich, but you are rich and don't return the money.
- You say you support middle-class tax cuts, then raise taxes on the middle class.
- You say you support tax cuts, but not when the economy is weak, but then vote against tax cuts when the economy is strong.
- You say tax increases strengthen the economy, but won't raise them even higher.

- You say the tax increases are only temporary, but then don't cut them when the economy stabilizes.
- You say that rich people don't spend their tax cut refunds, yet it is they who travel, add extensions to their homes, and buy new cars.
- You say rich people shouldn't get tax breaks, but they should get free prescription drugs.
- You say eliminating the death tax keeps the "big" money in the hands of the few, but you are one of the few.
- You complain that President Bush has lost jobs, but you protest when a "job-creating" Wal-Mart wants to move into your neighborhood.

You Know You Are a Liberal Hypocrite on Health Care When . . .

- You complain about the millions of uninsured, but do nothing about it when you are in power.
- You complain about the millions of uninsured, yet make it more difficult for people to become insured.
- You complain about the millions of uninsured, but support legislation making insurance less accessible.
- You support legislation limiting patient choice, while guaranteeing you have the most choices.
- You demonize "big" insurance as a special interest that only cares about profit, while allowing the number one special interest group, trial lawyers, to write malpractice legislation.
- You say you want to improve health care, but support legislation driving more and more doctors out of medicine.
- You denounce the pharmaceutical industry for putting profits over people, but make it difficult, if not impossible for them to invest in new research.
- You denounce U.S. companies for outsourcing, yet you want seniors to buy their medicine from Canada.
- You say that Europe and Canada have a better health-care system than the United States, but you never go or take your loved ones abroad for treatment.
- You insist on inexpensive insurance for the poor and working families—HMOs—yet you demand they give tier-one coverage.

You Know You Are a Liberal Hypocrite on Education When . . .

- You say public schools are #1, but you send your kids to private school.
- You say the children are our future, yet you condemn them to violent and drug-infested schools.
- You demand more money for the schools, and when the money is given and the results don't change, you say it wasn't enough.
- You say you support educational standards, but you are against firing teachers who can't write or speak basic English.
- You say you support educational standards, yet you don't demand students perform above failing levels.
- You say education is the way to success, yet you teach courses that have nothing to do with reading, writing, and arithmetic.
- You say money for education is scarce, but you waste the money you do have.
- You say teachers don't have fair contracts, yet many of them have paid sabbaticals.
- You ask for more money for education, but you promote students who can't read or write at their grade level.
- You say college campuses are places to learn and expand one's mind, then you deny conservative voices equal opportunity.

You Know You Are a Liberal Hypocrite on Abortion and Women's Rights When . . .

- You say you support women's rights, but you don't want to educate women on the effects of abortion.
- You accuse supporters of unborn children of "rolling back the clock on women's rights," but you defend Bill Clinton's treatment of women as "pieces of meat."
- You say "I am open-minded" but believe right-to-lifers are morons.
- You say you support abortion choice, but you oppose gun owners' choice, education choice, choice of doctors, choice on books to bring to school, choice to pray silently in school.
- You say you want to protect women, but you oppose any laws that give extra punishment to those who attack pregnant women.
- You say, "It's a woman's body," but you oppose adoption education.

- You say, "It's a woman's body," but you criticize the porn industry for exploiting women.
- You say you are marching "for women's lives," yet you support the killing of millions of unborn healthy baby girls.
- You say abortion is a medical decision, but you are silent when doctors botch abortions.
- You say, "Abortion is about a woman's right . . . with her body," but you support allowing a baby who was not killed during a botched abortion to starve to death.
- You say an abortion is "no different from removing a gallbladder," then you say that "abortion is between a woman, her doctor, and her G-d."
- You say there is nothing wrong with abortion, then you say it should be rare.

You Know You Are a Liberal Hypocrite on the Military When . . .

- You say, "I support our troops," then you compare them to Nazis.
- You say, "I support the military," but you condemn the military because a few were guilty of misconduct.
- You say, "I support the military," but you don't want them to fight overseas.
- You say, "I support the military," but then you say only poor people sign up.
- You say, "I want women, and gays, to have the right to join our military," then you say the only reason people sign up is for the benefits.
- You say "I support the military," but you bombard the media with demoralizing statements about the war's effort for cheap political gain.
- You accuse the U.S. military of abusive behavior, but you make excuses justifying or making a moral equivalence with terrorism.
- You say war is wrong when a Republican is president, but you approve of it when a Democrat is president.
- You say you support our troops, yet you accuse America of being imperialist.
- You blame President Bush for not doing enough to protect

America from terrorism, then you attack the president for not treating arrested terrorists "nicely."

You Know You Are a Liberal Hypocrite on Gun Ownership When . . .

- You say you support the Constitution, but you deny the rights guaranteed by the Second Amendment.
- You say you don't want to deny anybody the right to own a gun, but you support legislation restricting gun ownership.
- You say you support "privacy laws," but you support legislation requiring gun owners to report all guns they own.
- You say you support privacy between a doctor and the patient, but you want doctors to ask kids if their parents have guns in the home.
- You say people shouldn't have guns, but you have bodyguards who carry guns.

You Know You Are a Liberal Hypocrite on Race When . . .

- You say you want to help minorities, then you support programs that keep them down.
- You say you want to help minorities, then you deny them the chance to rise through the political ranks.
- You say you want to help minorities, but you condemn them to a life of misery in the country's worst schools.
- You say you want to help minorities, then you instill fear and old prejudices into their psyches.
- You say you want to help minorities, then you surround yourself with high-powered white people.
- You say you want to help minorities, then you diminish or mock the accomplishments of those minorities with whom you don't share an ideological bond.
- You say you want to help minorities, but you compare other groups' grievances to the black fight for civil rights.
- You say America is a racist country, but you support and encourage illegal mass black immigration to the United States.
- You say how much you care about black people, but you were silent when one million blacks were slaughtered in Africa.
- You attack Republicans for racially insensitive or misunderstood comments, but you are completely silent when Democrats make racist comments.

- You condemn racially insensitive comments against blacks, but you invoke the First Amendment when insensitive and scurrilous remarks are made against people of faith.

You Know You Are a Liberal Hypocrite on Patriotism When . . .

- You say "I want my country back," but you want to turn it over to the UN.

You Know You Are a Liberal Hypocrite on Truth When . . .

- You say that talk radio is dominated by conservatives, but you insist the print and news media are fair and unbiased.
- You say that Bill O'Reilly, Ann Coulter, and Sean Hannity are lying liars, but Al Franken, Janeane Garofalo, and Michael Moore tell the truth.

You Know You Are a Liberal Hypocrite on Energy When . . .

- You demand and call for energy conservation, but drive around in limousines and fly in private jets.

You Know You Are a Liberal Hypocrite on the United Nations and Our Allies When . . .

- You say Republican leaders should resign for mistakes in Iraq, but you make excuses or turn the other cheek when hundreds of thousands are slaughtered, and countless women are raped under Kofi Annan's watch.
- You accuse Republicans of going to war and spilling U.S. blood for oil, but you praise France, China, Germany, and Russia, who refuse to fight terror and tyranny and have large oil contracts with Iraq.
- You say the French have a right to hate America, but Americans don't have a right to hate the French.
- You say that we have betrayed our allies, but you deny it is they who have betrayed us.

You Know You Are a Liberal Hypocrite on Judges When . . .

- You say that judges who are rated highly qualified by the ABA and believe in rights for the unborn are "out of touch" with the mainstream, but judges who believe G-d and religious symbols should be removed from public forums are well qualified.

You Know You Are a Liberal Hypocrite on Political Organizations When . . .

- You support "People for the American Way," even though they are against the American way.

You Know You Are Liberal Hypocrite Al Franken When . . .

- You say you are "nice," but you make fun of and mock someone addicted to painkillers (and you have dabbled in white powder yourself in the past).
- You say you tell the truth, but you are caught in countless lies.
- You accuse others of misleading their audiences, but you do the exact same thing to your audience.
- You accuse others of insulting the intelligence of their readers, but you mislead your own readers by writing stories that completely misrepresent the truth.
- You say your show will represent a liberal perspective, but you spend your entire show with conservative-hating guests.
- You say you are honest and truthful, but you rarely interview guests with an opposing opinion.
- You say you do accurate and truthful research, but you leave out the information that contradicts your position.
- You say you hold yourself to an impossibly high standard when it comes to telling the truth, but you defend the integrity of Michael Moore's movies.
- You say you want us to win in Iraq, but you frequently interview authors who deride our war efforts.
- You ostensibly sob over the safety of our troops, but you produce parodies that mock them
- You berate Brit Hume over innocent comments made about the safety of our troops in Iraq, but you ignore the vicious comments made about our troops and military by Democrats.

39 The Al Franken "Flop-Out"

It's always amusing to see how seriously celebrities take themselves or overestimate their own importance or credibility. Hearing Al Franken say, "I'm often compared to Rush Limbaugh" is just such an example. What on earth are the similarities?

- Rush has more than six hundred stations. Franken has roughly fifty-three stations (as of June 2005).
- Rush has twenty million listeners. Franken—well, who knows? He claims his ratings are great, but radioequalizer.blogspot.com, which documents and cites Arbitron ratings, reports that Air America has less-than-stellar ratings.
- It doesn't matter which political party is in power—Rush is successful. Franken would be nowhere without Limbaugh, O'Reilly, Coulter, and other successful conservatives to trash.
- After just three months on the air and with talk radio still in its infancy, Rush Limbaugh had one hundred affiliates. After nearly six months on the air, Franken tells his audience that they are growing by leaps and bounds (more like anthills and speed bumps), adding new affiliates all the time—for a grand total of thirty-six.

Franken's "anti-Bush flop-out" has to have been one Franken's most embarrassing moments. In a takeoff from the movie *Network* and the Great American Shout Out, Franken dedicated the entire week of his radio show prior to the Republican convention in New York City in 2004 to promoting the "anti-Bush shout-out."

The plan was for listeners of the program to rally Bush-haters across the country to open their windows at the time President Bush was making his way to the podium at the Republican convention and yell out "Fuggetaboutit" or some similar form of "not in my backyard," depending on the dialect of each region of the country.

Franken spent one week promoting this idea on his show. In addition, he did several cable news interviews where he told the hosts and their audiences that anything under one hundred million people participating would be considered a failure. I found more than 780 stories on the Internet about this Franken project and his promotion of the historic event.

I didn't hear Franken gloating about the anti-Bush flop-out after the convention, so I decided to do my own research online. There were two news articles about it following the convention. The *New York Times* and *Los Angeles Times* didn't mention it. Neither did the *Washington Post* or the *Boston Globe*. The *Cape Cod Times* and the always hard-hitting *Jersey Journal* were right on top of it, though.

The *Cape Cod Times* reported the story on September 3, 2004, "'P' Town Shouts Against Bush."

> It wasn't loud enough to be heard in New York . . . but it was loud enough to be heard in, say, neighboring North Truro. . . . At least 100 people packed the red-brick concourse in front of Provincetown's historic town last night. . . .
>
> As a member of Outer Cape Peace and Justice Circle, [Kristine Hopkins of Provincetown] and other members of the peace organization have demonstrated against war and militarism every Saturday morning in front of town hall for more than two years.

So now it appears that even the few who came out for Franken's anti-Bush protest were regular protesters anyway. Anybody ever hear of the Outer Cape Peace and Justice Circle?

The *Jersey Journal* article wrote, in part, "At a small party in a

Jersey City apartment near Exchange Place, however, a half dozen people . . ." The participants in this historic event also included "a rat terrier and two orange tabby cats."

I tuned in to Franken's show the next day, as I always do, hoping to hear Franken himself talk about the *great success* of the anti-Bush shout-out.

Nothing. Not a word. Maybe he just forgot about it.

In contrast, when Rush Limbaugh sets out to mobilize his fans and supporters, they come out in droves. On May 23, 1993, CBS news reported, "The spectacle was enough to drive a stake through the heart of liberalism." This was in regard to Dan's Bake Sale, which drew what was reported to have been some sixty-five thousand people. They all flocked to Fort Collins, Colorado, for what was billed variously as "Rushstock '93" or a "right-wing love-in."

Another example of Franken's ability to "get his listeners out" occurred on Sunday, September 26, 2004. On the prior Friday, September 24, Al Franken had *American Candidate* hopeful Lisa Witter as a guest on his radio program. *American Candidate* was a political reality show on the Showtime cable network. The event became a national competition. By September 24 there were only three candidates left, with each candidate mobilizing their friends and organizations to call a toll-free number within a certain time frame after the Sunday show ended. The person with the lowest number of votes was eliminated.

So on Friday the twenty-fourth, Franken interviewed Witter, a consultant for MoveOn.org. He asked his listeners to call her toll-free number on Sunday so she could win. Sunday came and went, and Witter came in third place and was eliminated from the show. That's two for two, Al.

The winner and eventual *American Candidate* was Park Gillespie, an evangelical Christian and North Carolina Teacher of the Year. Park Gillespie is now running for Congress in South Carolina, challenging John Spratt in 2006.

A Not-So-Happy Birthday for Al

Everything I have written about Al thus far has been an honest and thoroughly researched exposé on Franken, who has spent the better part of the last few years challenging anybody to refute his charges against the Right. I think I've met and even exceeded the challenge. Although what I'm about to write is 100 percent truthful, it is still mean and out of character for me.

Every year Rush holds a leukemia cure-a-thon on his radio program, raising over a million dollars to help find a cure for this deadly cancer. Contributions come from his listeners, primarily conservatives. Or, as Franken likes to call them, coldhearted, zombielike morons.

So on May 20, 2005, Franken had a chance to show what compassionate progressives are made of and just how generous *they* can be. Certainly they must be a lot more generous than selfish, greedy conservatives are.

At the beginning of the program, he told his listeners that his birthday was the next day (May 21) and that in lieu of any gifts, he would like his supporters to make a contribution to the Wellstone Memorial, which is being built in Minnesota near the site of the crash that took the lives of Paul, his wife, Sheila, their daughter, the campaign staff, and the pilots. It would be a worthwhile, tax-deductible (no less) charity, indeed.

Before I tell you how much money was actually pledged, let's take a few moments to reflect on Franken's ratings, his popularity, the generosity of progressives, and how much one might expect a powerhouse like Franken to be able to raise.

- Franken is on fifty-three affiliates and growing by leaps and bounds (according to him).
- Franken beats Rush Limbaugh in the Portland, Oregon, market.
- Franken is beloved by Democrats, liberals, leftists, and progressives nationwide.
- Progressives are far more generous and compassionate than conservatives.
- Paul Wellstone was a hero to the common workingman—a progressive's progressive, if you will.

So how much did Franken raise? Drumroll, please. . . .

As the Friday, May 20, show came to a close, Franken's co-host, the adorable Katherine Lanpher, announced that 181 people (including Katherine herself) contributed a grand total of $8,200.

Well Al, there's always next year.

Oh, and just one more thought. You're going to need to raise a lot more than that to run for a Senate seat.

These embarrassing numbers do serve another purpose besides revealing how cheap leftists are. They also illustrate the reality behind Franken's ratings.

Anybody—just ask Air America management—can twist and spin numbers and data when discussing a network's ratings. You say Franken has poor ratings; he says he beats Rush Limbaugh in Portland, Oregon. You say he has few listeners; he says his show has more Internet hits than any other show. So whom do you believe? Who is to say that my data is more credible than his?

Well, Al (and Air America management and multimillion-dollar investors), if your number one star and featured talk-show host can only draw 181 donors for a worthy cause over a three-hour radio broadcast, I'll put my data up against yours any day of the week.

40 Franken: Wrong on America, Wrong on Israel

As reports came in that Yasser Arafat was knocking on death's door, Franken made the following statement on his radio program: "I am really angry at [Yasser] Arafat. He gave us [Ariel] Sharon."

I couldn't believe Franken could say something as stupid and outrageous as that. What do you mean, he gave *us* Sharon? Us? Who's "us"? Last time I checked, *our* leader was President Bush.

After years of homicide bombings and an unprecedented number of terror attacks against Israeli civilians, the Israeli people, who live in a democratic society, elected Ariel Sharon. They voted for someone *they* believed would be stronger on terror, not a terror appeaser like Ehud Barak, Jimmy Carter, or Bill and Hillary Clinton.

Furthermore, is that a sane reason for being angry at Yasser Arafat? What about the fact that he is the father of modern-day terrorism? Being angry at Arafat for Sharon is a lot like saying, "I'm really angry at Bin Laden. Because of him, we got Bush." But how can anyone explain Franken's way of thinking?

How should the families of Arafat's victims feel when they hear Franken, the new *front man* for the Democratic Party, suggest that Arafat's biggest crime was "giving us Sharon"?

Here are just a few examples of terror attacks against Israel that

Franken overlooks: the slaughter of eleven Israeli athletes during the 1972 Munich Olympics, the murder in 1973 of two American diplomats in the Sudan, the murder in 1974 of two dozen Israeli schoolchildren in Maalot, and the turning loose of young Palestinians as suicide bombers targeting civilians in Israel. To top it all off, over the years he has killed even more Palestinians than Israelis.

On November 9, 2004, Franken interviewed Senator George Mitchell, who had chaired a commission during the Clinton administration on how to bring a *just settlement* to the Israeli-Palestinian conflict. Franken asked Mitchell if "the Palestinians will be able to get their act together . . . in terms of stopping the terrorism they're perpetrating on Israelis, and will the Israelis be able to get their act together and really withdraw from Gaza and really get, uh, stop doing what they're doing to brutalizing people in the West Bank and stuff."

I like the "and stuff" part of the question.

Franken typifies the problem the Left has. He makes a moral equivalence between terrorists, who are enemies of society, and democracies like the United States and Israel, who fight back against terrorism. He makes a moral equivalence between Palestinian terrorism against innocent Israelis and the response to those attacks from Israel's Defense Forces (IDF).

Perhaps it is Franken's moral equivalency between good and evil that has led to his affinity toward UN Secretary General Kofi Annan. After the oil-for-food scandal broke, members of Congress, led by Senator Norm Coleman (R-MN), called for Annan's resignation. As in the past, Franken's interest in most issues was merely about how he could spin the story to attack Republicans. So, of course, he took Annan's side.

This isn't the first time Franken saw an opening to defend Annan. A week or so earlier, Rush Limbaugh had quoted Annan as singling out Israel for criticism in its "brutality" against Palestinians, when later in the speech he criticized Palestinian terror attacks against Israel as well.

Franken saw this misquote as yet another opportunity to berate resident dittohead Mark Luther for being "such a big fan of someone who doesn't tell the truth." Luther's response was, "Well, don't you agree that the UN is anti-Israel?"

"That's not the point!" responded an angry and impatient Franken.

But that was the point, and it remains the point. Going back to the early 1970s, following the UN resolution equating Zionism with racism, more than four hundred resolutions have been introduced in the UN against Israel while zero have been introduced condemning the terror attacks against Israel. This resolution lasted over twenty years before it was finally repealed, thanks in large part to the tireless efforts of John Bolton, whom Franken and the Democrats have demonized.

At a December 2004 luncheon and book signing for former Israeli ambassador to the UN Dore Gold, who was promoting his new book *Tower of Babble,* Gold recalled David Bar Ilan's comment, "In the UN Israel gets cited for jaywalking." This makes Franken's comments all the more distressing when he says, "I am pro-Israel."

Being "pro-Israel" doesn't mean you have to agree with Ariel Sharon, Israel's democratically elected prime minister. However, comparing his policies for protecting Israeli civilians and sovereignty with Palestinian terrorism is absolutely shameless.

Maybe he just loves Israel "in a grown-up way."

Everybody Is an "Expert" on Israel

There have been countless books, papers, and news columns explaining the reason for the instability in the Middle East.

"If only the Palestinians had a homeland of their own." "If America were more evenhanded, they wouldn't hate us." "If the Israelis were willing to be more flexible, we could have a peace treaty." "They hate us because of our support for Israel."

Don't believe a word of it!

The Arab world hates Israel because it is a Jewish state that exists in their midst. They did not seek a Palestinian homeland prior to the birth of Israel, and the only reason they claim to support one now is to use the idea as a propaganda tool against Israel.

Saddam Hussein paid the families of homicide bombers against Israel $25,000 per attack, but not a nickel for schools, hospitals, or housing.

When the homicide bombers began, the Palestinian leadership first said, "These are desperate acts. The Israelis are making us desperate." Soon they were recruiting potential bombers by telling them that seventy-two virgins awaited them if they blew themselves up. Suha Arafat, Arafat's widow, said that she wished she had sons, "so they could be homicide bombers."

See how their stories change? First these are desperate acts. Then they are the gateway to paradise and orgies.

They want to kill Jews, period! End of story!

It is precisely because America is great and a moral leader of the world, in spite of Moore's and Franken's objections, that we support Israel. America would not be America if we didn't.

When the so-called Oslo peace Accords were signed, the Palestinians promised to remove all language from their charter that called for the elimination of the state of Israel. They never did. As Israel made more concessions to the Palestinians at the heavy-handed urging of Bill Clinton, the attacks on Israeli civilians increased.

When Israelis became weary of Arafat's intentions and voted for Likud Prime Minister Benjamin Netanyahu, it did not sit well with Bill Clinton. How dare the Israeli people elect someone who would stand up to terror at a time when Bill Clinton could just taste the Nobel Peace Prize.

When the time came for Netanyahu to seek another term, Clinton made sure it wouldn't happen by dispatching James Carville to manage the campaign of the more flexible Ehud Barak of the Labor Party (equivalent to the left-of-center wing of the Democratic Party in the United States). In Clinton's mind, a Barak victory would guarantee a peace deal, no matter how flawed, and give him what he wanted: the Nobel Peace Prize.

So Barak was elected, deals were made, and more Israelis were killed.

In the end, Yasser Arafat rejected what was seen by many as the most generous offer they would ever see: a homeland of their own, with a piece of Jerusalem as their capital. And who advised Arafat to reject this once-in-a-lifetime peace deal? It was our "good friend" Prime Minister Jacques Chirac of France. He advised Arafat to hold out for more. I realize this must be a shock to those who thought that Chirac was our "friend and ally," whose goodwill President Bush had "squandered."

If the Arab world were truly interested in peace and stability, they could have it. But these leaders are despots, and they need the war, or at least the appearance of war, with the Jews to distract their citizens from their own corrupt governments.

President Bush recognizes the evil in the hearts of these Arab leaders, but Democrats like Clinton, Carter, Dean, Franken, and Moore only seem to sympathize with Israel when they are weak or vulnerable. When Israel is strong, they take it upon themselves to exert pressure to make them weaker.

The state of Israel is always in a heightened state of alert, and no Jimmy Carters, Bill Clintons, or Stuart Smalleys can say or do anything that will change that.

41 The Day After

Possibly the most painful day in liberal history was November 3, 2004. On that day an "illiterate, uneducated, draft-dodging, Bible-thumping, goodwill-squandering, unilateralist (and of course) lying Texas cowboy" defeated the suave, debonair, Vietnam veteran hero in the race for president of the United States of America.

The "experts," of course, wanted to know what went wrong.

After George Bush's Republicans had picked up seats in both the House of Representatives and the Senate in 2002, Democrats were left scratching their heads. Historically, midterm elections usually have resulted in a loss of seats for the sitting president's party.

The experts truly believed that talk radio and the conservative media had done them in. As then–Democratic leader Senator Tom Daschle said, "We had the right message, we just didn't get it out there." This reasoning contributed to the urgency for Democrats to launch their own radio network in 2004, which soon gave birth to Air America.

The op-ed section of the *New York Times* on November 5, 2004, contained four stories that tried to explain the results of the election and "where to go from here" for the Democratic Party. All four articles, incidentally, were written by liberals. Not even the article titled "Why They Won" was written by a conservative. Wouldn't common sense and fairness dictate that a Republican write "Why We Won"?

Let me save all of you experts, intellectuals, and pundits some time as to why you lost.

You lost because you can't run an intelligent, methodical plan when you're consumed with hatred and anger. It doesn't work. Ask any CEO or successful entrepreneur if they ever made a smart decision when they were angry.

Four years of bitterness and self-delusion trying to convince yourselves that George Bush was selected, not elected. Four years of blaming racist suppression of minority voters when there was just no evidence to corroborate those accusations.

Did you really think that Al Franken yelling and screaming every day that George Bush, Rush Limbaugh, and the rest of the conservative talking heads and pundits are evil lying liars was going to turn the blue states into red states?

Did you think that four years of screaming "Halliburton!" was going to convince people that the Bush administration is corrupt?

Did you really believe that Michael Moore, making the sleaziest piece of propaganda since Germany's Goebbels and Leni Riefenstahl to derail the Bush reelection would be taken seriously by patriotic Americans?

Even the tens of millions of dollars flushed down the toilet by mega-multibillionaire, self-hating Jew George Soros to defeat George Bush was an embarrassment.

And really, people, Al Sharpton and Howard "screamin' demon" Dean?

Liberals Attack the "Morals" and "Values" Voters

Being a political activist, I've learned that every person has a hot button. Look at how the slightest thing can set someone like Franken off.

On November 5, 2004, Franken lamented the so-called values Republicans claim to have: "I was talking about values. . . . I want to talk about values. . . . I am just sick of hearing . . . since the election you've been hearing a lot of gloating about values. . . ."

Just what is it about family values that has liberals so uptight?

What Else Went Wrong?

Democrats can't complain that they didn't get their message out. They had Al Franken. Okay, that was a low blow.

Democrats can't complain that Americans were misled by the Bush administration because Michael Moore put out a *dreck*-umentary exposing the Bush family's role in 9/11.

Democrats can't complain that they didn't have enough money in their coffers. George Soros and other rich Democrats poured in hundreds of millions of dollars to defeat President Bush.

Democrats can't complain they weren't organized, because they had a number of well-financed 527's like MoveOn.org and the Media Fund. The Media Fund alone spent more than $50 million on media buys.

Democrats can't complain that the candidates' wives didn't help, because Teresa's outbursts were called "refreshing."

Democrats can't complain that they didn't have a good candidate. They had a Vietnam veteran hero.

Democrats can't complain about minority turnout. Jesse Jackson and Al Sharpton got out the vote.

Anything else?

In Conclusion

As a political activist, I have attended many political speeches. During the question-and-answer period, there is always one person who asks, "What can we do to make a difference?" Writing this book is what *I* did to make a difference. The burden of defending our values and principles shouldn't rest on the shoulders of just a few.

When I first began communicating with Al Franken after his appearance on the *Donahue* show in which he blamed Rush and conservatives for the Wellstone debacle, I never dreamed it would lead to a full-blown exposé on one of the most dishonest pundits on the political scene.

Make no mistake. Al Franken is not his lovable *Saturday Night Live* character Stuart Smalley. He is vicious. He is mean. And yes, he is a wicked man. There are many religious teachings about people like Franken, whose sole purpose in life seems to be to engage in character assassination.

The media certainly have been caught napping on Al Franken. He laments that they are lazy and aren't thorough in their research. Had they done their jobs, Franken would not be where he is today: spewing vicious propaganda as a talk-show host. Because mainstream media have been so eager for a high-profile liberal to counter the O'Reillys, Coulters, Hannitys, and Limbaughs of the world, they allowed him to get away with it. Because of the media's laziness, a dishonest and manipulative Franken was elevated to the status of "truth-teller" when he is anything but.

Al Franken was right when he said that calling someone a liar is a serious charge. That is why people like O'Reilly take such offense at him. They have little patience when their accuser is a liar and a hypocrite himself and engages in smear tactics. Rush Limbaugh's promise to his fans was that he would not retire from radio until everyone agrees with him. Franken seems to have a different philosophy: Anyone who disagrees with him is a liar.

There was a time in the public arena that Americans could debate one another without fear of being stigmatized. We could agree to disagree and still be friends, but civil discourse is no longer a part of our culture. If you support tax cuts, you are a racist. If you believe in protecting unborn children, then you hate women. If you are a Republican, and a conservative no less, then you are mean-spirited and heartless.

Unfortunately, the Michael Moores and Al Frankens of the world have sullied the arena of public debate. Calling people liars and smearing their reputations with baseless, petty arguments does nothing to advance our country's interests (or the interests of good Democrats). It only works to further the careers of Franken and Moore. The price of their success, though, has been dividing us to the point where people feel alienated from one another. Being branded a liar can be as hurtful and damaging as being branded a racist. It still hurts to be called a racist, but because it has been so overused by the Left to attack those who disagree with them, particularly by the Jesse Jacksons and Al Sharptons of the world, it has lost some of its sting. It still stings, though, to be called a liar, particularly when you're not.

Because of this book, conservative readers are a little better equipped to engage their liberal friends. They no longer have to silently seethe while Franken gloats and smears the very people they support and admire. This book will challenge the media to allow the truth about Franken to be revealed.

If you are a liberal of the Alan Colmes variety, meaning an honorable and decent person who is a little confused on the issues (in my opinion), you and I are not enemies. We are just fellow Americans with different philosophical and ideological outlooks. Al Franken is not a liberal, though. He is a vicious smear merchant whose agenda is to silence conservatives who are in positions of influence.

Franken claims to be both a DLC Democrat and a liberal. I have e-mailed him that the two are opposites and inconsistent with each other. The DLC was created to distinguish itself from the liberal, or left wing, of the Democratic Party. Howard Dean himself has referred to the DLC as "Republican lite."

Franken e-mailed me back that he can be both, since Clinton and Gephardt are DLC Democrats, and that he has been invited to speak before their affairs. Does this make any sense? He says he has spoken before Republican audiences. Does that mean he is a liberal, a DLC Democrat, and a Republican?

Senators Joe Lieberman (CT) and Evan Bayh (IN) are moderate DLC Democrats. They wouldn't be caught dead with Michael Moore, Al Franken, or George Soros.

I have brought Moore's name into this book for several reasons. Bill O'Reilly has said that Franken, whom he refers to as Stuart Smalley, "is more dangerous than Moore," and Sean Hannity has referred to Moore and Franken as "the two biggest losers in the Democratic Party."

My take is that both of them are propagandists. They are deceitful. Moore is clearly anti-America. He believes that America is no better than any other country, that we are worse or more primitive than other Western nations. He is reported to have told an audience in London that "the dumbest Brit here is smarter than the smartest American."

Moore is a master at generating publicity for his works, though he does not seek the limelight for himself personally. He doesn't grant many television interviews—why would he? Then he would have to defend himself against questions about the truthfulness of his productions.

Franken is different. He is not anti-America per se, but he is, in my opinion, the kind of guy who won't lose much sleep if America takes a hit if it means bringing down a Republican administration. It would be seen as collateral damage, taking a loss for a greater gain. No matter what he says or where he says it, his objective is always the same: to pin the blame on a Republican. Even though the Kyoto treaty was rejected by the entire U.S. Senate under Bill Clinton, to him it was President Bush who "officially" walked away from it. Even though the United Nations oil-for-food scandal began in 1996 under Bill Clinton, the Congress was controlled by Republicans. It's that simple.

However, Franken has embraced Moore, and therefore he forfeits the right or authority to question other people's truths. Because he embraced Moore's *dreck*-umentary that portrayed our troops in a dishonest and negative light, he has forfeited the authority to say he "loves and honors our troops."

Because he embraces Bill Clinton's and Jimmy Carter's vision of the Middle East, he forfeits the authority to say he is a strong supporter of Israel. Because he did his radio show on Rosh Hashana, the holiest day of the year for Jews, declaring, "G-d would forgive me because I'm doing it for a good cause," he forfeits the authority to criticize devout Christians and Jews who do what they do in the name of G-d or religious observance.

Can Air America Succeed in the Marketplace?

Unlike leftists who try to silence conservatives, conservatives won't try to shut down Franken and Air America, nor should we. If it fails, it will be because they couldn't sustain an interested audience.

When I first began listening to Air America in July 2004, they had about twenty-five affiliates. As of this writing in September 2005, they have roughly seventy affiliates. As a business, almost tripling your production in less than two years isn't bad. But in the radio industry, it's nothing to gloat about.

When Rush Limbaugh began in the late 1980s, he was on one hundred stations after just three months of being on the air. And this was at a time when talk radio wasn't yet a proven commodity, let alone conservative talk radio. Franken, on the other hand, has been able to ride on the success of others before him, which certainly fits his trademark. Talk radio has already proven itself to be a multi-billion-dollar-a-year industry; but Franken's growth has been modest at best, even though he is viewed as the "go-to-guy" (for the Democratic Party) in liberal progressive talk radio.

Truthfully, there is no reason for him to be a complete failure in this market. After all, this is a country that has made frauds like Michael Moore successful, so why not one more? This is a country that bought more than one million copies of his last book, which did little more than "expose" Bill O'Reilly for misstating a Polk Award for a Peabody, Ann Coulter for not revealing her real age, Fox News for putting out a better product than CNN, and Sean Hannity for being an "Irish Ape man."

Franken's success as a radio personality does not, and will not, be a reflection of his on-air talent, which to date has been non-existent. Instead, it is a reflection on the ignorance of his audience, who view President Bush as a greater enemy than Saddam Hussein.

What Will They Say Now?

I hate it when I go to a terrible movie because of a great review. There should be an Oscar for critics who mislead people into seeing terrible movies. Is there a Peabody Award for writing deceiving movie reviews?

Franken's last book, *Lies and the Lying Liars Who Tell Them,* received rave reviews for its "truthfulness and honesty." The critics salivated and guffawed over his diligent research into the lying, "evil" conservatives. Now the truth is available for all to see. What will the critics say about Franken now? Here is what they said when his book was published:

- "Mr. Franken makes a bull's-eye out of Mr. O'Reilly . . . a bitterly funny assault." —*New York Times*
- "Franken uncovers countless lies, and he does it with brio." —*Washington Post*
- "Underneath the humor, though, there is a genuine anger at the Right, and a lot of fact-checking." —*Atlanta Journal-Constitution*
- "Franken does what many in my profession haven't done—present the truth and expose the lying liars." —*St. Paul Pioneer Press*
- "What sets *Liars* apart is how tightly researched it is, thanks to fourteen Harvard graduate students the author affectionately calls 'Team Franken.' . . . He provides facts, often drawn from official sources, that don't get in the way of the laughs." —*Los Angeles Times*
- "Franken is simply the most effective spokesman for the Democratic Party in America today." —*Sunday Oregonian*
- "Hilarious . . . *Lies and Lying Liars Who Tell Them: A Fair and Balanced Look at the Right* rings with the moral clarity of an

angel's trumpet . . . it presents well-substantiated arguments and damning examples of false accusations that conservatives have effectively used against Democrats. Also, and perhaps more importantly for conservative readers, it does so in an incredibly amusing way. . . . Franken repeatedly uses sharp analysis and humor to drive his point home." —Associated Press

- "Franken's by now infamous book is laugh-out-loud funny . . . and (refreshingly!) does not contain a single lie." —*Chico News & Review*
- "A compelling, fact-laden slam of the positions and posturing of conservatives. . . . Exhilarating." —*BusinessWeek Online*
- "Cast your mind forward to the morning of 3 November 2004. Imagine, just for a moment, that George W. Bush has gone down to ignominious defeat in the U.S. presidential election. . . . All across the nation, people are asking where it all went wrong for the chief executive who had seemed so immune from criticism for so long. And the answer, they all agree, is the moment that mighty Fox News Channel . . . was reduced to utter humiliation by a single pesky New York Comedian. [Franken] has indeed struck a blow against an information (and disinformation) machine that has played a crucial role in spreading and enforcing the White House's with-us-or-against-us mentality . . . a typically unabashed blend of razor-witted denunciation and old-fashioned gumshoe detective work directed at right-wing crazies both in and out of government." —*The Independent* (London)

Oh, blimey!

I should mention that these blurbs are from Franken's own Web site. I am not responsible if any of them are phony or false. Since they were posted on *his* site, I have to make the disclaimer.

I have never wished, and do not wish, Franken any harm, but he obviously has a lot of pent-up anger and bitterness. Smearing successful conservatives seems to be his outlet. Too bad, Al. Smearing other people is not an acceptable or responsible vehicle for a grown man to release his anger—at least in a civil society it is not.

You wrote in your book, Al, that liberals like yourself "love America in a grown-up way."

It's time to start acting like a grown-up, Al.

Acknowledgments

When I was younger, I was amazed at how new rock groups seemed to come out of nowhere and rise to the top of the charts on their first try. It wasn't until watching VH-1's *Behind the Music* many years later that I learned the hell these people went through for years before they got their first big break.

I didn't wake up one morning and decide to write a hopefully best seller on a most detestable human being. However, I did go through hell: listening to Franken's radio show every day. All kidding aside, I learned many important life lessons from a lot of people before even considering that I could write a book.

So I'd like to begin by thanking a whole lot of people who helped me grow and learn about what's really important and helped make me a better person.

First, I have to thank G-d for giving me the strength needed to overcome the hurdles we all go through in life.

I thank my father, who died in February 1987, for everything he taught me about having faith in G-d and being honest, and for telling me to "clean the streets before you accept charity." I'm not quite sure what drove him to teach me *that*, but it was something I never forgot.

I thank my mother, who always wanted what was best for me.

I thank my childhood friends, Akiva Goldman, Brian "Poko" Herschfus, Maurice Herschfus (of blessed memory), and Dr. Leon (also of blessed memory) and Mrs. Herschfus for everything you did for me before and after my father died. I also have to acknowledge Ezra Goldman for helping me with "crisis control" in building the business my father left behind. I also have to acknowledge the kindness and going beyond the call of duty to Gary Torgow, who helped my father at every turn.

I thank my diamond and emerald friends for the valuable lessons they taught me, with special recognition to Dr. Morris Charytan.

I thank the political leaders in Nassau County, New York, from both the Republican and Conservative Parties, for giving me, an unknown with no experience, the opportunity to fulfill a lifelong dream of running for Congress, although my dream was to win.

I thank all those who volunteered for my campaign: Team Skorski—Simmie, Howie, Bruno, Jim, Beth, Joseph, Barry, MD, Mickey, Charlie, Abe, Chris, Steve, Howard, Tony, Billy, David, Jonathan, Avery, Eliezer, Ralph, Michael, David, Seth, Becky, Jason, Hal, Perry, Beryl, big Darren, little Darren, Jeremy, and Gershon.

Extra special thanks to Myrna Zissman, David Lyons, Bruce Ventimiglia, Bob Fegaro, Mike D., Joel Klein, Kellyanne Conway, Joseph Frager, Dr. Solomon Schwartzstein, and Rabbi Kaufman. To Jason Maoz, editor of the *Jewish Press,* who has allowed me to contribute to the paper whenever I felt the need to vent.

Special thanks also goes to those radio talk-show hosts who interviewed me following the launch of stopfrankenlies.com; Geoff Metcalf, BQ Cullum, and Barry Farber.

I would also like to acknowledge those sites who have taken the time to monitor and report on Franken's untruths: Frankenlies.com, lyingliar.com, and frankenwatch.blogspot.com.

And of course I have to thank all those without whose support this book may never have seen the light of day:

To Joseph Farah of World Net Daily, who had the vision to see that a book of this nature would have its place in the arena of ideas way before Franken had reached any kind of star power.

To my personal editor Martin Wooster for cleaning things up for me. My agents at Writer's Reps for believing in me. To Chris Bauerle who worked with me to make the book deal move forward. To Stacie Bauerle, who is incredibly talented in so many ways. To my editor Ron Pitkin, for his patience and support.

Even before I hooked up with WND, I had a few friends who believed in me and pushed me to write and write and research and write; like Debbie Schlussel. My great friend, Michael Benjamin—the "Agent 007" of politics and founder of savenewyork.org and future of New York's Republican Party. To David Bossie and Brian Danza of Citizensunited.org, a very important conservative action group. To John Fund, who helped put me in touch with a lot of the right people. To Brent Bozell for taking an interest in my book. Tim Graham, also of the MRC, who spent time with me on the phone getting me the information I needed to refute Franken's assault on Bernie Goldberg. To FactCheck.org for taking my calls and assisting me whenever I had questions. To Dr. Larry Hunter, who advised me on issues pertaining to Social Security . . . and who knows a lot more than Senator Harry Reid and Al Franken. And yes, I even have to thank FAIR for taking my calls and not hanging up on me, even after I told them I was doing research on Al Franken. I have to thank Tony Snow, one of the most righteous men I know, who always took my calls. I also want to thank my good friend Dick Morris, whom I met when I was running for Congress and who has stayed in touch with me ever since. Another good friend, Larry Ward, the smartest political Internet guy on planet Earth, from Political Media Group, who helped me in all kinds of ways I can never repay. And to my PMG compadre, Sanders.

Last, what would I have done and where would I be without the support of my wife and three beautiful daughters, Nicole, Alli (Balli), and Julia (Mulia)?

And, of course, my in-laws. There's nothing like Jewish Hungarian in-laws.

INDEX

C

Q

R

S